# HOLY GROUND:
# A STUDY OF THE AMERICAN
# CAMP MEETING

*Garland Reference Library of Social Science (Vol. 717)*

*Religious Information Systems Series, Vol. 5*

# Religious Information Systems
## J. Gordon Melton
## General Editor

Religious Bodies in the United States:
A Directory
by J. Gordon Melton

Religious Information Sources:
A Worldwide Guide
by J. Gordon Melton and Michael A. Kószegi

Magic, Witchcraft, and Paganism in America:
A Bibliography
Second Edition
by J. Gordon Melton and Isotta Poggi

The African-American Holiness Pentecostal Movement:
An Annotated Bibliography
by Sherry Sherrod DuPree

The Cult Controversy:
A Guide to Sources
by J. Gordon Melton

Encyclopedic Handbook of Cults in America
Revised and Updated
by J. Gordon Melton

Islam in North America:
A Sourcebook
by Michael A. Kószegi and J. Gordon Melton

# HOLY GROUND:
# A STUDY OF THE AMERICAN
# CAMP MEETING

by
**Kenneth O. Brown, Ph.D.**

RELIGIOUS INFORMATION SYSTEMS

**Garland Publishing, Inc.**
**New York & London**
**1992**

BV
3798
.B76
1992

**Library of Congress Cataloging-in-Publication Data**

Brown, Kenneth O., 1943–
    Holy ground : a study of the American camp meeting / by Kenneth O.
Brown.
        p.    cm. — (Garland reference library of social science ; v.
717)  (Religious information systems series ; vol. 5)
    Includes bibliographical references and index.
    ISBN 0–8240–4837–7
    1. Camp-meetings—United States—History. 2. Camp-meetings—
United States—Bibliography. 3. United States—Church history.
4. United States—Church history—Bibliography. I. Title.
II. Series. III. Series: Religious information systems series ;
vol. 5.
BV3798.B76    1992
269'.24'0973—dc20                                                    92–9742
                                                                     CIP

Printed on acid-free, 250-year-life paper
Manufactured in the United States of America

# CONTENTS

**Part Three**

**A Working List of Camp Meetings, Bible Conferences,
    Chautauquas, Assembly Grounds,
    and Christian Retreat Centers**

# FOREWORD

Camp meetings originated on the southern frontier during the Great Revival (1787–1805) in response to an environment in which population was widely scattered and church facilities were few. Because of their duration and because those in attendance could camp on the site, camp meetings drew crowds of several hundred or even a few thousand from distances that otherwise would have prevented many from attending a religious service. Although the term "camp meeting" did not come into general use until about 1802, the first identifiable camp meeting appears to have been organized in the Carolinas or Georgia during the last decade of the eighteenth century. The most famous of these early camp meetings took place in August 1801 at Cane Ridge, Kentucky, where attendance estimates range from 30,000 to 100,000.

The earliest camp meetings were under Methodist auspices, but soon involved representatives of the Presbyterian, Baptist, and Methodist denominations. After 1805, however, camp meetings were sponsored mainly by the Methodists and, although never institutionalized by them, were an important part of Methodist practice, especially in the Midwest and South until the 1840s.

Camp meetings were held annually in most districts, usually in the late summer. In the least settled areas, they took place under "brush arbors"—large natural canopies formed by overhanging branches—around which participants camped in canvas tents. In more settled regions, services might be sheltered by a wooden shed, with cottages providing comfort for the participants. Camp meetings usually lasted four days, with services scheduled from early morning until late at night.

By the 1840s, as many areas became more densely populated, camp meetings began to seem less necessary to sustaining religion. Local churches increasingly became the centers of religious activity as church leaders turned mainly to indoor "protracted meetings" for their revival efforts.

After the Civil War camp meetings were revived by the newly resurgent holiness movement within Methodism. A National Camp

Meeting Association for the Promotion of Holiness and a widely circulated newspaper, *The Christian Standard*, undergirded the cause. Many new campgrounds, often beside the sea or in the mountains, were built to promote the call to personal holiness. Their summer assemblies which mixed preaching and recreation continued well into the twentieth century. Two other movements in American religious life took up the camp meeting in the Victorian period—the Chautauqua movement and the Bible Conference movement. Many current Christian retreat centers trace their origins to nineteenth-century camp meetings.

The general story of camp meetings has been told many times. However, until Ken Brown came along little effort had been made to track down the locations and document the history of the countless individual camp meetings. His *Holy Ground* identifies more than 1,800 surviving sites across the country. An introductory essay sets them in historical context and expands our knowledge of their status and role in America's religious history. An extensive bibliography gathers together for the first time a wealth of surviving camp meeting literature, including apologies, sermons, biographies, and histories of individual camp meetings.

*Holy Ground* is a rich new resource for the study of religion in America.

Kenneth E. Rowe
Professor of Church History
Librarian, Methodist Archives and History Center
Drew University
Madison, New Jersey
December 1991

# PREFACE

The idea for this book started in 1968 while I corresponded with Dr. Delbert R. Rose, then professor of Biblical theology at Asbury Theological Seminary in Wilmore, Kentucky. I had asked for his list of holiness camp meetings, and he wrote back suggesting I compile such a list for the state of Ohio. I did, and that effort has since grown to international proportions, and now includes a broad ecumenical base of denominations, associations, and independent organizations.

The years have taught me the limitations of such a study, and I make no claim that the lists or bibliography included in this book are exhaustive. Indeed, they are not. Consequently, this volume is offered as an introductory working tool, one which, I hope, may be able to expand the field of camp meeting studies and research.

For over one hundred years the claim has often been made that the camp meeting is dying out; nothing could be further from the truth! The camp meeting as an institution began to change and grow almost from the day it was founded, and the modifications not only expanded its ministry, but practically guaranteed long life as well. Unfortunately, sometimes even its friends had difficulty accepting the changes, but in spite of their cries of protest, the camp meeting, including its many variations, has developed into one of the most powerful institutions of the modern church.

# INTRODUCTION

The camp meeting has made a lasting impression on the life of American religious history. While scholars have been uncertain about its origins, evidence suggests that it first appeared in the backwoods of Carolina and Georgia during the last decade of the eighteenth century. Since that time over a quarter of a million annual encampments have been held, with the total number of religious services easily reaching into the tens of millions. No accurate estimate of attendance can be given, but it is obvious that the camp meeting has touched the heartbeat of American society.[1]

The title of this book may seem strange. It could bring to mind several Biblical scenes, including Moses at the burning bush, Joshua near the city of Jericho, or the Tabernacle during the wilderness wanderings of the ancient Jews. Those familiar with the camp meeting setting will quickly recognize that such Biblical images were deliberately used to name some encampments, and in this way the campground itself became a theological statement, historical and eschatological at the same time. It looked back to an age when God hallowed the very ground with presence, but it also encouraged people to pray and believe that God would again break into human existence, bringing glory and salvation into their lives.[2]

John B. Jackson has recognized the importance of this principle of holy ground, and has argued that the sacred grove is a very important aspect of the American landscape. In *The Necessity for Ruins*, Jackson included a chapter on "The Sacred Grove in America," in which he claimed that for Christians, action, human or divine, sanctified the place. This helped him understand the existence of almost numberless little hamlets across the country, especially in the South, with the name "Grove" in them. For him the term "grove" in an American place-name almost always carried deep significance, for it recognized the site of a revival, camp meeting, or church.[3] Jackson's keen observation may be right, for a large number of camp meetings have included the term "grove" in their name. Several sites quickly come to mind, such as Ocean Grove, New Jersey; Asbury Grove, Massachusetts; Bismark Grove, Kansas; God's Holiness Grove,

Pennsylvania; and Beulah Grove, Ohio. These, as well as many other encampments, have recognized and symbolized "holy ground," a place set apart, where God may still act in the lives of people.

Religious historians have only begun to recognize the vast contribution of the camp meeting to American society. While the subject is usually discussed, or at least mentioned in the important histories, dictionaries, and encyclopediae of American Christianity, few major studies of this institution have been made, and no one has seriously looked at its impact on modern culture. This is all the more surprising when one considers the number of denominations which presently sponsor annual encampments, the number of independent camp meetings which are held each year, and the growing influence of such related movements as family camping and Christian conference centers.

In 1955 Charles Johnson published his classic work, *The Frontier Camp Meeting*, and it immediately became the primary reference for scholarly research. As the title implies, however, Johnson focused on the frontier, and limited his study to the first four decades of the nineteenth century.

Several new works have appeared more recently which help expand our knowledge of the camp meeting. In 1974 Dickson Bruce published *And They All Sang Hallelujah*, an interpretation of the camp meeting as a part of southern "plain folk" religion. However, it is also limited to the years 1800–1845. In 1978 Ellen Jane Lorenz published *Glory Hallelujah*, a study of the "campmeeting spiritual," based on her Ph.D. dissertation, "A Treasure of Campmeeting Spirituals." In 1987 Ellen Weiss published *City in the Woods*, a new approach to camp meeting history. This interesting volume probes the story and architectural design of the encampment at Martha's Vineyard, Massachusetts, one of the oldest camps in the East.

Over the years the camp meeting material has grown to become a corpus in itself. It includes almost innumerable broadsides, brochures, and pamphlets, histories of individual campgrounds, postcards, stereoscope views, published bylaws, and reports of the associations, sermons, biographies, some scholarly studies, denominational histories, theses, and a considerable number of periodical articles. In all this material, however, there is no tool which attempts to draw these various strands together. The layperson or scholar has no reference work to consult which will provide historical and bibliographical information or list the encampments for a single state or denomination.

This volume is that research tool. It probes in depth the origins of the camp meeting, and offers an alternative to the popular thesis that James McGready held the first planned encampment in Kentucky at the end of the eighteenth century. It lists nearly two thousand live camp meetings around the country and in some foreign lands, and includes historical and denominational information on each, where possible. Furthermore, it offers a bibliography of the camp meeting material, placing a special emphasis on the history of individual encampments.

## Definitions

It will be helpful for the reader to study the following definitions of terms which are used throughout this book.

1. *Stand* One of the earliest outdoor religious forms, often called the "preacher's stand." Usually somewhat elevated, it consisted of a pulpit and an overhanging roof for protection from the weather.

2. *Brush Arbor* The earliest encampments often consisted of a brush arbor, a crude overhang of branches or brush, constructed to protect the preacher or the people from the extremes of weather. It sometimes resembled a lean-to, or tent, and has been so depicted in some of the earliest drawings. It also has been called a "harbor," because of its basic function of shielding people from the weather.

3. *Camp Meeting* This is an elusive term, one that may predate the American Revolution. In previous popular usage it referred to a self-styled outdoor religious gathering in which the people sustain themselves while camping on the grounds for the duration of the services. Today, this term is difficult to define due to the variety of usage. One may read about the district camp, the state camp, the general camp, the work camp, the children's camp, the youth camp, the family camp, the indoor camp, the drive-in camp, etc. These are all part of the meaning of the term "camp meeting" for today's church. It is not necessarily held outside, nor do the people necessarily camp or otherwise sustain themselves on the grounds. The district or state camps are those conducted by or for a specific geographical area in a given church, while the general camp is sponsored by or for the whole denomination. A work camp is conducted in order to make necessary improvements and repairs to the facilities. The "indoor camp meeting" may be either denominational or interdenominational, and is held in a tent, a church, or civic building. It provides no camping facilities whatsoever. The "drive-in camp meeting" is so called because people must drive in to the campground for the services. It provides no

camping facilities, and the only building on the grounds will be the tent or tabernacle. Union Camp Meeting in Chillicothe, Ohio, is a perfect example, for the only building on the grounds is the tabernacle.

4. *Tent* The employment of tents for outdoor religious services began very early, and predates the camp meeting. The obvious meaning of the word applies to its usage by encampments, for people often worshiped under a huge canvas tabernacle, as well as ate and slept in canvas tents. However, some campgrounds improved the "tent city," as the canvas quarters were called, by adding wood floors or sides. Such "tents" are still used each year at many campgrounds, such as Ocean Grove, New Jersey.

5. *Cabin* As camps became settled in one location, some people built their own cabins in which to live, or to house the preachers. Some cabins were lavish, consisting of several stories, and some camp grounds had literally hundreds of them. While most camps still use cabins for temporary housing, some have been winterized as permanent dwellings. The fancy Victorian ones can still be found at places like Martha's Vineyard, Massachusetts.

6. *Tabernacle* The main sanctuary on any campground is called the tabernacle, the structure in which the campers gather for preaching or sacramental services. The tabernacle might be made of wood, metal, or canvas, or it may be a natural amphitheater open to the weather, such as the one at Old Orchard Beach, Maine.

7. *Camp Shed* This is another term for tabernacle, used mostly in the South. The old southern camp sheds often have no sides, allowing cool breezes free access on hot summer days. A good example is the ca. 1850 camp shed at McKenzie's Camp Ground, operated by local African Methodist Episcopal Zion churches in Catawba County, North Carolina.

8. *Tent Meeting* In the strictest sense a tent meeting is a portable revival, with the big tent the focal point of the meetings. These revivals are often called "camp meetings, "and over the years have been the genesis of many permanent encampments. A good example is the annual "tent camp" held at Bobo, Indiana.

9. *Holiness Camp Meeting* This term is difficult in one sense because there are various interpretations of the term "holiness." Generally speaking, a holiness camp meeting is one in which the doctrine of the holy life is preached and taught as a specialty, usually

including an emphasis on the doctrine of entire sanctification as a second work of grace. A good example, and one of the largest campgrounds in the nation, is the Indian Springs Camp Meeting in Flovilla, Georgia.

10. *Pentecostal Camp Meeting* This term, which was once used to describe holiness camps, has now come to have a very specialized meaning. A pentecostal camp meeting is one which usually features the doctrines of the pentecostal and/or charismatic movement, especially speaking in tongues and divine healing. A good example, one of the oldest and largest pentecostal campgrounds in the country, is the Pleasant Grove Camp Meeting in Durant, Florida, now sponsored by the Pleasant Grove Assemblies of God Church.

## Acknowledgments

I want to publicly offer my thanks to the many people who have helped me research this topic over the years. It is not possible to name the pastors, camp meeting presidents, secretaries and evangelists, editors and other denominational officials, librarians, and archivists who have responded to my letters, phone calls, and personal visits. And yet without their generous assistance this project could not have been written.

I owe a special debt to my longtime friend, Dr. Delbert R. Rose, who in 1968 suggested this field to me as an area for scholarly research. I am especially grateful to my wife, Charlotte, and our two sons, Jonathan and Nathan. They have been willing to listen to my ideas, and accompany me on "camp meeting trips" through two dozen states. They were such patient souls, willing at moment's notice to go visit another campground.

I am grateful to my esteemed friends, Dr. Kenneth E. Rowe, Methodist Librarian at the United Methodist Archives and History Center in Madison, New Jersey, who helped proof this manuscript, and Dr. Charles Yrigoyen, General Secretary for the General Commission on Archives and History of the United Methodist Church. They provided assistance whenever I asked, and never hesitated to make available the resources at their disposal. I owe a very special thanks to two of my friends at Asbury Theological Seminary, in Wilmore, Kentucky, Dr. William Faupel, Director of Library Services, and Dr. David Bundy, former Acquisitions Librarian. They strongly encouraged this research and publication, and even helped provide storage for my material during times of relocation. I must thank three camp meeting enthusiasts, collectors, and researchers who helped me beyond measure. Dr. Ellen Weiss and Harry McClarran generously shared their research files with me, and James Robertson made available his collection of camp meeting postcards and stereoscope views. Finally, I want to thank the people of Diamond United Methodist Church for encouraging their pastor to research and write this book. I am very grateful to my personal friend and parishioner, Dr. David Orbin. He taught me how to use the computer and helped me get this manuscript ready for publication. He truly saved me many long hours of work.

## An Appeal

In most of my camp meeting articles I made an appeal to the reader for help, and I would include that here. If you have information which will add to, correct, or improve any of the material in this book, *please* contact me. I am always looking for brochures, pictures, histories, and other camp meeting material.

Dr. Kenneth O. Brown, Pastor
Diamond United Methodist Church
Hazleton, PA 18201

## NOTES

1. Very frugal estimates establish the figure for the number of services. Since 1870, most camps lasted between eight to ten days, and often had six services or more per day.

2. The Biblical references are Exodus 3:1–4:18; Joshua 5:13–15; Exodus 40:1–38. Some also cite the ancient Feast of Tabernacles as Biblical authority for the camp meeting and similar outdoor religious exercises.

3. John B. Jackson, *The Necessity for Ruins*. Published by the author. 1980, pp. 77–79.

1. Photo of historical marker for Grassy Branch Camp Meeting at the Rehobeth United Methodist Church, North Carolina.

2. Photo of jail at Ball's Creek Camp Meeting, North Carolina.

3. Stereoscope view of the National Holiness Committee, taken at the 1869 National Camp Meeting in Round Lake, New York.

4. Postcard view of early holiness camp meeting tent in Vermont.

5. Stereoscope view of Ocean Grove Camp Meeting, New Jersey, with the Reverend Elwood Stokes in the foreground.

6. Stereoscope view of tents at Ocean Grove Camp Meeting, New Jersey.

7. Postcard view of entrance to Spiritualist Camp Meeting, New York.

8. Postcard view of entrance to Camp Sychar, Ohio.

9. Postcard view of Hollow Rock Camp Meeting, Ohio.

10. Postcard view of Spring Grove Camp Ground, Vermont.

11. Postcard view of tabernacle at Martha's Vineyard, Massachusetts.

12. Postcard view of Old Orchard Beach Camp Meeting, Maine.

13. Postcard view of Montrose Bible Conference, Pennsylvania.

14. Postcard view of coliseum building at Iowa Chautauqua, Pennsylvania.

# Part One
# Origins and Development
# of the Camp Meeting

# ORIGINS AND DEVELOPMENT OF
# THE CAMP MEETING

The camp meeting has been like the giant, Atlas, among the institutions developed by American Christianity. It has served as a school for revivalism, church planting, missions, Christian education, national reform, and Christian political action. Moreover, it has been a model for the Chautauqua, the Christian resort, the family camping movement, Christian conferences, and even community planning and development. Perhaps no other single institution of the church has carried such a burden, and carried it so well. Frontier Methodist Bishop Francis Asbury once referred to the camp meeting as a "harvest time," but little did he know how bountiful that harvest would be.[1]

Scholars have disagreed for years over the founding of the camp meeting. The classic book on this subject has been Charles A. Johnson's *The Frontier Camp Meeting*, published in 1955. He suggested that the problem is mainly one of definition, and offered several antecedents, including the outdoor preaching of Whitefield and the Wesleys, the long-standing tradition of outdoor sacramental services, which sometimes met in barns or open fields, the "Big Meetings" held by the Pennsylvania Germans, and the Methodist quarterly meetings, which often had to meet out of doors. At least two other ancestor/antecedents also deserve mention, the European "Holy Fairs," and the "tents," "stands," and other pulpits of what some called the "outdoor church" which sprang up on the American frontier.[2]

One particular antecedent deserves special recognition, the outdoor services of the Separate Baptists in Virginia. This includes the work of evangelists James Read and Samuel Harriss, who may have had men camp on the ground during their 1769 sacramental meetings, and John Waller, who appears to have called his services "camp meetings," even drawing up a special set of rules to govern them.[3] However, as Charles Johnson observed, and Catherine Cleveland before him, there are major differences between these services and the camp meetings which followed. In the Virginia meetings, women were not allowed on the grounds after certain hours, and the campers were dependent on the local populace for sustenance.[4]

These ancestors and antecedents highlight the tremendous precedent for outdoor religious services that existed in Europe and on the American frontier. Moreover, they force the issue of definition. Were the European "Holy Fairs," or the outdoor preaching services by Whitefield and the Wesleys' "camp meetings"? In America, were the outdoor sacramental occasions, German "Big Meetings," services held at stands or tents in the woods, or Methodist quarterly gatherings "camp meetings"? And if not, why not? What was the difference? When and where, and under whose leadership did outdoor religious services actually become camp meetings? The answer to these and similar questions will help settle some of the annoying historical problems relative to this subject.

No standardized definition of the term "camp meeting" has yet been developed. Although Charles Johnson did not offer a formal definition of the term, it becomes obvious that for him it must include outdoor religious exercises in which anyone may camp independently on the grounds, and it included popular usage as well as a standardized pattern. It is important to recognize five basic elements within the context of this "working definition":

1.  outdoor religious exercises;
2.  everyone may camp on the grounds;
3.  the campers independently support themselves;
4.  the camp meeting method gains wide popular recognition;
5.  the camp meeting method becomes standardized into a pattern.

This is an almost foolproof definition for Johnson's purpose, for it excluded the antecedents, and all but guaranteed a founding date during the "Great Revival" in Kentucky, circa 1800. On the one hand, with this definition Johnson could affirm the relative unimportance of questions regarding the date and place of the very first camp meeting. On the other hand, however, it enabled him to claim with confidence, "In the year 1800 the camp meeting sprang into being, was almost instantly universalized along the southwestern frontier, and almost as rapidly standardized into a pattern."[5]

Such a definition, working or otherwise, faces serious difficulty, for while it recognizes antecedents, it also deliberately limits them, and makes broad assumptions based on those limitations. It places an inordinate weight upon the supposed standardization of the camp meeting during the Great Revival, and confidently assumes that nothing similar could have taken place earlier or elsewhere. Moreover, it demands that wide popular recognition be used as one of the main criteria of definition, an impossible requirement. It begins to appear that this definition was constructed with the Great Revival in mind.

Such a definition also just happens to fit very neatly into the consensus of scholarly opinion, for historians have claimed for years that the "Great Revival" in Kentucky served as the birthplace of the camp meeting.[6] Many scholars have given the credit to the Presbyterians, and the man most often linked with this revival effort is Presbyterian evangelist James McGready.[7] Others have honored the Reverend Barton W. Stone for conducting the "first planned camp meeting" at the Cane Ridge Meeting House near Paris, Kentucky, in the summer of 1801.[8] A few historians have said the credit rests with the Methodists, and the minister most often named is the Reverend John McGee. This thesis has much to commend it, but it has not yet gained wide popularity.[9]

There can be no doubt that the Great Revival in Kentucky catapulted the camp meeting onto the national stage as a revival method of major importance. Nor can there be any doubt as to the role of such ministers as James McGready, Barton W. Stone, John and William McGee, William McKendree, Bishop Francis Asbury, Peter Cartwright, James B. Finley, and a host of others who widely promoted this new means of mass evangelism and made it such a rousing success. But doubt must be cast upon any definition, working or standard, which uses the items outlined by Johnson as the criteria of formulation and in effect locks out any further need of research.

## The First Camp Meeting

One of the so-called "antecedents" of the camp meeting makes an exceptionally strong case as the first encampment ever held. Incredibly, it is still conducted by Methodists in western North Carolina. Added to this are six other live Methodist camp meetings, two in North Carolina, three in South Carolina, and one in Georgia, all of which may predate the Great Revival in Kentucky and share the honors of being called the very first camp meeting.

The oldest of these appears to be the Effingham County Camp Meeting, near Springfield, Georgia. The 1989 brochure announced the "199th Annual Camp Meeting," indicating 1790 as the founding year. According to an undated history of the encampment written by N. Hinton Morgan, Gideon Mallette and George Powledge built the first campground near Turkey Branch Creek about 1790. Mallette, a Methodist local preacher, had come to the area in 1785, and later established the Turkey Branch Methodist Church. The location of the camp meeting was on ground that had belonged to Powledge since 1789, and in 1802 he sold the two hundred-acre plot to Mallette.[10] In the years that followed, the encampment grew so large that the "tents" lined all four sides of the property. In 1864, when General Sherman's army marched through the area, they burned the buildings and utterly destroyed the campground. For the next two years, meetings were held under a brush arbor on the lot of Turkey Branch Church. In 1866 Colonel Edward Bird gave ten acres of land at Springfield, Georgia, and the people built a spacious tabernacle, capable of seating 1,000 people. In 1907 this, too, was replaced, and the camp relocated once more, this time to a lovely ten-acre plot outside the town of Springfield, Georgia. The annual camp meeting has been held here since that time.[11]

The Rock Spring Camp Meeting, near Denver, North Carolina, has been in continuous operation at various sites since 1794. Charles Johnson recognized it as one of the oldest claimants, but in light of his criteria of definition it had to be rejected. The standard Methodist history mentions Rock Springs as an "accident," and attempts to explain its early continuous story in the light of "Quarterly Meetings." In 1985, during a special service of recognition, the original location was designated a "United Methodist Historic Site." The North Carolina Annual Conference of the United Methodist Church recognized it as "the first camp meeting grounds in North Carolina . . . probably the first camp meeting in the United States."[12] A small but growing number of scholars have given support to that statement, and it forces a reinterpretation of camp meeting origins.

The founding of Rock Springs Camp Meeting is woven into the life work of a pioneer Methodist minister, the Reverend Daniel Asbury. Born on February 18, 1762, in Fairfax County, Virginia, Asbury, no relation to Bishop Francis Asbury, came to North Carolina in 1787, and stayed for nearly forty years. As a youth he had been captured and adopted by the Shawnee Indians, but during the Revolution they traded him to the British, who imprisoned him in Detroit. He planned a daring escape, and on February 23, 1783, after an absence of five years, returned to his home in Virginia. It is said that even his mother did not recognize him.[13]

Asbury seemed to lose all interest in religion during his years of captivity, and after he came home opposed the work of the churches, especially the local Methodists. They, however, were able to gain his confidence, and after a long spiritual struggle, he became converted. Believing his life to be forever changed, he joined the local Methodist society, and began to exhort in the public services. Sensing his call, and recognizing his gifts, the local leaders quickly brought him to the attention of the itinerant preachers. They encouraged him to become a minister.

Joining the Methodist Conference in 1786, Asbury served several appointments in rapid succession, the custom of that day. In 1789 he and young John McGee received appointment to the Yadkin Circuit, and so successful were their labors that within three months a new circuit had to be formed. The Bishop placed Asbury over the new Lincoln Circuit, covering the territory west of the Catawba River, and in less than a year he reported 189 members. In 1790 he again received appointment there, and so rapidly did the circuit grow that at the next conference he reported a total membership of 441.[14]

A cluster of nearly a dozen Methodist families formed the nucleus of this new circuit. In 1787 these people had moved from Virginia and settled in Lincoln County, North Carolina, near the Catawba River. As they journeyed to their new home, they conducted outdoor services along the way and often made the forest ring with their singing and shouting. The group had no regular pastor, and even after establishing their new homes often worshiped out of doors along the banks of the Grassy Branch Creek. In the fall of 1788 a Methodist preacher from Virginia came to visit them, and they secured permission for him to preach in the local German church. He preached with exceptional zeal and fervor, and some of the Methodists, especially the widow Morris, began to shout aloud the praises of God.

> The congregation was panic-stricken; the old German ladies pressed their way to Nancy L. Morris, the widow's daughter, and exclaimed in the utmost fright, "Your Mother has a fit, indeed she has; and she is going to die!" The daughter, not at all alarmed, answered with surprising calmness, "She will soon recover from them."[15]

Daniel Asbury and John McGee found this group of ardent Methodists in 1789, and organized them as a preaching point on the newly established Lincoln Circuit. While working with the people, Asbury became acquainted with Nancy L. Morris, and married her on January 4, 1790. In 1791 this group built the first Methodist church west of the Catawba River, now known as Rehobeth United Methodist Church. Three years later they held an outdoor revival, and it has become one of the best known claimants for the honor of being the first camp meeting ever held.[16]

In 1794 Daniel Asbury, Herbert Harwell, Samuel Harwell, John Edwards, John Turbefield, and Benjamin Stacy consulted together, planned to build a "stand" and "tents," and hold an outdoor revival meeting on the grounds of the Grassy Branch Methodist Church in Lincoln County. In some ways those plans were not new or unusual, because outdoor services had been held in that locality for many years. According to Foote's *Sketches of North Carolina*, "stands" and "tents" had been used for religious purposes in the Carolinas as early as 1742 in places where there were no church buildings. Moreover, evidence now suggests that by the 1790's outdoor religious exercises may have become somewhat common all over the frontier.[17]

It appears, however, that the outdoor revival at Grassy Branch brought important and permanent changes to this type of religious service. Daniel Asbury and his associates planned in advance to build stands and tents because they expected large crowds, far more than the little log church could hold. But these Methodists also actually planned to "tent out" on the grounds of the church for the duration of the services, and that idea forever altered the appearance and use of the outdoor revival. This "camping out" for services may have been going on for several years at this location, some say since 1789. Be that as it may, these leaders appear to have actually planned the encampment of 1794 in advance in order to help coordinate and promote the revival.

The 1794 revival at Grassy Branch probably far exceeded the dreams of its planners. For one thing, at least three hundred persons were converted under the preaching of Daniel Asbury, William McKendree (who later became Bishop), Nicholas Watters, William Fulwood, John McGee, and Dr. James Hall (a noted local Presbyterian). Daniel Asbury's widow later wrote that her daughter was baptized during the revival, and others claimed that its very success prompted the appointment of another meeting for the next year. One record even indicates the leaders referred to the services as a "camp meeting."[18]

These outdoor revival meetings were held at this same location for the next three years. By 1798 the congregations had grown so large that the meeting had to be moved in order to find a better water supply for drinking and refrigeration. While the sources are unclear as to exact dates and location, the people seem to have developed a permanent site by 1815 near Denver, North Carolina, called Robey's Campground. The meeting moved once again in 1829, but this time the Lincoln Circuit bought a forty-five-acre plot, named it Rock Springs Campground, and the services have been held there since that time.[19]

The evidence is very strong to support the claim that slaves attended and participated in the Grassy Branch Camp Meeting of 1794, and in successive encampments after that. These black Christians had to conduct their own services, with their own preachers, in their own quarters; in effect, they had to hold their own separate camp meeting. Bishop Francis Asbury encouraged Methodists to minister to the slave population, who in turn eventually founded their own campground, perhaps as early as the first quarter of the nineteenth century. This encampment also had to relocate several times, but it found a permanent home in 1879, on land deeded to the trustees by Mary E. Tucker. The modern ancestor of that early slave encampment is Tucker's Grove Camp Meeting, named in honor of its benefactor, and located near Machpelah, North Carolina. It has been operated continuously by the African Methodist Episcopal Zion Church since 1876, and is listed on the National Registry of Historic Places. It claims to be the oldest continuously operated black camp meeting in the nation; it can also claim joint honors with nearby Rock Springs as one of the first camp meetings ever held.[20]

While Daniel Asbury assisted in the development of the Grassy Branch Camp Meeting, evidence suggests he also busied himself in conducting other encampments nearby. There may have been a camp meeting at the Bethel Methodist Church in 1795; the record is unclear. However, in 1796 he and Dr. James Hall conducted the Great Union Camp Meeting at Shepherd's Cross Roads in Iredell County, and reported at least five hundred conversions. Methodist minister Thomas Mann, appointed to the Union Circuit that year, simply wrote "Camp Meeting" in his journal.[21]

There are three live encampments in South Carolina whose history takes them back to the last decade of the eighteenth century. The oldest of these, Cypress Camp Meeting, located near Ridgeville, South Carolina, is said to date from 1794. On October 28, 1984, this encampment celebrated its 190th anniversary in conjunction with the bicentennial of American Methodism. A memorial plaque in the tabernacle informs the reader that Cypress was established on October 28, 1794. Cattle Creek Camp Meeting, near Branchville, South Carolina, was founded about 1795. To date no official history of either campground has been written, although one is being prepared for Cypress by a local historian.[22]

The Indian Field Camp Meeting, located near St. George, South Carolina, also dates from about 1795, and is listed in the National Registry of Historic Places. Local Methodists held the first encampment on ground which belonged to Enoch Pendarvis, and the meetings grew so rapidly that it became necessary for the camp to relocate. In 1800 the campground moved to its present location, and established its unusual twelve-sided grounds in 1830, patterned after the Levitical Harvest Festivals of the ancient Israelites. John Gavin and William Murray deeded the land to the trustees in 1838, and the present tabernacle was built in 1848 and restored in 1970.[23]

One other camp meeting must be mentioned which also predates the Great Revival. Evidence suggests that the Reverend John Page, pastor of the Greene Methodist Circuit in Tennessee, conducted a camp meeting on his parish in 1796. This may have been the first encampment ever held in that state, the forerunner of many hundreds yet to come, and a full year before any of the sacramental services conducted by James McGready. It is claimed that Page got the idea from John McGee.[24]

## A New Interpretation

The popularly accepted thesis claims that the very first camp meeting was held on the Kentucky frontier about the year 1799 or 1800 as part of the sacramental services conducted by Presbyterian minister James McGready. Although unplanned and spontaneous, this type of meeting was quickly recognized for its potential as a tool of mass revivalism, and it became one of the major factors in the spread of the Great Revival. This terse statement, or one similar to it, has appeared in almost all the standard historical and reference literature on the subject of American religion for over a century.[25] Unfortunately, some of its information is incorrect and/or misleading. It leans too heavily on the Great Revival for definition and historical interpretation, and fails to credit or recognize the earlier work of the Methodists in the Carolinas and Georgia. Other than the revival, it has no other means to explain the evolution of the camp meeting.

In the light of the camp meetings listed previously, and there may well be others, it is no longer possible to support unequivocally this popular thesis. While the Great Revival can help explain the meteoric rise of the camp meeting on the American religious landscape, the evidence will no longer allow the claim that the revival, or the ministry of James McGready, led to the birth of the camp meeting. If one includes the continuous service of the six live encampments in Georgia and the Carolinas, there may have been as many as forty-one separate camp meetings held by the Methodists before McGready conducted his famous 1799 sacramental services.

Nor is it possible any longer to define the camp meeting in terms of the popularity and standardization it achieved during the Great Revival. Those earlier southern encampments meet these criteria locally, and more. Standardization took effect almost instantly, for from the beginning the services were held out of doors, under stands and tents, with the people camping and sustaining themselves on the very grounds. These elements did not change; in fact, they were repeated year after year. These meetings did not gain national attention, but their local popularity can still be measured in at least three ways: annual repetition, numerical growth, and a large number of conversions.

It is important at this point to add to the list of criteria which make up a working definition of the term "camp meeting." Earlier historians have stressed the sacramental aspect of the antecedents and initial meetings of the Great Revival, and this element is extremely important. It is equally important, however, to recognize and emphasize two other criteria: proclamation and revival. While it may be argued that these elements were an integral part of the Great Revival, it must be admitted that the antecedents emphasized something else as their primary goal, whether it be the business and administration of a Methodist quarterly meeting, or the worship and liturgy of the Presbyterian sacramental occasion. James McGready held outdoor services on the Kentucky frontier, but their nature and primary purpose were sacramental. Although it may be said that McGready was a revivalistic preacher himself, and therefore all his meetings were evangelistic, the outdoor services of 1799 were by his own admission sacramental occasions.[26]

The same cannot be said for the early outdoor meetings held by the Methodists in Georgia and the Carolinas. While at least one baptism was administered at Grassy Branch Camp Meeting in 1794, it still must be recognized that preaching and revival, not the celebration of the sacraments, were the essential purpose of the services. This is not meant to suggest that the Presbyterian sacramental occasions were seldom revivalistic, or that the Methodist revivals never included the sacraments. Nor does this imply that the early camp meetings stressed only revival preaching and had no place for the celebration of sacrament. Such statements simply are not true. The encampments often included the services of holy communion and baptism, and the frontier sacramental occasions glowed with revival fires. This is precisely the reason why the camp meeting influenced so many lives over the years. It combined the elements of sacrament, revival, and proclamation in such a way that it quickly became what Charles Parker has called the "first sustained oral mass communication" in American history.[27] Consequently, these elements—sacrament, proclamation, and revival—must be recognized as three of the major components for any working definition of the camp meeting and its ancestral antecedents.

In addition to these essential elements of definition, the early southern Methodist encampments also demand a new interpretation for what has been called the "rise" of the camp meeting. Some scholars have seen significance in the fact that such leaders of the Kentucky revival as James McGready, John and William McGee, Barton Stone, and William McKendree came from North Carolina. There is tremendous significance in that, for at least two of them, John McGee and William McKendree, were among the preachers at the Grassy Branch Camp Meeting in 1794. In fact,

John McGee stayed in the area until 1798, witnessing and perhaps contributing to the growth and development of Grassy Branch. He then moved to Tennessee, and a year or so later joined his brother William on a now-famous preaching tour which enabled them to make major contributions to the revival then brewing on the Kentucky and Tennessee frontier.

### John McGee

It is becoming increasingly evident that more attention needs to be paid to the efforts of John McGee in the outbreak of the Great Revival. This takes nothing away from the work of James McGready, Barton Stone, or any other key leader, but evidence indicates that McGee, not McGready, suggested and introduced the camp meeting as an integral part of the great revival on the Kentucky frontier. He had spent the last decade in western North Carolina, and had seen for himself the power and effects of the outdoor camp meeting revival. He knew Daniel Asbury personally, and not only preached at Grassy Branch, but undoubtedly helped organize other camp meetings in the area. He had worked side by side with such Methodist celebrities and pioneers as Bishop Francis Asbury, William McKendree, and others who were among the best revivalists American Methodism had to offer. In fact, he was a Methodist revivalist himself.

John McGee was born June 9, 1763, in Orange County, North Carolina, the son of Colonel John McGee and his second wife, Martha McFarlane McGee. Evidence indicates that the McGees, also spelled McGhee, were emigrants from northern Ireland who settled in Anson County, North Carolina, about 1750. The family quickly climbed the social ladder. In 1753 McGee served as constable for Orange County, and in 1757 received commission as Justice of the Peace. Meanwhile, he farmed, and sometime between 1750 and 1755 began to operate the local "ordinary," a combination grist mill, inn, trading post, and store. He also received appointment to command a company of local militia, and served as "Captain of the Rangers" in 1760. While he may have seen action in the regular army, his rank of colonel probably came from this local service.[28]

Most sources indicate that the McGees had a Presbyterian background, probably due to the strong influence of Martha. It has been claimed that they attended services at the church which David Caldwell pastored, and their son, William, did enter the Presbyterian ministry after attending Caldwell's "Log College." Further evidence may be seen in the fact that Colonel McGee willed an acre of ground, and a little meeting house, "for the use of a presbayren Society" [sic] and regular traveling ministers. It has been assumed that this meant the local "Presbyterian Society" and its ministers.[29]

Colonel McGee appears to have provided very well for his family, having acquired considerable wealth over the years. When he died on December 13, 1773, it is said that more than 500 persons were indebted to his estate. He left property, money, and slaves to all his children, John inheriting the Richland Plantation, one slave, 100 pounds in money, and a watch. Just a few months before Colonel McGee died, his brother, Andrew McGee, passed away in Dorchester County, Maryland, leaving the property there to his nephews, John and William McGee. Young John was just ten years old.[30]

After the Colonel's death, Martha McGee, John's mother, married a Mr. William Bell and gained considerable fame during the Revolution. The Reverend Eli Caruthers told her story in his *Interesting Revolutionary Incidents and Sketches of Character*, and it has often been repeated. She spied on the British troops, and provided information for General "Lighthorse Harry" Lee. It is said that she made things difficult for the troops of British General Lord Cornwallis when they came to Bell's Mill seeking provisions. For these and other acts of heroism, Martha has been given considerable recognition, all justly earned. For example, in 1928 the Alexander Martin Chapter of the Daughters of the American Revolution erected a monument to this "Revolutionary Heroine" in the Guilford Courthouse National Military Park.[31]

It appears that young John McGee also fought in the American Revolution as a boy-soldier, serving as a private in Captain John Johnstone's militia company, under Brigadier General John Butler. A few years later, according to family legend, John and his brother Samuel bought a merchant ship, and lived independent lives, perhaps sailing the seas themselves, until it wrecked. McGee was obviously a wealthy young man. He had substantial inheritance from both his father and uncle, and while he may not have squandered his wealth like the storied prodigal son, he admitted in his later years that he had been "a wild young man," given to dissipation.[32] All that changed, however, when John met the Methodists.

The evidence suggests that John McGee may have become acquainted with Methodism in the mid-1780s while visiting his brother Samuel in Maryland. It has been said that in Baltimore he heard the preaching of Captain Thomas Webb, Revolutionary War soldier turned Methodist minister, known to lay his sword on the pulpit before he spoke. Under the ministries and influence of the Methodist preachers McGee became convinced of his need for a changed heart. He soon claimed that God had answered his prayer and forgiven his sins, making him a Christian. Although raised a Presbyterian, McGee, profoundly affected by this new religious experience, joined the Methodist Episcopal Church.[33]

Within three days of his conversion experience, McGee claimed the call to ministry, and began traveling with the circuit preacher, speaking in public services. He wrote his mother about the great change in his life, and told her "he had become a preacher among the Methodists." Rather than being pleased, however, the news so distracted her that she actually considered disowning him. Consequently, he stayed in Maryland, and did not return home for nearly two years.

Tension filled the air when John McGee finally went home to see his family in North Carolina. He had expected a cool reception from his mother, and got it. She expected a rabid fanatic; he was not. His younger brother, William, just finishing preparations for the Presbyterian ministry, finally persuaded a very stubborn Martha McGee to allow her Methodist minister son to lead the family evening prayers. John did well. In the days that followed, the news flashed throughout the neighborhood that John McGee had come home a Methodist preacher, and a large crowd gathered the next Sunday to hear him preach on one of his favorite themes, "The New Birth." Interestingly, a revival broke out under his preaching, and during the services that followed many of his old friends and acquaintances were converted, including two members of the family—his mother and brother.[34]

Although received on probation by the Methodist conference in 1788, McGee did not accept appointment as an active circuit rider until 1789, when he served with the Reverend Daniel Asbury on the Yadkin Circuit. Events followed quickly after that, and he served several circuits while completing the required course of study and finishing the steps which led to ordination. In 1792 he was ordained an elder in the church, and about the same time married Martha Johnson of South Carolina. Probably due to his marriage, he "located" in 1793, Methodist jargon for withdrawing from the active traveling ministry. This does not mean that he withdrew from the church, or that he stopped preaching; he did neither. The denomination understood and appreciated the needs of a family, and required a married man to "locate" rather than travel as a circuit rider.[35]

McGee continued to preach on a local basis, and in 1798 moved his family to what is now Smith County, Tennessee. He may have wanted to live near his brother William, a Presbyterian minister who had moved to that area two years before. John purchased extensive land holdings, including a plantation near Dixon Springs, Tennessee, where he settled his family. Here he farmed during the week, continued his work of ministry, and raised a son and four daughters, two of whom later married ministers. Even with these heavy responsibilities, McGee still took time to pursue his calling. He preached in local churches, took evangelistic tours, and served on the general church level. For example, in 1815 and 1816 he was appointed "Presiding Elder" (district superintendent) of the Cumberland District, a large territory which included middle Tennessee and parts of southern Kentucky.[36]

Although no one has written a biography of John McGee, and no photograph of him is known, several primary sources do exist which paint a fascinating portrait of this pioneer revivalist and his work. His son-in-law, the Reverend Thomas Joyner, described him as follows:

> Mr. McGee was below the medium size, but formed for activity and durability; was a model of industry, energy, and economy; provided bountifully for his own household, sustained the institutions of the church, and his hand was ever open to the calls of charity. He was a good citizen—loyal to the Government, and obedient to the powers that be—and an ardent admirer of the democratic institutions of the country.
>
> Mr. McGee possessed a strong and vigorous intellect, clear perception, sound, discriminating judgement, and a mind well stored with varied useful knowledge; was thoroughly versed in the Scriptures, understood the doctrines and usages of the Church, and was well prepared to explain and defend them. His manner in the pulpit was mild, plain, and methodical: he never attempted embellishment, but, when fired by the divinity of his theme, frequently rose to the sublime, and carried his hearers with him to the mount to take a view of Canaan, and his applications and exhortations were often overwhelming to the unconverted.[37]

The Reverend John Carr, a pioneer Methodist minister in Tennessee, who knew McGee personally, wrote:

> I have often listened to his preaching with a great deal of interest; and he preached most forcibly the scriptural doctrine of a change of heart. . . . He was well educated in the English branches, and had a fine address, and a keen, sharp voice. He was a bold defender of Methodism, and was one of the most energetic and useful preachers of his day. [He] excelled as a farmer as well as a preacher . . . one of the most successful preachers of his day.[38]

Much of this material can be verified by other primary sources. McGee's initial personal wealth came from his father and uncle, and their wills are on file in North Carolina and Maryland, respectively. His personal will was registered in Smith County, Tennessee, and provides ample testimony to the care he gave his family and church. He left land and money to each of his children, the home plantation, with all its furniture, utensils, and equipment, to his wife, Martha, and $200 to the Missionary Society of the Methodist Episcopal Church. He died on June 16, 1836, following the amputation of his arm due to the complications of a tumor. He was 75 years old.[39]

## John McGee and the Great Revival

The story of the Reverend James McGready and the Great Revival has been so well told and documented as to need no repetition here.[40] The same can be said for the Reverend Barton Stone and the great Cane Ridge sacramental meeting.[41] The same, however, cannot be said for the contribution of the Reverend John McGee, who, although perhaps best known for his preaching during that time of spiritual upheaval, has been assigned a minor role by many historians. Unfortunately, it is easy to make that mistake, for on the surface of things it would appear that all McGee did was visit and preach a few times.

There are at least two strands of historical tradition regarding the outbreak of the Great Revival on the Kentucky frontier, and each has variations to it. The most commonly accepted view holds that James McGready and a few other Presbyterian ministers served as the catalyst of the revival, assisted at times by many visiting preachers, including the McGee brothers. The second tradition claims that John McGee, assisted by his brother, William, actually set up the chain of events which led to the outbreak of the revival, with the work of McGready and other ministers being secondary.

Both traditions agree that in the year 1800 John and William McGee decided to take a preaching tour which would extend as far north as Ohio. According to the second tradition, the McGees set up a loosely organized itinerary of two-day preaching appointments at various places, beginning with the Red River Meeting House on McGready's parish. They left the details of these services to be worked out by the local ministers, and McGready announced this first one as a sacramental meeting. When the McGees arrived, they found McGready with two Presbyterian minister friends, John Rankin and William Hodge, and a huge crowd of people. While all five ministers preached in these services, the revival broke wide open under the preaching of John McGee.[42]

The common tradition says that McGready had labored for three years to bring revival to his small parish, and finally had begun to see results. Consequently, he planned a sacramental meeting for June at the Red River Meeting House, no doubt praying that God would continue to revive the people. News may have reached the McGees that manifestations of a revival had begun to appear, and they obviously wanted to see it and participate themselves. It must have seemed natural to include the Red River sacramental occasion in their trip and, fortunately, they arrived in time to take part in the services. William McGee had known McGready and the other ministers back in Carolina, so he introduced his brother, and both were invited to preach.[43]

There are several primary sources available for the historian to piece together the tapestry of events which led to the revival explosion in the summer of 1800. Of course, care must be exercised in using these sources, and each must be allowed to speak for itself, making its own unique and valuable contribution. Moreover, each account must be interpreted from its own particular theological point of view. For example, McGee cannot accurately be explained from James McGready's Presbyterian standpoint, and vice versa. Furthermore, the language of each text must be carefully studied so that nothing may be read into or out of what the author meant to say. And, finally, it must be admitted that each source has omissions which are difficult to explain, and may contain errors of judgment or memory.

The earliest extant sources may be listed as follows:

1. John McGee's letter, dated October 27, 1800;[44]
2. James McGready's letter dated October 23, 1801;[45]
3. James McGready's letter to the *Methodist Magazine*;[46]
4. James McGready's "A Short Narrative," published in *The New York Missionary Magazine*;[47]
5. John McGee's letter, "Commencement of the Great Revival," published in the *Methodist Magazine*;[48]
6. John Rankin, "Autobiographical Sketch";[49]
7. T. Marshall Smith's *Legends of the War of Independence*;[50]
8. Captain Wallace Estill's account of the Gasper River services.[51]

McGee's early letter is tantalizingly brief, while the McGready material omits at least one very crucial fact, the participation of John McGee. The rest of the source material is either memoir or third-party accounts, and must be handled accordingly. The 1820 McGee letter cites 1799 instead of 1800 as the year he and William made their famous preaching tour. Rankin does not name John or William McGee, but quite obviously has them in mind, and corroborates events cited by McGee. The account by Captain Estill is an attempt to establish the Gasper River meeting as the first camp meeting. Marshall Smith provides many details not included in the other sources, but it is third-party material written over fifty years after the events described. The author, however, claimed to have heard much of it from the lips of John McGee.[52]

According to these sources, the services at Red River began on Saturday, June 21, and continued through Monday, June 23, 1800, with nearly 500 people in attendance. William McGee preached on Saturday, preparing the hearts of the people for the sacrament on the next day. However, things broke loose on Monday, "the great day," as McGee and McGready called it.[53] A woman shouted while William Hodge preached a powerful, moving sermon based on Job 22:21. He later said that he never before preached with such freedom and power of speech.[54] After a brief intermission John McGee rose to preach, and Smith wrote that he came to the pulpit singing,

> Come, holy spirit, heavenly dove
> With all thy quick'ning powers
> Kindle a flame of sacred love
> In these cold hearts of ours.[55]

All accounts say that a woman shouted at the beginning of John McGee's service, but Smith claimed *two* elderly women shouted, Mrs. Pacely, seated at McGee's far left, and Mrs. Clark, seated to his right.[56] He left the pulpit to go shake their hands, when the glory of God seemed to break out almost violently on the people. Some fell to the floor, screaming and praying for mercy, while others shouted aloud the praises of God. William McGee went down on the floor of the pulpit, and John almost fell himself, so strong did the power of God come upon him. In the fervency of the hour, he "went through the house shouting and exhorting with all possible ecstasy and energy, and the floor was soon covered with the slain."[57] Although McGready, Hodge, and Rankin had seen emotional outbursts before, and a few persons had actually fallen to the ground while they preached, these ministers stood aghast at what they witnessed at the Red River Meeting House. Never had they seen such extraordinary behavior in the house of God, and they consulted together as to what should be done. John Rankin advised McGready and Hodge to allow the service to run its course, lest they interfere with the work of God.[58] John McGee, long used to sudden and almost overwhelming displays of religious emotion, assured them that this represented a mighty outpouring of the Spirit of God. Rankin later wrote,

> On seeing and feeling his confidence, that it was the work of
> God, and a mighty effusion of his spirit, and having heard that he was
> acquainted with such scenes in another country, we acquiesced and
> stood in astonishment, admiring the wonderful works of God.[59]

These services at Red River created a sensation among the people, and the news spread rapidly over the surrounding territory that something extraordinary had taken place. At least three estimates of the number of conversions have been made, none of which seems exceptional, considering the size of the congregation and the overpowering presence of God.[60] In an effort to continue the spirit of revival, other services soon followed. McGready wrote that the next "remarkable outpouring of the Spirit of God" took place at the Gasper River Meeting House on the fourth Sunday in July.[61] McGee and Smith, however, offer an alternative view. Smith claimed that the McGees kept themselves busy with special services every week, at least for the month of June, and probably throughout the summer. McGee's early letter seems to agree.

After Red River the brothers held a meeting the next weekend at the Beech Meeting House, Sumner County, Tennessee, not far from Nashville. It attracted huge crowds, and nearly one hundred people professed conversion. The next weekend they preached at the Muddy River Meeting House, near Russelville, Tennessee, and here the revival truly caught fire. People came by the wagonload, prepared with victuals to stay for the duration of the services, and several hundred found spiritual help. Smith quoted Samuel Wilson as saying,

> My preacher also, Rev. James McGready, was for a time there among
> those crying for mercy, and never before, as he often told me
> afterwards, felt a scriptural assurance that he was born of God.[62]

John McGee later referred to Muddy River as a camp meeting.

Obviously, there is some disagreement among the sources regarding the sequence of the various meetings held during the summer of 1800. McGready wrote that five weeks separated the Red River and Gasper River services, but offered no explanation as to how they sustained the revival spirit. Rankin said they were only two weeks apart, and the early McGee letter appears to agree. However, McGee's later memoir letter and Smith's *Legends* claim that Muddy River came before the Gasper River services. Unfortunately, these seemingly conflicting accounts have led to a considerable amount of misunderstanding. Some scholars have accepted only the McGready reports, and have made little effort to reconcile them with the other material. The result is a very biased, one-sided treatment of one of the most important revivals in American religious history. When these sources are collated, it becomes apparent that ministers from various denominations conducted special services on a regular basis throughout that summer at several different locations. The services differed to some extent, that is, some were Presbyterian sacramental occasions, some were Methodist quarterly meetings and others were simply weekend evangelistic services. However, they all contributed to the ground swell of the movement, and finally caused the revival to explode into action on the Kentucky and Tennessee frontier.

Perhaps these services reminded John McGee of the camp meetings in which he had participated back in western North Carolina. With the arrival of summer the season was just right for people to sleep in their wagons or camp on the grounds, and a revival spirit already had been manifest. Several of the ministers had assembled, making it easy to divide the work of preaching among them. Advertising would not be difficult either, because the people were already talking about events at Red River, and they most certainly would tell the general public what had happened. The leaders would have to widely advertise the next meeting, and place heavy stress on the necessity of provisions for camping. It appears that McGready took care of the majority of those details. He urged the members of his churches to tell their friends, and "had it proclaimed far and wide . . . that he expected the people to encamp on the ground." Moreover, he sent "pressing invitations to ministers at distance," asking them to "come and see this strange work."[63] Word of mouth proved the best advertising for these services, and as summer wore on, interest grew until the crowds finally numbered in the thousands.

It is the thesis of this book that John McGee proposed the idea of a camp meeting in order to facilitate and spread the revival spirit that broke out in the summer of 1800, and he probably suggested the plan at the Red River meeting in June. He could then attend to his itinerary, preaching and promoting the revival among the Methodists, while McGready and his friends did the same among the Presbyterians. It was no accident that these denominations came together, or that the people brought wagons full of provisions to the Muddy River and Gasper River services, and arrived prepared to stay for several days. Someone suggested the idea to them, and *only* John McGee had prior knowledge as well as experience, having participated in the Grassy Branch Camp Meeting years before. When revival fires grew hot at Red River, under McGee's preaching by the way, Rankin reported that he [McGee] calmed their fears by telling the ministers "he was acquainted with such scenes in another country." Although Rankin does not name that other country, McGee undoubtedly meant North Carolina. He could not have meant his own work in Tennessee, due to its near proximity, for the other ministers, especially William McGee, would have known about such services and participated in them. John McGee obviously meant the camp meetings in North Carolina, and the spiritual genius of the man shows through in that he quickly realized how useful and productive that revival method could be in the present circumstances, and applied it to them with resounding success.[64]

Some scholars have been puzzled by the fact that James McGready did not claim the honor of being the founder of the camp meeting. John McGee did not claim that honor either, and both men should be praised for their honesty, because it belonged to neither one. This helps explain why scholars have been unable to pinpoint precisely when (or how) the founding of the camp meeting took place during the Great Revival; it did not begin then. John McGee transplanted the idea from the Carolinas to Kentucky and Tennessee, and worked hard to help insure its success in this new locale. In his own contexts, James McGready was also willing to work with this novel method of revivalism, and used it to help ignite the flame of the Great Revival. Both have earned a unique place in the history and tradition of the revival, and richly deserve the credit for their work.

The camp meeting and the Great Revival seemed made for each other. The revival needed what John Boles has called a "catalytic agent"[65] for its spontaneous spiritual combustion, and the camp meeting needed a springboard from which it could leap into the American consciousness. Once they found each other, both became part of the great "spiritual volcano," as Leonard Sweet has described it, that erupted on the frontier in 1800.[66] Scholars have pointed out many factors which contributed to the almost unbelievable success of the camp meeting (and the revival) during that early period, including its novelty, the social and spiritual needs of the people, the setting, the boisterous services with fiery preaching and exhortation, huge crowds singing, shouting, and praying, and especially the physical phenomena and exercises, such as falling, dancing, barking, and the almost legendary "jerks." People flocked to these meetings by the tens of thousands, and some claimed the millennium had begun.[67] In August 1801 as many as twenty-five thousand persons, including the Governor of Kentucky, attended the meeting at Cane Ridge near Paris, Kentucky. Many churches and ministers participated, and the evidence indicates that there were separate services for blacks.[68] Reports soon appeared in religious journals as far away as England, making the revival, and the camp meeting, a household word in America.

The versatility of this kind of revivalism became almost immediately apparent. It could be adapted to the particular needs of the frontier as well as the more staid ways of New England. It seemed not to know denominational barriers, and often helped bring the churches together, if only for a short while. It was mobile, and yet could become permanent at the same time. Mobility and ease of organization made the camp meeting indispensable to the wandering itinerant preachers, and they took it everywhere. Most early ones were conducted by streams or rivers to supply the need for water, refrigeration, and, perhaps, some relaxation. An area could quickly be cleared, a brush arbor erected for preaching, split logs smoothed and arranged for seats, and the camp meeting was on!

These rustic encampments, with their sensational and acrobatic emotional expression of religion, seemed to seize the American mind at the beginning of the nineteenth century. They helped scatter the red-hot coals of the Great Revival far and wide, and became festivals to celebrate the mighty work of God in a given community. Charles W. Ferguson has called them a "frolic of faith," and along with others has recognized the changes that these meetings helped bring to the American community.[69] However, as this revival fanned out in nearly every direction, powerful adverse reactions quickly surfaced. Not everybody appreciated the camp meeting, or the radical religious practices it espoused. Even before the initial wave of revival had passed, negative feelings grew so intense in some denominations that the ministers refused to use this new form of revivalism any longer.[70] Consequently, within the first decade or so after the Great Revival, the camp meeting almost became a Methodist institution.

## Methodism and the Camp Meeting

The leaders of the Methodist Episcopal Church, including Bishops Francis Asbury and William McKendree, understood the critical importance of the camp meeting. They saw it not only as a technique of revivalism, but also as a vital medium for church growth, and promoted its development on a large scale. Nathan Hatch may be correct that Asbury exaggerated the annual attendance figures for the encampments of 1811, but, even using Hatch's figure of 1.2 million attendance, at least a tenth of the total American population was reached that year.[71] Asbury's cry was "Camp meetings!,"[72] and they became a major vehicle of expansion for Methodism in the nineteenth century. Especially was this true for the first few decades, causing Methodist historian Cullen Carter to refer to the period 1800–1812 as "the greatest outpouring of the Holy Spirit since Pentecost."[73] In just twelve years the membership figures for the western region rose from a total of 2,801 to nearly 31,000. The number of annual encampments grew to about five hundred by 1811, and nearly one thousand by 1820. Asbury believed the millennium had begun.[74]

The camp meeting quickly proved how mobile and malleable it could be, and many methods of operation and organization became popular. It also very early demonstrated the power of its permanency, and proved the critics wrong by its lasting durability. No one knows where or when the first campground, with permanent arbor and tents, was built. It is almost a certainty that the Methodists can claim this honor, and the first logical choice would have to be one of the six southern encampments mentioned previously. Wherever it started, the idea of constructing permanent camp meeting sites rapidly spread. By 1810 Bishop Asbury encouraged the practice, and his letter to Jacob Gruber describes the construction of an early camp shed:

> If our encampments could be paid in every circuit and the bottom part of a meeting house (built) about 100 feet long and equal width, fences up about 5 feet high, a good floor, strong back benches, partition in the middle, passage on the sides, strong gates that would be the holy place, as much as one seat space left before the pulpit for mourners. In the front seat let all the officials sit. If the ground was floored it would be dry very soon for publick [sic] worship.[75]

Charles Johnson has shown that three basic designs were used in the layout of the frontier encampment, the circular, the oblong square, and the open horseshoe, with the circular being most popular.[76] Fortunately, descriptions and drawings of these early campgrounds have been preserved. For example, in 1809 Benjamin Henry Latrobe, an American architect and engineer, visited a camp meeting in Virginia, and sketched one of the earliest portrayals of the open horseshoe style.[77]

Jesse Lee included a detailed description of an oblong square in his 1810 history of Methodism, shedding considerable light on its set-up and organization. He told his readers that there were other "forms" for these meetings, but this was the only one he had used or seen in operation.[78] These early designs obviously became the pattern for the first permanent camp sites. Later campgrounds expanded them into far more elaborate schemes, such as the twelve-sided "biblical" plan of the Indian Field Camp Meeting in 1830. By mid-century, some camp meetings actually began to look like towns, and a few hired famous landscape designers to submit drawings for their development. For example, in 1866 Robert Morris Copeland helped design Oak Bluffs as a resort subdivision of the famous Wesleyan Grove Camp Meeting located on the island of Martha's Vineyard, Massachusetts. Copeland also drew the 1872 plans for the Shelter Island

Grove Association, a Methodist encampment located on Long Island, New York. Ellen Weiss claims,

> They took the pervasive American event, the camp-meeting revival
> in the woods, and brought it to spectacular conclusion in a form
> which has something to do with that pervasive American residential
> habit, the suburb. Both, after all, were intended as societies of the
> like-minded, with a strong family ideology, living in nature.[79]

Kirk Mariner has argued that a Methodist minister, the Reverend William Penn Chandler, refined some of the basic organizational needs of the camp meeting, and may have been the first to adapt a floor plan naming streets, etc. He also used special revival techniques, with two public altars, one for men and one for women, and kept records of attendance and the number of conversions. Moreover, he enforced the law on the campers, Methodist law, backing it up with a camp meeting jail.[80] Mariner is undoubtedly correct in his observation that "the camp meeting was to be a small, self-contained, and visibly godly state while it was in session."[81] The reason for that is not hard to discover, for the encampment itself had already become a powerful theological and eschatological symbol of the presence of God; it was holy ground. Reports about Chandler's success drew praise from Bishop Asbury, and not only fueled his desire to have more such meetings, but also may have provided a model of organizational style for others to use.[82]

The vision for the development of permanent campgrounds, with structures such as sheds, board tents, and other living quarters, succeeded in measure far beyond the limit of its dreamers. While it actually may have begun during the latter part of the Great Revival, the proliferation of these camps has continued to the present day. Nor did the establishment of such grounds spell the disintegration of the frontier camp meeting, as Charles Johnson has suggested.[83] Instead, it actually provided a new paradigm which enabled church leaders to adapt the camp meeting to the changes of society, and not let it atrophy as the frontier disappeared. This new vision brought new life and purpose to the camps, and new meaning of community for the church, for as the years passed loyalty and affection grew up around "the old campground." The people built crude, sturdy buildings from hand-hewn timber, sided and roofed with clapboard or shingles, and some of these sheds and cabins continued in use for more than three generations. A few of the sheds were huge. The Reverend Peter Cartwright, pioneer Methodist circuit rider and camp meeting preacher, said that some early sheds were capable of offering shelter to as many as five thousand persons.[84]

While none of the earliest sheds or tents has survived, historical architects have demonstrated that the style of the buildings continued almost unchanged through the years. Some early tents were built like a "party-wall dogtrot," an architectural form similar to the modern day row house, and one may still be seen at Spring Hill campground in Mississippi.[85] Ellen Weiss has suggested that the great open southern camp sheds "constitute an American building type," a "powerful architectural form from a vernacular tradition."[86] Of the camp sheds she examined which were listed on the National Registry of Historic Places, the oldest appeared to be the tabernacle at Rock Springs, North Carolina, built in 1832.[87]

The issue of permanent early campgrounds is a difficult one to explore. For one thing, thousands of such sites have existed around the country, and no exhaustive list of them has ever been made. Some were simply grounds donated by a local farmer where the meeting could be held on an annual basis. Such places often carried the name of the donating family, such as "Robey's Campground," in North Carolina. Others had a far more elaborate construction, consisting of a shed or tabernacle, and an area laid out for campers, perhaps including permanent tents and cottages. Most died out nearly a century or more ago, and their locations have been lost or forgotten. A few are still remembered by such signs as "Camp Ground Road," but now usually only the oldest local residents can recall that a camp meeting once stood nearby.

There are nearly 120 live encampments around the nation which were established in 1876 or earlier. Most of these were founded by Methodists, even those which claim interdenominational status. Some have become the property of other churches, and a few were founded by other denominations. The following table will provide an overview of these historic camp meetings.

| Name | City | State/Prov. | Year |
|------|------|-------------|------|
| Adams Camp | Auburn | MS | 1815 |
| Alton Bay Conference Center | Alton Bay | NH | 1863 |
| Asbury Grove Camp | South Hamilton | MS | 1859 |
| Ball's Creek Camp | Maiden | NC | 1853 |
| Battle Ground Camp | Battle Ground | IN | 1870 |
| Bay View Assembly | Petrosky | MI | 1875 |
| Bentleyville Camp | Bentleyville | PA | 1867 |
| Berwick Camp | Berwick | Nova Scotia | 1872 |
| Bethel Camp | Carrolton | GA | 1868 |
| Bethel Camp | Carthage | TX | 1860 |
| Bethlehem Camp | Climax | NC | 1854 |

| *Name* | *City* | *State/ Prov.* | *Year* |
|---|---|---|---|
| Brandywine Summit Camp | Delaware County | PA | 1865 |
| Camp Greene | Greene | RI | 1871 |
| Camp Sychar | Mt. Vernon | OH | 1870 |
| Camp Witwen | Prairie du Sac | WI | 1853 |
| Camp Woods | Ossining | NY | 1804 |
| Carey's Camp | Philips Hill | DE | 1875 |
| Carthage Camp | Carthage | TX | 1860 |
| Cattle Creek Camp | Branchville | SC | 1790 |
| Chautauqua Institution | Chautauqua | NY | 1874 |
| Cherry Run Camp | Rimersburg | PA | 1862 |
| Chester Heights Camp | Chester Heights | PA | 1872 |
| Claremont Union Camp | Claremont | NH | 1873 |
| Clear Lake Camp | Clear Lake | IA | 1875 |
| Connecticut Camp | Southington | CT | 1869 |
| Crystal Springs Camp | Dowagiac | MI | 1860 |
| Cypress Camp | Ridgeville | SC | 1794 |
| Dempster Grove Camp | New Haven | NY | 1875 |
| Des Plaines Camp | Des Plaines | IL | 1859 |
| Dimock Camp | Dimock | PA | 1862 |
| Douglas Camp | Douglas | MA | 1875 |
| Durley Camp | Greenville | IL | 1870 |
| East Livermore Camp | East Livermore | ME | 1847 |
| Ebenezer Camp | Center Point | AR | 1822 |
| Eleazer Camp | Madisonville | TN | 1840 |
| Emory Grove | Glyndon | MD | 1868 |
| Empire Grove Camp | East Poland | ME | 1834 |
| Felder's Camp | McComb | MS | 1810 |
| Frost Bridge Camp | Waynesboro | MS | 1850 |
| Hedding Camp | Epping | NH | 1862 |
| Herndon Camp | Herndon | PA | 1874 |
| Hertz Grove Camp | Bonfield | IL | 1853 |
| Holbrook Camp | Holbrook | GA | 1838 |
| Hollow Rock Camp | Toronto | OH | 1818 |
| Indian Field Camp | St. George | SC | 1795 |
| Iowa Conference Camp | Birmingham | IA | 1874 |
| Cedar Springs Camp | Cedar Springs | IA | 1853 |
| Jacksonville Camp | East Machias | ME | 1865 |
| Jonesville Camp | Jonesville | VA | 1810 |
| Kavanaugh Camp | Crestwood | KY | 1875 |

| Name | City | State/ Prov. | Year |
|------|------|------------|------|
| La Grange Tabernacle Camp | Leighton | AL | 1870 |
| Lake Creek Camp | Smithton | MO | 1843 |
| Lakeside Assembly Grounds | Lakeside | OH | 1872 |
| Lancaster Camp | Lancaster | OH | 1872 |
| Landisville Camp Meeting | Landisville | PA | 1867 |
| Laurel Park Camp | Northampton | MA | 1872 |
| Lawrenceville Camp | Lawrenceville | GA | 1832 |
| Lebanon Camp | Lebanon | GA | 1845 |
| Lena Camp | Lena | IL | 1870 |
| Little Texas Camp | Tuskegee | AL | 1828 |
| Loudsville Camp | Cleveland | GA | 1838 |
| Lumpkin Camp | Dawsonville | GA | 1830 |
| McKenzie's Camp | Catawba County | NC | 1850 |
| Maine District Camp | Richmond | ME | 1870 |
| Malaga Camp | Newfield | NJ | 1869 |
| Marietta Camp | Marietta | GA | 1837 |
| Martha's Vineyard Camp | Martha's Vineyard | MA | 1835 |
| Methodist Camp Grounds | Chappel | TX | 1858 |
| Morrison Camp | Rome | GA | 1868 |
| Mossy Creek Camp | Cleveland | GA | 1833 |
| Mott's Grove Camp | Catawba County | NC | 1850 |
| Mt. Gilead Camp | Atlanta (Ben Hill) | GA | 1824 |
| Mount Moriah Camp | Matthews | GA | 1827 |
| Mt. Olivet Camp | Dillsburg | PA | 1862 |
| Mt. Tabor Camp | Mt. Tabor | NJ | 1866 |
| Mt. Zion Camp | Griffin | GA | 1834 |
| National Camp | Glendale | TN | 1873 |
| Ocean Grove Camp | Ocean Grove | NJ | 1869 |
| Old Lebanon Camp | Ackerman | MS | 1850 |
| Old Orchard Beach Camp | Old Orchard Beach | ME | 1870 |
| Patterson Grove Camp | Huntington Mills | PA | 1835 |
| Pine Log Camp | Dalton | GA | 1842 |
| Pitman Grove Camp | Pitman | NJ | 1870 |
| Plainville Camp | Plainville | CN | 1865 |
| Pleasant Hill Camp | Franklin County | TX | 1873 |
| Poplar Springs | Canon | GA | 1832 |
| Red Rock District | Paynesville | MN | 1868 |
| Redding Springs Camp | Weddington | NC | 1854 |

| Name | City | State/Prov. | Year |
|------|------|------------|------|
| Rock Springs Camp | Denver | NC | 1794 |
| Round Lake District | Round Lake | NY | 1867 |
| Ruggles Camp | Tollesboro | KY | 1873 |
| Salem Camp | Benton | AR | 1838 |
| Salem Camp | Covington | GA | 1828 |
| Salem Camp | Jackson County | MS | 1826 |
| Santa Claus Camp | Santa Claus | IN | 1849 |
| Seashore Methodist Assembly | Biloxi | MS | 1870 |
| Seaville Camp | South Seaville | NJ | 1864 |
| Shady Grove Camp | Harleyville | SC | 1860 |
| Sherman's Camp | Sherman | IL | 1871 |
| Shiloh Camp | Carrolton | GA | 1867 |
| Shiloh Camp | Pilahatchie | MS | 1832 |
| Shingleroof Camp | McDunnough | GA | 1831 |
| Simpson Park Camp | Romeo | MI | 1864 |
| South Union Camp | Ackerman | MS | 1872 |
| Spring Creek Camp | | TN | 1850 |
| St. Paul's Camp | Harleyville | SC | 1860 |
| Sterling Camp | Sterling | MA | 1852 |
| Stoverdale Camp | Hummelstown | PA | 1872 |
| Sulpher Springs Camp | Morristown | TN | 1820 |
| Tabernacle Camp | Brownsville | TN | 1826 |
| Tabernacle Camp | Columbus | AL | 1828 |
| Tabernacle Camp | Marquette Heights | IL | 1852 |
| Tarentum Camp | Natrona Heights | PA | 1849 |
| Tarentum Camp | Tarentum | PA | 1849 |
| Tattnal County Camp | Reidsville | GA | 1820 |
| Thousand Island Park | Orleans | NY | 1875 |
| Torrence Chapel Camp | Troutman | NC | 1867 |
| Tucker's Grove Camp | Machpelah | NC | 1794 |
| Unity Grove Camp | Reform | AL | 1842 |
| West Chazy Camp | West Chazy | NY | 1842 |
| White Oak Camp | Thomson | GA | 1842 |
| Willimantic Camp | Willimantic | CT | 1860 |
| Winnepesaukee Camp | The Weirs, Laconia | NH | 1868 |
| Yarmouth Camp | Yarmouth | MA | 1819 |

The question has persisted in scholarly circles as to why Methodism so informally claimed the camp meeting, and yet relied upon it so heavily through the years. Russell E. Richey has suggested that Methodism adopted the camp meeting as a kind of "historical drama" of its own history, a method by which the church could draw upon and share the spiritual vitality that created it. Born amid the spirit of revival, the camp meeting provided Methodism with a medium with which it could safely evolve and yet maintain its original image of revival. "In short," Richey suggests, "the camp meeting allowed Methodism to change while appearing to remain the same."[88]

Richey's keen observation has much to commend it, for the Methodists quickly discovered how well this new measure of revivalism blended in with their styles of organizational structure and their vision for society. They could take the camp meeting idea nearly anywhere, and almost did. Moreover, they could apply it to practically anything, and almost did that, too. The Reverend Lorenzo Dow, eccentric independent Methodist pioneer preacher, took the idea to England, and in spite of bitter opposition by British Methodist authorities, inspired the first British encampment at Mow Cop in 1807. In 1842 the Reverend Apollos Hale, a Methodist minister captivated by William Miller's second advent preaching, helped organize the first Second Advent Camp Meeting in the United States, drawing up to ten thousand worshipers. Miller delivered his famous lectures, and within two years his followers conducted more than one hundred such gatherings annually. Thirty years later the Reverend William B. Osborn, far-sighted Methodist minister and founder of Ocean Grove, New Jersey, established holiness resorts like Ocean Grove in Florida, Niagara Falls, the great Northwest, and eventually Australia and India. The camp meeting became a worldwide institution.[89]

At about the same time, a few church leaders applied the camp meeting idea to two prominent social issues, temperance and the women's movement. The National Temperance Camp-Meeting Association was officially organized at the 1874 session of the Maine Temperance Camp Meeting, held at Old Orchard Beach, Maine. Deliberately patterned after the famous national holiness association, this new organization conducted temperance encampments at various sites around the nation for several years.[90] Mrs. Mary D. James linked these two issues and in 1877 helped organize the Women's Gospel Temperance Camp Meeting at Ocean Grove, New Jersey. Great crowds gathered to hear a powerful battery of women speakers which included the first president of the Women's Christian Temperance Union, Mrs. Annie Wittenmyer.[91] In 1880, Mrs. O. M. Fitzgerald and other women holiness leaders founded the Women's Union

Holiness Camp Meeting, which met annually for many years at Mt. Tabor, New Jersey.[92]

These particular usages of the camp meeting came from Methodists and former Methodists who saw and appreciated the role the institution could play in their efforts to impact society with the gospel of Christ. Other new innovative ideas also appeared during that time, some from the Methodist community, some from without, and all served to bring a new kind of ministry to the old campground. These innovations have brought lasting change to the institution of the camp meeting, and have expanded its ministry in ways that the church at large can enjoy and use yet today.


## Modern Camp Meeting Developments

Change has affected the camp meeting since its beginning in the backwoods of Georgia and Carolina. Within twenty years of its founding new concepts were introduced which would make the encampment a permanent fixture on the American landscape. The bifurcation of mobility and permanency had undoubtedly become fairly well established between 1815 and 1825, and helped make possible the remarkable growth and vitality of the institution in the years ahead. The camp meeting could be used on an annual transitory basis, and at the same time become an established religious organization in any given community. It followed the frontier, yet did not become a frontier institution because in many instances it planted roots in the native soil of the very communities it served.

Those who have studied the camp meeting have often been perplexed by this seeming double paradox, and have gone to great lengths in order to explain it. However, much of the problem stems from the false assumptions which have been made about the camp meeting and its history. For example, it has been assumed that the early encampments were always and only crude transient frontier meetings, and nothing else. It was a "frontier camp meeting."[93] It has been assumed that no permanent campgrounds were constructed in the Midwest before the 1830s, and Charles Johnson has gone so far as to suggest an 1850 date for the beginning of camp sheds in Georgia. He is at least twenty years too late.[94] It often has been claimed that the camp meeting slipped into a serious state of decline before the Civil War, and was literally in danger of dying out. Methodist historian William Warren Sweet thought so, and Johnson agreed, calling this period a "collapse," a "disintegration." He offered several possible explanations, including the disappearance of the frontier, the rise of permanent campgrounds, the growth of the protracted meeting as a means of revivalism, and the publication of camp meeting manuals.[95] Some have claimed that the Methodists actually over-organized the institution, causing its demise, while others have suggested it began to "die out" due to the awful spiritual lethargy which ran rampant before and after the Civil War.[96]

Many campgrounds did die during those years, just like many individual churches, due to the ebb and flow of society. If the population shifted, and people moved away, or if the interest of the churches waned and the base of support died, the local encampment might cease to exist. However, the camp meeting most certainly did not begin to disintegrate, or die out as an institution; instead, it began to change and adapt to the needs of society. If there ever was a "frontier camp meeting," it started a process of semi-metamorphosis almost as soon as it came into being, certainly before the frontier disappeared. Some contemporaries bitterly complained about this turn of events, but wise church leaders understood and appreciated the need for such modifications. They realized that unless the camp meeting could grow to meet a changing society it would not and could not survive, and the church would lose a powerful and constructive resource.

Shortly after the Civil War several major developments took place, each one affecting the use and application of the camp meeting. These adaptations and alterations were applied with amazing success, and each may be considered a genre in its own right. It is difficult to separate these different modifications chronologically; they are all entwined to some degree, so the following outline has been imposed:

1   the camp meeting as a religious resort;
2.   the holiness camp meeting;
3.   the Bible and Prophecy Conference;
4.   the Chautauqua Institution;
5.   the denominational camp meeting;
6.   the pentecostal camp meeting; and
7.   the family camping movement.

## The Camp Meeting as Religious Resort

The Wesleyan Grove Camp Meeting at Martha's Vineyard, Massachusetts, appears to have paved the way for what Charles Parker has called the "Methodist religious resort."[97] Railway and steamship lines vastly improved public transportation, and as the middle class began to travel for vacations, camp meeting resorts were soon established as a religious alternative to such places as Newport, Rhode Island; Coney Island, New York; and Atlantic City, New Jersey. Some of the new camp meeting resorts developed a full schedule of summer programs which included Chautauqua, weeklong services for children and youths, a Bible Conference, special patriotic rallies, and the annual camp meeting. Such programs often featured nationally known speakers and attracted enormous crowds. It is said that as many as 300,000 persons visited the Ocean Grove, New Jersey, complex in 1883.

Charles Parker has suggested that by establishing such summer Christian resorts, as many as sixty new campgrounds were founded by the sea along the Atlantic coast from Maine to Florida, and near lakes, woodlands, and mountains from the East Coast to the Midwest. In actuality, visionaries like the Reverend William B. Osborn extended the Christian resort idea nationwide, and between 1860 and 1890 the Methodists founded camp meeting resorts from coast to coast. Nor were they alone in this process. Stanford E. Demars has shown that during the same time frame other religious groups, such as the Baptists and the Christian Church of California, also established camp meeting resorts. When considered together, these, too, extended coast to coast.[98]

Over the years many of these campgrounds have developed into incorporated municipalities. Places like Martha's Vineyard, Massachusetts; Ocean Grove, Pitman Grove, and Mount Tabor, New Jersey; Ocean Park and Old Orchard Beach, Maine; Round Lake and Shelter Island, New York; Lakeside, Ohio; Mount Lebanon, Pennsylvania; Rehoboth Beach, Delaware; Mountain Lake Park, Maryland; and Pacific Grove, California, have become actual communities in their own right. Most are now inactive, as camp meetings go, but some still conduct an annual encampment.

One other development may have come out of the rise of the camp meeting resort, the formation of the camp meeting association. Present research has not established when the first one was established, but these associations became very popular after the Civil War, and literally sprang up all over the nation. Acting as a governing body for the campground, many became incorporated and some performed as if they were actual municipalities, passing laws and governing life in the camp meeting community. This led to sore trials later, and raised the question of the separation of church and state, as in the famous case involving Ocean Grove, New Jersey. Most of the associations leased land to the cottage-holders, and so maintained control over the property. Some, however, such as the camp meeting in Pitman, New Jersey, actually sold lots outright, consequently losing control of the property and, eventually, their own destiny.[99]

## The Holiness Camp Meeting

The formation of this specialized encampment was heavily influenced by the earlier work of Methodist lay evangelists, Phoebe, Sarah, and Walter Palmer, who for over fifty years promoted the doctrine of Christian perfection. Phoebe, the leader of this lay trio, developed an "altar theology," and used the slogan "the altar sanctifies the gift" to exemplify and simplify her teaching for the masses. The Palmers became virtual legends in the upcoming holiness revival, partially due to the scope of their work. Sarah and Phoebe established an informal parlor meeting for holiness, the famous "Tuesday Meeting," whose extended ministry covered at least seventy years. The three of them preached and taught at churches and camp meetings in the United States, Canada, and Great Britain. Walter and Phoebe owned and edited one of the famous religious periodicals of the day, the *Guide to Holiness*, and its life covered more than sixty years. They also published books and other holiness literature, and helped influence thousands of persons in the quest of the holy life.[100]

Founded in an effort to propagate the Methodist doctrine of Christian perfection, the "holiness camp meeting" appears to have been the brainchild of the Reverend John A. Wood, a Methodist pastor and author of the religious best seller, *Perfect Love*. The idea quickly caught fire in the hearts of the "friends of holiness," and at a meeting in Philadelphia they laid plans to conduct the first encampment at Vineland, New Jersey, in July 1867. The committee chose "The National Camp Meeting for the Promotion of Christian Holiness" as the official name, and some 10,000 persons came on Sunday to hear renowned Methodist Bishop Matthew Simpson preach. More than 25,000 gathered for the second National Camp Meeting at Manheim, Pennsylvania, in 1868, and leaders advertised the encampment at Round Lake, New York, in 1869 as an "expected pentecost." By 1870 these gatherings had become a grass roots movement which claimed thousands of followers, and made the ministers national celebrities.[101] The National Association, as it came to be called, elected the Reverend John S. Inskip, a Methodist pastor and former Civil War Chaplain, as its first president, and under his fiery and aggressive leadership holiness camp meetings were held coast to coast. He and the Reverend William McDonald, vice president of the association, crisscrossed the nation as a team of holiness evangelists, preaching, teaching, and promoting their cause in numerous ways.[102]

The national camp meetings and the work of the National Association served as the prototype for a larger ministry yet to appear.

Permanent interdenominational holiness camps were introduced shortly after the Vineland meeting, and it seems that Ocean Grove, New Jersey, founded in 1869, might have been the first.[103] Camp Sychar, located near Mt. Vernon, Ohio, founded in 1870, appears to be next, followed by well over a thousand permanent holiness camps founded since that time.[104] Interestingly, the rise of the camp meeting resort seemed to coincide with the burgeoning popularity of this new holiness revival, and several such resorts were founded by holiness leaders. Along with these encampments and holiness resorts must be considered the almost innumerable transient holiness camps which various groups have conducted over the years. All of them have been established as specifically holiness camp meetings, and as such constitute a genre all their own within the context of camp meeting studies.

The question is sometimes asked, "Which one of these is the oldest holiness camp meeting?" Circumstances make that question a difficult one to answer, for some camps must use a double schema of dates. The Hollow Rock Camp Meeting near Steubenville, Ohio, is an excellent example. It has claimed to be the oldest holiness encampment, indeed, it has claimed to be the oldest continuous camp meeting in the country. It is neither. Several other continuous camps are older than its 1818 founding date, and the holiness association did not take over the grounds until 1877.[105] By that time several other permanent holiness camps had already been established. Hollow Rock did quickly emerge as one of the premier holiness camp meetings in the nation, and always drew thousands of persons to its services. It, along with hundreds of other camps, helped bring the holiness movement before the public eye and keep it there.

From this very successful beginning, the National Association expanded its ministry in many ways. It touched the soul of several denominations, and even spread its influence overseas.[106] It encouraged the formation of other holiness associations, and promoted the work of holiness evangelists and other holiness ministries, such as holiness publishing houses, holiness missions and mission agencies, and holiness training schools and colleges. They even called this living kaleidoscope the "holiness movement," and it eventually led to the formation of several holiness denominations. The Bishops of the Methodist Episcopal Church, South, criticized the movement, however, claiming these people had holiness as a "watchword." The leaders meant to; it was their specialty.[107]

Perhaps for the first seventy-five years of its history, the holiness movement could be compared to a huge expanding spoked wheel, with the holiness camp meeting as the hub. In 1924 the Reverend Joseph H. Smith, dean of holiness preachers and evangelists, and soon to be president of the National Association wrote:

> The Camp Meeting is still the unit and the center of the Holiness Movement. Neither the convention, nor the evangelist, nor the paper, nor the training school, nor the college; no, nor the Holiness church is *it*. These are but auxiliaries, some of them but incidents and the best of them but products of the Holiness Camp Meeting.[108]

By this Smith meant that the camp meeting served as a channel and clearinghouse for nearly every agency of the holiness movement. The mission agencies, the publishing houses, the schools, and even the evangelists themselves were products of the holiness camps, and depended on them for their support. "In fact," Smith wrote, "all these auxiliaries and adjuncts of the Holiness Movement center in and radiate from the Interdenominational Holiness Camp Meeting." And he said, "We repeat the *Camp Meeting is the unit of the Movement*."[109]

Smith's comments clearly reveal how some leaders felt about the holiness camp meeting in its relationship to the holiness movement at large. The National Association started on a campground, and its leaders declared from the beginning that conducting holiness camp meetings was one of its primary functions. The Reverend Henry Clay Morrison, an outstanding southern Methodist holiness evangelist who founded the *Pentecostal Herald* and Asbury Theological Seminary, wrote that the holiness camps were one of the greatest facts in the modern holiness movement. He called them "conservators of orthodoxy," and claimed that they drew at least one-half million persons each summer. This may help explain the almost exalted position of the camp meeting in the strategy and thinking of many holiness leaders, and why some believed the holiness movement might actually save the camp meeting as an institution for the church.[110]

The holiness camp meeting is still an active and growing part of the holiness movement and the American religious scene. It most emphatically is not dying out; new ones are founded almost every year. To better understand this genre, it has been divided into three categories: denominational, associational/organizational, and interdenominational encampments. The denominational camps include all the self-styled churches within the holiness movement, from the most radical groups with the strictest standards, to those most liberal with seemingly the fewest standards. These holiness churches conduct hundreds of encampments each year, and the list grows as the denominations increase in number. The associational/organizational camps are conducted by groups that may appear to be a denomination, but who do not consider themselves as such. These groups sponsor as many as seventy-five camps each year. The interdenominational camps may be conducted by members of several churches or associations and organizations, but they are operated on a completely independent basis. These camps once formed the backbone of the holiness movement, and there are still hundreds of them held on an annual basis. It is, perhaps, a matter of debate as to their status in that movement today.

## The Bible and Prophecy Conference Movement

The Bible and Prophecy Conference movement in the United States has been heavily influenced by the Prophecy Conference and Higher Life movements in Europe, and special recognition must be given to the Mildmay Prophecy Conference and the Keswick Convention. The latter, founded in 1875, could trace its history to the American holiness movement through the work of such leaders as Robert P. and Hannah W. Smith, who helped ignite the holiness revival in England and on the continent.[111]

In the United States the Bible and Prophecy Conference movement held much the same place for early fundamentalists as the camp meeting did for the friends of holiness. While no history of the movement has yet appeared, Ernest Sandeen, Timothy Weber, George Marsden, and David Beale have briefly told its story in the context of the revival of premillennialism that swept across Europe and America during the last half of the nineteenth century. Revival is the key word to describe that movement, too, for it had a powerful effect on American evangelical denominations through the work of such prominent evangelists as Dwight L. Moody and "Billy" Sunday. In fact, Moody is sometimes given the credit for founding the first Bible Conference assembly in the United States, his famous Northfield Bible Conference, founded in 1880.

Although some scholars have difficulty trying to explain it, a large number of Methodists joined the new premillennial revival. These included many key leaders of the holiness movement, and they, along with others, helped bring the Bible and prophecy conferences to the camp meeting platform.[112] The Believer's Meeting for Bible Study, later to become the world-famous Niagara Bible Conference, "the mother of them all," as Sandeen says, met a few times on campgrounds, including Old Orchard, Maine, and, in 1900, Asbury Park, New Jersey, part of the Ocean Grove camp meeting complex. This was nothing new to Ocean Grove. Methodist evangelist Leander W. Munhall had established an "Inter-denominational Bible Conference" there in 1888, and brought some of the foremost teachers and preachers of premillennialism into that bastion of postmillennialism.[113]

Interestingly, 1900 proved to be the last year for the Niagara Bible Conference, and holding a session at the popular Asbury Park/Ocean Grove may have been a last ditch effort to save it.

The camp meeting and Bible/prophecy conference movements have interacted with and influenced each other in a number of ways over the years. The physical structure and setting of the campground undoubtedly served as the pattern for some permanent Bible conference grounds. They often looked alike, including the tabernacle, cottages, kitchen, and dorms, and had the same setting, designed for spiritual emphasis in a relaxed atmosphere. The Montrose Bible Conference is a good example. Founded by Dr. Reuben A. Torrey in 1908, tucked away in northeastern Pennsylvania, it resembled any one of a hundred camp meeting grounds.[114] By the early 1900s several such established conference grounds had appeared around the country, all of them vying for the patronage of vacationing fundamentalists. Some changed their name to "assembly"; others called themselves "Christian retreats." Both revealed a heightened perspective of ministry, and none became more famous than Winona Lake, Indiana. Purposely established to combine the best in Bible and prophecy conference, Chautauqua and assembly, it drew thousands of visitors each year to hear the preaching of a "Billy" Sunday or the music of a John Philip Sousa.

The Bible and prophecy conference exerted tremendous theological influence in some circles of the camp meeting movement, and there premillennialism gained more than just respectability; it became a militant creed. Americans had seen premillennial camp meetings before, as in the case of the Second Advent Camp Meeting, held by the Millerites in 1842. But by the turn of the century the campground had once again become a battleground, and again the war of words centered around the second coming of Christ. The National Association refused to allow premillennialism to be preached or taught at any of the camp meetings it sponsored, and called the issue a "side track."[115] Opponents responded in kind, and the holiness movement, like the fundamentalist movement before it, experienced polarization over the eschatological issues of the day.[116]

Like the camp meeting, the Bible and prophecy conference movement changed over the years. Some conferences never did establish permanent grounds, and the Niagara Bible Conference may be the best example. Others did, but were still forced to adapt to the changing times, and perhaps the best illustration of that is Winona Lake, Indiana. Founded in 1894 by Dr. Solomon Dickey, a Presbyterian minister, deliberately patterned after Moody's Northfield Bible Conference and the Chautauqua Institute, this location became the foremost fundamentalist resort in the Midwest. By the 1920s it could boast the Winona Lake School of

Theology, the annual Bible/Prophecy Conference, and a Chautauqua program that often filled the huge 7,500 seat "Billy Sunday Tabernacle." Within twenty years, however, progress, in the name of paved streets and a modern disposal system, had so strapped the institution with debt that it faced bankruptcy and had to be reorganized. In 1938 it was chartered as "Winona Lake Christian Assembly, Inc.," and continues its ministries today under that name.[117]

The Bible conference and assembly grounds still maintain an active role in the life of the church. Most have upgraded their programs to include family camping, and offer sessions for children, youths, and adults throughout the year. Others also include specialty ministries, sponsoring meetings for women only, workshops on missions and evangelism, marriage enrichment seminars, etc. While a large number of the Bible conference and assembly grounds are controlled and operated by independent organizations, most sites are owned and sponsored by the various denominations. Counting them together, there may be as many as one thousand such locations around the country.

### The Chautauqua Movement

If the holiness camp meeting must be seen as a specialty for the promotion of the doctrine of the holy life, then the Chautauqua must also be viewed as a specialty, and might be called "the Sunday School camp meeting." Interestingly, that very idea occurred to Lewis Miller, prominent Ohio Methodist layman, inventor, and educator, and he expressed it to some friends while attending the 1872 session of the Ohio State Camp Meeting for the Promotion of Holiness.[118] He and the Reverend John H. Vincent, later to become Bishop, had been working on plans for a national educational institute which would provide serious training for Sunday School teachers. At the Ohio encampment, Miller told a few friends that he had considered using the camp meeting idea as the setting for the proposed institute, and they approved. One of the ladies had attended the Fair Point Camp Meeting on Chautauqua Lake, New York, and highly praised that location to Miller. He soon visited the site, realized the possibilities, and joined its governing body as a trustee. Within a year Miller convinced John Vincent of the feasibility and practicality of using those campgrounds as the site for their newly proposed institute. By October 1873, the official committee had been formed, and it immediately began to plan the first

Sunday-school Teachers Assembly to be held at the Fair Point Camp Ground in August 1874.[119]

The success of the first assembly proved to Miller and Vincent the worth of their dreams, and the Chautauqua became famous overnight. It was definitely *not* a camp meeting, and its designers deliberately planned it that way. Some leaders criticized that move severely. Methodist holiness advocate Joseph H. Smith called the Chautauqua a "perversion" of the camp meeting, and based his views mostly on the complete lack of evangelistic emphases.[120] Miller and Vincent, however, had visioned Chautauqua differently, and purposely planned it as a religious educational institute. They used the camp meeting idea because they realized that the grounds inspired relaxation and recreation, and provided a perfect setting for such an assembly. Crowds had thronged the place, and put up with leaky roofs, tent living, and rules such as "No giggling after ten o'clock—no chopping of wood before six."[121]

Although founded by Methodists, and on a Methodist campground, Chautauqua quickly became a national institution in its own right, one that knew no denominational barriers. The camp meeting grounds which housed the first assembly became the campus of the world-famous Chautauqua Institution, and its growth has been dramatic. Starting with just fifty acres and a few rustic buildings, Chautauqua now covers more than 700 acres, and its landscape is dotted with modern buildings constructed over the years by various denominations. The program quickly grew into an eight-week summer course, and then expanded to include such things as a series of public lectures, concerts, entertainment, and the famous CLSC. The Chautauqua Literary and Scientific Circle, a guided reading course designed for persons with limited educational opportunities, ultimately enrolled nearly one million persons from around the world.[122] Like the camp meeting, the Chautauqua idea quickly leap-frogged around the nation. The Methodist encampments at Petrosky, Michigan, and Lakeside, Ohio, were among the first to adopt the summer assembly programs and have a Chautauqua on their grounds. Other camps quickly followed suit, as did some community sites, and by 1904 at least 150 independent Chautauquas had sprung up across the country. Within five years some entrepreneurs considered taking the institute on the road, but none was truly successful until Keith Vawter designed and implemented what came to be called the "circuit Chautauqua." This traveling show moved by train from town to town, putting on the Chautauqua program each night under a huge canvas tent. The communities bought a packaged contract deal, guaranteed the funding, and booked "the greatest aggregation of public performers the world has ever known."[123] By 1921, about the peak of the circuit movement, nearly one hundred Chautauqua circuits served 9,597 communities, and sold almost forty million tickets.[124]

Theodore Morrison has referred to the circuit Chautauqua as a "social phenomenon" of American culture. On that platform millions of Americans heard some of the most famous, controversial, and inspirational speakers of the day, such as three-time presidential candidate William Jennings Bryan, Senator Albert Beveridge, labor leader Samuel Gompers, and the Reverend Russell Conwell, famous for his speech, "Acres of Diamonds." On that platform Americans also watched plays and operas, saw the newest developments in science and industry, enjoyed all sorts of vaudeville acts, and listened to every conceivable form of music. Legend even has it that the male barbershop quartet originated on the Chautauqua circuits. They called it "culture under canvas," and Americans feasted on it for nearly thirty years.[125]

Chautauqua still exists at many locations around the country, including the original site on Chautauqua Lake in New York, now called the "Chautauqua Institution." It still sponsors religious and cultural events, and conducts a yearly convention at one of the Chautauqua sites. An association has been formed, and the *Chautauqua Network News* keeps the membership informed regarding events, news, and publications.

## The Denominational Camp Meeting

The denominational camp meeting probably began with the Methodists, although as Charles Johnson has pointed out, "It was never an official institution of that denomination."[126] However, as Russell Richey demonstrated, the camp meeting did become a "national quasi-official institution" of Methodism because of the essential revivalistic continuity it provided between the quarterly meeting and the annual conference, and he called that a "unity of revival and machinery."[127] Many modern denominational camps offer strong support to Richey's thesis, for they often accomplish the same result. They, too, provide a unity of "evangelism and organization," and offer the denomination a vehicle with which it can continue to expand, and at the same time maintain the original image of revival. Some churches have district as well as national encampments, with the organizational work of the denomination being done in session at the campground, often just prior to the annual camp meeting.[128] Some denominations have taken the process even further, and have established the encampment as the official "space" of the church. The campground serves not only as the locus for revival, it is also the location of the district center, and perhaps the denominational headquarters. For these churches the camp meeting indeed has become holy ground.[129]

It is uncertain when the denominational encampment first appeared as a genre in its own right. While the Methodists certainly conducted more camps than anyone else, it is clear that many denominations sponsored and conducted camp meetings during the nineteenth century, including the black Methodist churches, the Presbyterians, the Millerites, the Wesleyan Methodists, the Free Methodists, the Seventh-day Adventists, the Church of God, the Universalists, and the Spiritualists. Present evidence suggests that the Seventh-day Adventist Church may have conducted the first truly denominational general encampment at Wright, Michigan, in September 1868, and many others soon followed.[130] The Wesleyan Methodists, Presbyterians, and Free Methodists held encampments much earlier, but it appears that they had the same quasi-official relationship to their denominations as the earlier Methodist camp meetings did. It may be that the rise of the National Camp Meeting Association in 1867, and the plethora of interdenominational holiness camps which followed, provided the impetus for the holiness denominations to establish official encampments of their own. It is known that some of the later holiness churches, such as the Pillar of Fire Church, the Church of the Nazarene, the Churches of Christ in Christian Union, and the Pilgrim Holiness Church, established the camp meeting as an official institution within the denomination. Pentecostal churches, such as the Apostolic Faith, the Assemblies of God, and the Pentecostal Fire Baptized Holiness Church, did the same.[131]

The denominational encampment is perhaps the strongest arm of the camp meeting movement in the world today. It is not known exactly how many annual camps the various churches do conduct, but the number is without question well above two thousand, and this does not count children's or youth camps. Most of these are small, with an average attendance of less than one thousand per service. However, their overall impact has been tremendous, and they will undoubtedly continue to benefit the churches who use them.

## The Pentecostal Camp Meeting

The pentecostal camp meeting has been an integral part of the revival which produced the modern pentecostal charismatic movement, and that story has been so well told as to need no repetition here.[132] Practically every pentecostal evangelist and denomination used or participated in camp meetings and it became part of the standard fare in pentecostal revivalism. Evidence suggests that some pentecostal preachers conducted encampments even before the famous Azusa Street Revival in Los Angeles. Charles Parham certainly did, as in the case of the 1905 Apostolic Faith camps in Columbus, Kansas, and Houston, Texas, and there were probably others. However, for obvious reasons, perhaps all the permanent pentecostal camps should date after the "American Jerusalem," as Vinson Synan has called the spiritual earthquake which struck the Azusa Street Mission in April 1906.[133]

The tremors of the Los Angeles revival spawned several new pentecostal denominations, and they in turn began holding pentecostal camp meetings all over the nation. Mrs. Florence L. Crawford founded the Apostolic Faith Mission in Portland, Oregon, and the new organization held its first encampment in 1907.[134] Others quickly followed suit, with the Pentecostal Holiness Church sponsoring at least five encampments by 1910, and Parham's loosely organized Apostolic Faith conducting at least fifteen camps by 1913.[135] Like the holiness movement before it, the pentecostal movement used the camp meeting as a key ingredient in revivalism, and by the 1920s pentecostal encampments, transitory and permanent, were held all over the country by roving evangelists as well as newly formed denominations.

The question of the oldest continuous pentecostal camp meeting is bound to be asked and, like that regarding the oldest holiness encampment, this, too will be difficult to answer. Some may point to the Pleasant Grove Camp Meeting, near Durant, Florida, founded in 1885, or the Falcon Camp Meeting, near Dunn, North Carolina, founded in 1900. Neither camp, however, was founded as a pentecostal encampment; both were taken over by pentecostals at a later time, and a double dating schema must be used for each.[136] The Apostolic Faith camp meeting in Portland, Oregon, was founded by pentecostals who came directly from the Azusa Street revival, and has a continuous history at several locations since 1907. It may well qualify as the oldest continuous pentecostal encampment.

The pentecostal camp meeting as a genre should also be divided into three categories, and for the same basic reasons as those used with the holiness encampments. The categories are denominational, associational/organizational, and interdenominational. While it is not known how many pentecostal camps are conducted each year, the first two categories are probably the largest, and the total number may exceed two thousand. Moreover, as with the holiness camp meeting, this one, also, is most assuredly not dying out. New ones have been organized almost annually, and this trend will undoubtedly continue.


## The Family Camping Movement

Family camping actually started with the very first camp meeting, because the pioneers took provisions to camp on the grounds with their families. No one knows when the first Children's Meeting or Youth Services took place, but they probably developed on an informal basis, dictated by the need of children to have services planned and held at their level of understanding. James McGready had reported conversions of youths and children at the sacramental occasions he conducted in 1799 and 1800, and eyewitnesses claimed many children were also converted at Cane Ridge in 1801.[137] It is known that Martha Inskip and other women holiness leaders conducted services for children at the National Holiness Camp Meetings, probably from the beginning, and Martha became nationally known as the "Children's Apostle." She kept an active file on some 3,000 children who had attended the camps, and also wrote a regular column for them in the *Advocate of Christian Holiness*. These women deserve credit and recognition for their pioneering efforts in the field of Christian children's camping.[138]

Christian camping for children appears to have begun in 1880 when the Reverend George W. Hinkley of West Hartford, Connecticut, took seven boys from his parish to Gardner's Island, near Wakefield, Rhode Island, for a camping trip. The idea blossomed almost overnight, first with Christian organizations like the Young Men's Christian Association. The YMCA started its camping program in 1885, and by 1911 had begun to take it worldwide. Following this example the Boy Scouts of America, Camp Fire Girls, and Girl Scouts of America popularized camping for children and youths, resulting in a fantastic numerical growth of campsites around the nation. In 1914 the International Sunday School Association held a summer program at Lake Geneva, Wisconsin, and from it emerged what eventually became a national movement of church camps for children and youths.[139]

Today children's and youths' camping is still a ministry of its own as well as a part of the family camping movement. It is also big business. It has expanded far beyond the usual concept of camp meeting, and thousands of children's and youths' camps have sprung up around the nation, perhaps most of them within the last fifty years. Almost all of the American denominations now sponsor an active camping program during the summer, even those churches who earlier withdrew their support of the camp meeting, and many of these programs are conducted at church-owned facilities. Affected by the YMCA camps, and perhaps scouting programs as well, the church camp often consists of outdoor and indoor summer sports, water sports, hiking, all types of crafts, games, and, of course, religious instruction and services designed specifically for the age group at hand. At least one United Methodist annual conference has expanded its summer program to include all ages, and calls it "camping and leisure ministries."[140] This kind of ministry has become so vital to the church that many denominations now employ full-time camping personnel, and a few seminaries have begun to include camping ministry courses in their curricula.

In the early 1950s, some camp leaders on the West Coast felt the need for an organization which would encourage and promote the work of Christian camps and conference centers. Their interest led to the founding of the Christian Camps and Conferences Association in 1959, with Graham Tinning as the first executive director. In 1963 this organization became international in scope, and in 1968 changed its name to "Christian Camping International." Its growth has been phenomenal, and today it counts nearly 5,000 members in an active ministry that spans the globe.

> CCI is an alliance of 12 camping associations around the world that includes: CCI/Australia, CCI/Brazil, CCI/Canada, CCI/Japan, CCI/Korea, CCI/Latin America, CCI/New Zealand, CCI/Philippines, CCI/Southern Africa, CCI/Republic of China, CCI/United Kingdom, [and] CCI/United States.[141]

CCI/USA is the "only inter-denominational national association of Christian camping leaders in the U.S.A.," and has endorsed the stringent regulations of the American Camping Association which must be met before an encampment can be registered as an "ACA Accredited Camp," an "ACA Approved Site," or a "CCI/USA Certified Member." Maintaining headquarters in Wheaton, Illinois, CCI/USA is dedicated to the ministry of Christian camping, and is divided into six camping regions. It publishes the *Journal of Christian Camping*, and member camps, those who affirm the association's statement of faith and pay the annual fee, are included in the *Official Guide to Christian Camps and Conference Centers*. The 1990–91 edition contained a listing of 985 camps and conference centers.[142]

# Conclusion

The camp meeting is a unique institution, and was the first American sustained oral mass communication.[143] It has been a workhorse in its response to the ecumenical and denominational needs of the church. From a backwoods outdoor revival in Georgia or Carolina, its ministries have become a powerful dynamo to American religion, pumping spiritual energy into practically every aspect of church life. It has served as a platform from which the church could reach out to society through several media: revivalism, missions, church planting, Christian education, national reform, recreation, and even political action. It has also served as a model for the Chautauqua, the Christian resort, the Bible conference, the family camping movement, and the Christian conference centers. In certain ways it even contributed to community planning and development.

No one knows how many camp meetings, assembly grounds, Bible conferences, and Christian retreat centers actually do exist, but if the count included children's, youths', and the specialty camps (denominational, associational/organizational, and interdenominational}, the total number might well exceed six or seven thousand encampments per year. If one attempts to count services and estimate attendances, these camps easily affect many millions of lives annually. Obviously, the enlarged vision and use of the camp meeting has made a profound impact on the life of religion in America. It has touched practically every part of the church, and all its outreach ministries. Now this institution is approaching its two hundredth anniversary. With such a history, and such a ministry, it has well earned the right to celebrate.

# NOTES

1. Asbury had some inkling how plenteous this harvest would be, however, for he wrote Jacob Gruber that the camps drew three to four million persons annually! See his letter to Gruber in J. Manning Potts, editor, *The Journal and Letters of Francis Asbury*, 3 volumes. London: Epworth Press, 1958, 3:453.

Interestingly, Asbury is usually quoted as the first to use the term "camp meeting." See Charles Johnson, *The Frontier Camp Meeting*. Dallas: Southern Methodist University Press, 1955, p. 83, 280; and John B. Boles, *The Great Revival 1787–1805*. Lexington: The University of Kentucky Press, 1972, p. 55. Asbury used the term in a letter to Thornton Fleming, dated December 2, 1802. See Asbury, *Journal and Letters*, 3:251. There is an earlier reference in "William Ormond Jr.'s Journals," dated September 2, 1805, and again October 28, 1802, 4:56, 59. I am indebted to Duke University Archives, Durham, N.C., for these references. See also the statements regarding the Thomas Mann diaries in footnote 21.

2. See Johnson, *Frontier Camp Meeting*, p. 25 ff. Regarding the German "Big Meetings," John B. Frantz uses the phrase "German Awakening" in "The Awakening of Religion among the German Settlers in the Middle Colonies," in *William and Mary Quarterly*, April 1976, pp. 266–288, based on his unpublished doctoral dissertation, "Revivalism in the German Reformed Church in the United States to 1850, with Emphasis on the Eastern Synod," University of Pennsylvania, 1961. See also Stephen L. Longnecker's unpublished doctoral dissertation, "Democracy's Pulpit: Religion and Egalitarianism among Early Pennsylvania Germans," Johns Hopkins University, 1989, especially chapters 5 and 6, pp. 121–233. For an excellent treatment of the European holy fairs see Leigh Eric Schmidt, *Holy Fairs, Scottish Communion and American Revivals in the Early Modern Period*. Princeton: Princeton University Press, 1989, 59–68. For the "outdoor church" see John W. Barber, *Historical, Poetical and Pictorial American Scenes; Principally Moral or Religious*. New Haven: J. W. Bradley and J. W. Barber, 1852, p. 154. For "stands" and "tents" see footnote 17.

3. See Johnson, *Frontier Camp Meeting*, p. 27; see also Robert B. Semple, *History of the Baptists in Virginia*, revised and extended by G. W. Beale. Lafayette: Church History Research and Archives, 1976, pp. 17–23. For an early sketch on Waller see James B. Taylor, *Virginia Baptist Ministers*, 2 volumes. New York: Sheldon and Company, 1860, 1:78–85.

4. Johnson, *ibid*.; see Catherine Cleveland, *The Great Revival in the West 1797–1805*. Chicago: The University of Chicago Press, 1916, pp. 52–53.

5. Johnson, *ibid*., p. 40.

6. Rather than offer a huge list of American church history texts, let me challenge the reader to find historians who make a statement to the contrary. There are few.

7. Of course, Presbyterian historians have made this claim for many years. See, for example, James Smith, *History of the Christian Church, from Its Origin to the Present Time: Compiled from Various Authors, Including a History of the Cumberland Presbyterian Church, Drawn from Authentic Documents*. Nashville: Cumberland Presbyterian Office, 1835, p. 571 ff.; Robert Davidson, *History of the Presbyterian Church in the State of Kentucky*. New York: Robert Carter, 1857, p. 131 ff.; E. H. Gillett, *History of the Presbyterian Church in the United States of America*, 2 volumes. Philadelphia: Presbyterian Publication Committee, 1864, 2:158–170; B. W. McDonnold, *History of the Cumberland Presbyterian Church*. Nashville: Board of Publication of Cumberland Presbyterian Church, 1899, pp. 10–15; Ben M. Barrus, Milton L. Baughn, and Thomas H. Campbell, *A People Called Cumberland Presbyterians*. Memphis: Frontier Press, 1978, pp. 37–49; Ernest Trice Thompson, *Presbyterians in the South*, 3 volumes. Richmond: John Knox Press, 1963, 1:130–155. A few Methodist scholars have rightly complained about the Presbyterian neglect or outright bias against Methodist presence in the founding of the camp meeting. See, for example, R. N. Price, *Holston Methodism, From Its Origin to the Present Time*. Nashville: Publishing House of the M.E. Church, South, 1912, p. 363. Others, however, have accepted the Presbyterian thesis, seemingly with reservations. See Emory Stevens Bucke, general editor, *The History of Methodism*, 3 volumes. Nashville: Abingdon Press, 1964, pp. 509–510.

These Presbyterian historians have influenced many others. See, for example, "Camp Meeting Origins," in the Methodist periodical, *Western Christian Advocate*, September 13, 1839, p. 81; Smith's history is the cited source. See J. H. Spencer, *A History of Kentucky Baptists*, 2 volumes. Cincinnati: published by the author, 1886, 2:508–509. His only sources for camp meetings are the histories by Smith and Davidson. See William Warren Sweet, *Religion on the American Frontier—1783–1840*, 3 volumes. New York: Cooper Square Publishers, Inc., 1964, 2:85. His source is Davidson. For other historians, see Robert Baird, *Religion in America*. New York: Harper and Brothers, Publishers, 1856, pp. 432–433; Winfred Ernest Garrison and Alfred T. DeGroot, *The Disciples of Christ, A History*. St. Louis: Christian Board of Publication, 1948, p. 99; Robert T. Handy, *A History of the Churches in the United States and Canada*. New York: Oxford University Press, 1977, pp. 166–167; and "The Return of the Spirit: the Second Great Awakening," in *Christian History*, Volume VIII, No. 3, Issue 23, 1989, p. 25. Modern camp meeting studies almost invariably point to a Presbyterian heritage for the camp meeting, giving minor credit to the Methodists and Baptists. See Charles Johnson, *Frontier Camp Meeting*, p. 32 ff.; John B. Boles, *The Great Revival*, p. 55; Dickson D. Bruce, *And They All Sang Hallelujah, Plain-Folk Camp Meeting Religion, 1800–1845*. Knoxville: The University of Tennessee Press, 1974, p.

51; and Ellen Weiss, *City in the Woods, The Life and Design of an American Camp Meeting on Martha's Vineyard.* New York: Oxford University Press, 1987, p. 3.

8. See W. P. Strickland, editor, *Autobiography of Peter Cartwright, the Backwoods Preacher.* New York: The Methodist Book Concern, 1900, p. 31. See William H. Milburn, *The Pioneers, Preachers and People of the Mississippi Valley.* New York: Derby and Jackson, 1860, pp. 357–361. Modern scholars have made this claim, also. See Mendell Taylor, *Exploring Evangelism.* Kansas City: Beacon Hill Press, 1964, p. 411.

9. Often Methodist historians credit both John and William McGee for the "rise" of the camp meeting, thus giving the nod to Presbyterians as well as Methodists. Some, however, place the honor only on the Methodists; see Albert M. Shipp, *The History of Methodism in South Carolina.* Nashville: Southern Methodist Publishing House, 1884, p. 27; W. L. Grissom, *History of Methodism in North Carolina from 1772 to the Present Time.* Nashville: Publishing House of the M. E. Church, South, 1905, pp. 328–330; Paul Neff Gerber, *The Romance of American Methodism.* Greensboro: Piedmont Press, 1931, pp. 170–175; Elmer T. Clark, *Methodism in Western North Carolina.* Nashville: Parthenon Press, 1966, pp. 30–31; Alva W. Plyler, "The Early Circuit Riders of Western North Carolina," in *Historical Papers of the North Carolina Conference Historical Society and the Western North Carolina Conference Historical Society.* Greensboro: North Carolina Christian Advocate, 1925, pp. 101–102; W. L. Grissom, "Some First Things in North Carolina Methodism," an address presented before the North Carolina Conference Historical Society in 1908, on file at Duke University special collections, Durham, North Carolina.

10. See "Effingham County Camp Meeting" file on record at Methodist Archives and History Center, Madison, N.J. It includes materials used to establish this encampment as a United Methodist Historic Site, and contains a copy of the deed, statement of history, brochure, etc. See also the "Effingham County Camp Meeting" file in author's personal collection, which contains brochures, correspondence with Ernest Seckinger, and a copy of N. Hinton Morgan's "History," written in the 1950s. See Ernest W. Seckinger, Sr., "Effingham Camp Ground: Then and Now, A History," in *Historical Highlights,* Spring 1990, pp. 54–67. He argues convincingly for the "possibility" of the 1790 founding date. It must be admitted that at the present time the documentary evidence is not strong enough to establish firmly the 1790 date. See Harold Lawrence, *A Feast of Tabernacles.* Published by the author, 1990, p. 42. However, there is strong local oral tradition regarding this date, and it must not be disregarded.

11. See files above, and Lawrence, *Feast of Tabernacles,* pp. 41–42.

12. See Bucke, *History of Methodism,* 1:509. See the article, "Grassy

Branch Camp Meeting Named Historic Site," in *North Carolina Christian Advocate*, August 27, 1985.

13. It has been claimed that Daniel Asbury was related to Bishop Francis Asbury, but no documentary evidence has been found to support that statement. See *Journal of Francis Asbury*, 1:3–4, note 2.

For biographical material on Daniel Asbury see William L. Sherrill, *Annals of Lincoln County, North Carolina*. The Observer Printing House, 1937, pp. 89–90. See Herbert Asbury, *A Methodist Saint, The Life of Bishop Asbury*. New York: Alfred A. Knopf, 1927, pp. 6–7. See also James Osgood Andrew, "Daniel Asbury," in William B. Sprague, ed., *Annals of the American Pulpit*. New York: Arno Press and the New York Times, 1969, 8:127–129; "Daniel Asbury," in M. H. Moore, *Sketches of the Pioneers of Methodism in North Carolina and Virginia*. Nashville: Southern Methodist Publishing House, 1884, pp. 167–180; Louise Queen, "Daniel Asbury," in Nolan B. Harmon, general editor, *The Encyclopedia of World Methodism*, 2 volumes. Nashville: Methodist Publishing House, 1974, 2:58–59. See also the sketches of his life in A. M. Chreitzberg, *Early Methodism in the Carolinas*. Nashville: Publishing House of the Methodist Episcopal Church, South, 1897, pp. 87–88; Albert Deems Betts, *History of South Carolina Methodism*. Columbia: The Advocate Press, 1952, p. 171; Elmer T. Clark, *Methodism in Western North Carolina*. Nashville: The Parthenon Press, 1966, pp. 28–29; Grissom, *Methodism in North Carolina*, pp. 278–280; Shipp, *Methodism in South Carolina*, pp. 263–266; and Plyler, "Early Circuit Riders," p. 101.

14. See his pastoral record in *Minutes of the Methodist Conferences, Annually Held in America from 1773 to 1813 Inclusive*. New York: Published for the Methodist Connexion in the United States, 1813. See also his obituary in *The Methodist Magazine*, October 1826, p. 368. See biographical file, "Daniel Asbury," in author's collection, which contains a copy of his will and correspondence regarding his life and ministry. See biographical file, "Daniel Asbury," at the United Methodist Archives and History Center in Madison, New Jersey, which contains correspondence regarding his life and ministry. He is mentioned in the *Journal and Letters of Francis Asbury*. An abstract of Daniel Asbury's will can be found in Mitchell W. Thornton, *North Carolina Wills: A Testator Index, 1665–1900*, 3 volumes. Raleigh: published by the author, 1987, 3:35. Asbury's death notice is listed in Carrie L. Broughton, compiler, *Marriage and Death Notices from Raleigh Register and North Carolina State Gazette, 1799–1825*. Baltimore: Genealogical Publishing Co., 1975, p. 173. According to his gravestone, located in the cemetery of the Rehobeth United Methodist Church, Daniel Asbury died on May 15, 1825. The stone also says, "Nancy L. Morris, wife of Rev. Daniel Asbury, Died 1862, aged 92 years." An old stone plaque in the vestibule of the Rehobeth church has the following inscription: "Rev. Daniel Asbury, the pioneer of Methodism in Western North Carolina, was born February 18, 1762, died May 15, 1825. He organized this circuit in 1789; and the same year organized the first Methodist Church in the state west of the

Catawba River. The first church building was erected here in 1791. The first camp meeting was held here in 1794."

15. Shipp, *Methodism in South Carolina*, p. 261.

16. See Sherrill, Moore, Shipp, Grissom, and Clark in note 13 above; see anonymous "History of Rehobeth Methodist Church," in author's collection; see also "Grassy Branch Camp meeting" file on record at the United Methodist Archives and History Center in Madison, New Jersey, which contains materials used in application as a United Methodist Historic Site. Materials include deed. One source claimed the founding date should be 1791, the date of the first outdoor services at the site. See Lavens Thomas II, *Religious Education in the Methodist Episcopal Church to 1870*, quoted in John James Powell, "The Origin and History of the Methodist Camp Meeting Movement in North Carolina," B.D. Thesis presented to Duke Divinity School, Durham, N.C., 1944, p. 10. See also Charles Wesley Kimbrell, "The Camp Meeting as a Factor in the Growth of Early American Methodism, 1794–1844," a B.D. thesis presented to the Duke Divinity School, Durham, N.C., 1937, p. 11.

17. For stands and tents being used for outdoor services see Harold James Dudley, ed., *Foote's Sketches of North Carolina*. Dunn: Twyford Printing Company, 1965, p. 440; Paul A. Wallace, ed., *Thirty Thousand Miles with John Heckewelder*. Pittsburgh: University of Pittsburgh Press, 1958, p. 235. Methodist minister, William Ormond, Jr., preached from "a stand near the road in the woods," and "Bro. D. Asbury Exhorted." See the "William Ormond Journals," July 28, 1802, 4:52, Duke University Archives, Durham, N.C.

For the founding of Grassy Branch Camp Meeting, see the letter of Dr. Albert M. Shipp in *Southern Christian Advocate*, October 30, 1872, p. 170; see also Shipp, *History of Methodism in South Carolina*, pp. 271–272.

18. See "Camp Meeting" file in the North Carolina Conference Archives of the United Methodist Church, Charlotte, N.C. See also the Shipp letter, which refers to documentary evidence, an eyewitness account of the first Grassy Branch encampment, written by Mrs. Daniel Asbury. Unfortunately, the "Papers" referred to in the Shipp letter cannot be located.

19. The historical material available on the Rock Springs Camp Meeting is impressive, and growing all the time. It can never again simply be considered an "antecedent" of the camp meeting, as Charles Johnson called it. See Shipp, *History of Methodism in South Carolina*, p. 272; and the Shipp letter in the *Southern Christian Advocate*, October 30, 1872, p. 170; see works cited by Sherrill, Grissom, Clark and Plyler. See W. A. Massebeau, "The Camp Meeting in South Carolina Methodism," an address presented before the Upper South Carolina Conference Historical Society on November 4, 1919, and the South Carolina Conference Historical Society on November 25, 1919, and published by order of these societies (no publication data, n.d.), pp. 6–7; Elizabeth Simpson Smith, "Camp Meetin' Time," in *Historic Preservation*, April–June,

1978, pp. 20–23; Jenny Copeland, "The History of the Rock Springs Campground," a research paper presented to the class "Early Methodism" at Duke Divinity School, Durham, North Carolina, Fall semester 1986, pp. 7–9; Mrs. Vagie D. Smith, "A Brief History of Rock Springs Camp Meeting," handwritten manuscript in author's file; Liz Chandler, "Terrell Old-Timer Keeper of Community's History," in the Sunday edition of *Catawba Valley Neighbors*, August 25, 1985. A sketch also appears in the Rock Springs Camp Meeting booklets; see Lily Estelle Sigmon, "History and Traditions of Rock Springs Camp Ground," in *Rock Springs Camp Meeting, 158th Annual Session*, booklet history published in 1987 by the Rock Springs Camp Meeting, Denver, North Carolina, p. 4. See also Mrs. Gabriel Sigmon, "History and Traditions of Rock Springs Camp Ground," in *Rock Springs Camp Meeting, 142nd Annual Session*, booklet history published in 1971 by Rock Springs Camp Meeting, Denver, North Carolina, no pagination.

20. I am well aware that this is another situation where the documentary evidence is not exceptionally strong, and research must stand upon local oral tradition. However, this tradition is very old, and deserves consideration. Even the county histories support the claim that slaves were included at the Rock Springs Camp Meeting: see Clarence W. Griffin, *The History of Old Tyrone and Rutherford Counties*. Asheville: 1937, p. 590. For a historical statement re: Tucker's Grove Camp Meeting, see "Tucker's Grove Nomination Forms," National Registry of Historic Places, Washington, D.C. See also "Tucker's Grove Camp" file in the author's collection.

21. See Shipp, *History of Methodism in South Carolina*, p. 272. See "Camp Meeting" file at the North Carolina Conference Archives of the United Methodist Church, Charlotte, N.C. See particularly the material marked: "Campmeetings, Landmark, Jan. 16, 1880," for the quote from the journal of the Reverend Thomas Mann. Unfortunately, these early years of the Mann diaries seem now to have disappeared. The statement from the Mann diary is also mentioned in the Shipp letter to the *Southern Christian Advocate*, October 30, 1872. p. 170.

For the work of Presbyterian minister Dr. James Hall see Dudley, *Foote's Sketches of North Carolina*, pp. 315–336. Hall died on July 25, 1826. This source says nothing about Dr. Hall preaching at Grassy Branch Camp Meeting in 1794. This is not at all surprising, however, for this is a Presbyterian history, and Foote believed that McGready established the camp meeting as part of the revival in Kentucky. He believed the first camp meeting in North Carolina (and the whole South) was held at Hawfields, in October 1802; see p. 227.

22. A history of Cypress Camp Meeting is being prepared by Mrs. Mattie Lee Browning, historian for the encampment. It is on the National Registry of Historic Places. Bishop Asbury visited this area several times; see his *Journal*, 2:318, for example, and see notes 125, 127, and 128. I am indebted

to Maynard Davis for "Brief History of Cypress Camp Ground," and information regarding the memorial plaque in the tabernacle. Much of the evidence for this camp is local oral tradition as well. See "Cypress Camp Meeting" file in author's collection.

The Cattle Creek Camp Meeting also has a strong local oral tradition for its history. Bishop Asbury visited here, too; see his *Journal*, 2:318. Massebeau, "The Camp Meeting in South Carolina Methodism," thought Cattle Creek had been established as a Presbyterian camp meeting about 1819, later taken over by the Methodists; see p. 23. Local history does not support his view.

23. See "Indian Field Camp Meeting" file in author's collection, which includes correspondence with trustees, brief historical statements, and brochures. The Indian Field Camp Meeting is listed in the *Encyclopedia of World Methodism*, 1:1208, where an incorrect founding date of 1838 is given. Betts, *History of South Carolina Methodism*, provides the correction, for with a picture of the tabernacle on p. 340, he observes that it was moved to its present location in 1838. Bishop Asbury preached at the early Indian Field location, see his *Journal*, 2:318, but he did not specifically call it a campground. For further historical information see Doug Scott, "History of Indian Field Camp Meeting," an unpublished historical paper furnished me by Dr. J. Gavin Appleby, late chairman of the Board of Trustees. Dr. Appleby wrote the brief "History of Indian Field Campground," which is printed on the back of the camp brochures. See also the several newspaper articles in author's file.

24. R. N. Price, *Holston Methodism*, 1:356–357. See also Mary Thomas Peacock, *The Circuit Rider and Those Who Followed*. Chattanooga: Hudson Printing and Lithographic Co., 1957, p. 24. She uses as source an article in the *Southwestern Christian Advocate and Journal*, September 28, 1839, which gave Page the credit for the origin of the camp meeting.

It is certainly possible that other early claims will surface as camp meeting research matures. Kirk Mariner has mentioned that Thomas Smith may have held an 1800 encampment on the eastern shore of Maryland. See Kirk Mariner *Revival's Children, A Religious History of Virginia's Eastern Shore.* Salisbury: Peninsula Press, 1979, p. 42.

25. The reader is encouraged to check *any* standard reference source, secular or religious. See, for example, *The New Schaff-Herzog Encyclopedia of Religious Knowledge*, the *Dictionary of American History*, the *Mennonite Encyclopedia*, the *Presbyterian Encyclopedia*, the *Cyclopedia of Methodism*, and the *Encyclopedia of World Methodism*. The new resource material is no better. For example, see Eerdman's two resource volumes, *Handbook to the History of Christianity* and *Handbook to Christianity in America*. See also *The New International Dictionary of the Christian Church*, the *Encyclopedia of Religion in the South*, and the *Dictionary of Christianity in America*. This incorrect and

misleading information started as early as *Appleton's Cyclopedia of American Biography*, published in 1888, and continues to the present.

26. The Presbyterians referred to these services as "sacramental occasions," and McGready used that language when speaking of them. So did others. See the letters in William W. Woodward, *Surprising Accounts of the Revival of Religion in the United States of America*. Philadelphia: 1802. Some are extracted and reprinted in Lon D. Oliver, *A Guide to the Cane Ridge Revival*. Lexington: Lexington Theological Seminary Library, 1988, pp. 29–34.

There is no full biography on the Reverend James E. McGready, and while articles on him abound, factual data are scarce. He appears in the *Dictionary of American Biography*, 12:56–57, *Annals of the American Pulpit*, 3:278, *Who's Who in American History*, Historical Volume 1:417, *The Wycliffe Biographical Dictionary of the Church*, pp. 256–257, *The Dictionary of American Religious Biography*, pp. 274–275, *Dictionary of Christianity in America*, pp. 687–688, and *Encyclopedia of Religion in the South*, pp. 437–438. Scholars have long been content to assign him "the leading role" in the drama of the Great Revival. John Boles certainly does that, as did Johnson and Cleveland before him, and much of their source material came from the Presbyterian historians cited previously. A sketch of McGready's life may also be found in the *Minutes of the Redstone Presbytery* and *Minutes of the Washington Presbytery*, on file at the Presbyterian Archives and Department of History in Philadelphia, Pa. See also their biographical file on him, and the "James McGready" file in the author's collection. See John Opie, Jr., "James McGready: Theologian of Frontier Revivalism," in the December 1965, issue of *Church History*, pp. 445–456. See the histories by Smith (with a sketch on pp. 672–673), Davidson, Gillett, Sweet, and Thompson; see *Foote's Sketches*, pp. 367–414. Of special importance is Lucien V. Rule, "Glimpse of Rev. James McGready, 'Thunder-bolt of God,'" an old undocumented article in the author's collection. Rule quotes a 1941 letter from Mrs. J. A. Priest, McGready's great-great-granddaughter. She mentioned that Mrs. Agnes McGready (James's wife) died on January 18, 1800, at the age of 44. She also had family documentation that claimed James McGready died December 28, 1818, at the age of 55. This would make his birth year 1763. She also wrote that McGready had been born in Scotland, and came to Pennsylvania at a very early age. In 1792 he married, and shortly after moved to North Carolina. These facts are significant because it has been believed that he was born in Pennsylvania in 1758, and died in 1815 or 1817.

Recently I tried to locate McGready's tombstone in Henderson, Kentucky. According to local historians, he had performed marriages in Henderson county as early as 1800, and moved his family there sometime in 1809. His intense revivalistic preaching continued unabated, as did his aggressive attempts at public reform. The story is told how he once brought charges against three rather prominent citizens for public profanity, one of whom was General Samuel Hopkins, a local hero during the American

Revolution. The three culprits meekly paid their fines, and McGready continued his efforts to revive the community. For these and other stories see Maralea Arnett, *The Annals and Scandals of Henderson County, Kentucky, 1775–1975*. Corydon: Fremar Publishing Company, 1976, p. 313; Edmund L. Sterling, *History of Henderson County, Kentucky*. Evansville: Unigraphic, Inc., 1965, pp. 105–106 [reprint of 1887 edition]; and *Henderson, A Guide to Audubon's Hometown in Kentucky*. New York: Rhode Printing-Publishing Company, n.d.

  Unfortunately, as is sometimes the case, the local community has all but forgotten this most illustrious minister. One looks in vain for a historic marker in or around Henderson, Kentucky, which would commemorate his life and work. Instead the Reverend James McGready lies in an unknown and unmarked grave, still waiting the local organization which will give him the recognition he so richly deserves. Obviously, further research must be done on the life and work of this famous revivalist.

  27. Dr. Charles A. Parker, correspondence with author, October 9, 1987.

  28. The Presbyterians have James McGready; the Methodists have John McGee. Price called him "the hero of the revival of 1800," see *Holston Methodism*, 2:126. Unfortunately, he has been largely neglected by the scholarly world, and his name does not appear even in the standard Methodist sources, such as the *Encyclopedia of World Methodism*. I am greatly indebted to his ancestors for much of the material here, especially the correspondence of Marshall Curtis and Mrs. Helen B. McKnight. See also Helen Bowling McKnight, *My McGee and Joyner Families*. Huntsville: published by the author, 1983; and Helen Bowling McKnight, "John McGee—Methodist Circuit Rider and Camp Meeting Evangelist," a historical paper on file at the State Library and Archives, Nashville, Tennessee. See "John McGee" file at the Methodist Archives and History Center in Madison, New Jersey, which contains letters regarding genealogy.

  See also the "John McGee" file in author's collection. A life sketch of John McGee can be found in John B. McFerrin, *History of Methodism in Tennessee*, 2 volumes. Nashville: Publishing House of the M.E. Church, South, 1888, 1:291–302; Moore, *Pioneers of Methodism*, pp. 237–248; John Carr, *Early Times in Middle Tennessee*. Nashville: The Parthenon Press, 1958, pp. 53–54. See also Grissom, *History of Methodism in North Carolina*, pp. 330–332; and Clark, *Methodism in Western North Carolina*, pp. 51–52.

  For information on John McGee's father, see correspondence in "John McGee" file, author's collection. See also McKnight, *My McGee and Joyner Families*, pp. 1–15.

  29. See copy of "Abstract of Will of John McGee, merchant," dated November 22, 1773, in *My McGee and Joyner Families*, pp. 11–12.

  30. *Ibid.*, p. 4. Also see correspondence between author and Marshall Curtis, May 7, 1990.

31. See E. W. Caruthers, *Interesting Revolutionary Incidents and Sketches of Character.* Philadelphia, 1856, pp. 304–340. See Mcknight, *My McGee and Joyner Families,* p. 21 ff.

32. McKnight, *My McGee and Joyner Families,* pp. 49–50; see the Curtis correspondence with author, May 7, 1990; see also the sketch by his son-in-law, the Reverend Thomas Joyner, in McFerrin, *Methodism in Tennessee,* pp. 208–209. The Reverend John Carr wrote that McGee had admitted to being a "wild young man." See Carr, *Early Times in Middle Tennessee,* p. 53.

33. See especially Carr, *Early Times in Middle Tennessee,* pp. 53–54, and Moore, *Pioneers of Methodism,* pp. 239–240.

34. See especially Moore, *Pioneers of Methodism,* pp. 240–241, and Carr, *Early Times,* p. 54. This runs directly contrary to the Presbyterian accounts, which claim that William McGee was converted under the ministry of James McGready. See James Smith, *History of the Christian Church,* p. 84, where it is said that William was converted during the McGready revival at David Caldwell's "Log College." Davidson, *History of the Presbyterian Church in Kentucky,* p. 263, says the same, and his source is Smith. John Opie, Jr., makes this claim in "James McGready," p. 447, and his source is Davidson. Ernest Trice Thompson, *Presbyterianism in the South,* p. 131, claims that both McGee brothers were converts of the McGready revival, and his source appears to be Davidson. This information is plainly incorrect. Even Beard states that John McGee had a profound influence on his brother, William. See Richard Beard, *Brief Biographical Sketches of Some of the Early Ministers of the Cumberland Presbyterian Church.* Nashville: Southern Methodist Publishing House, 1867, p. 19. The evidence appears incontrovertible that William McGee was converted under the ministry of his brother, John McGee.

For more information, see the "William McGee" file at the Presbyterian Archives and Department of History in Philadelphia, Pa., and the "William McGee" file in the author's collection. See especially the chapter on him in McKnight, *My McGee and Joyner Families,* p. 83 ff.

35. For his pastoral record, see the *Minutes of the Methodist Conferences 1773–1813;* see his file in the author's collection. The date of his marriage is not known.

36. McKnight, *My McGee and Joyner Families,* p. 59.

37. As quoted in McFerrin, *Methodism in Tennessee,* 1:299–300.

38. Carr, *Early Times in Middle Tennessee,* p. 54.

39. Moore, *Pioneers of Methodism,* pp. 247–248; McFerrin, *Methodism in Tennessee,* 1:301–302.

40. See Cleveland, Johnson, and Boles, for example, and the various works on the history of revivalism, such as Bernard A. Weisberger, *They*

*Gathered at the River.* Boston: Little, Brown and Company, 1958, pp. 20–38.

41. The best bibliographical study is Lon D. Oliver, *A Guide to the Cane Ridge Revival.* See also the newest study, Paul Conkin, *Cane Ridge, America's Pentecost.* Madison: The University of Wisconsin Press, 1990. This work, however, relies too much on the Presbyterian sources, and reflects a heavy bias in that direction. While John McGee is recognized, having preached once at Red River in 1800, he is also accused of later trying to claim the credit for igniting the "spark" of the revival. Conkin simply is convinced that James McGready masterminded the beginning of the revival in Kentucky.

For Barton Stone see *Barton Warren Stone: Early American Advocate of Christian Unity.* Nashville: The Disciples of Christ Historical Society, 1954.

42. See T. Marshall Smith, *Legends of the War of Independence.* Louisville: J. F. Brennan, Publisher, 1855, pp. 371 ff.

43. See the Presbyterian histories by J. Smith and Davidson; this tradition appears to be founded on them.

44. Published in Lorenzo Dow, *Extracts from Original Letters to the Methodist Bishops, Mostly from Their Preachers and Members in America Giving an Account of the Work of God since the Year 1800.* Liverpool: Printed by H. Forshaw, 1806, p. 10. There is also an early John McGee letter in William W. Bennett, *Memorials of Methodism in Virginia.* Richmond: published by the author, 1871, but it is a detailed account of the 1801 Red River sacramental service. However, it *does* illustrate John McGee's continued participation in the revival.

45. Entitled "Narrative of the Commencement and Progress of the Revival of 1800," published in James Smith, editor, *Posthumous Works of the Reverend and Pious James M'Gready,* 2 volumes. Louisville: printed by W. W. Worley, 1831, 1:ix–xvi.

46. Undated letter published in the *Methodist Magazine,* London, 1803, pp. 181–184.

47. Entitled "A Short Narrative of the Revival of Religion in Logan County in the State of Kentucky, and in the adjacent settlements in the State of Tennessee, from May, 1797, until September 1800," published in *The New York Missionary Magazine and Repository of Religious Intelligence,* Volume IV, 1803, pp. 74–75, 151–155, 192–199, 234–236.

48. Published in the *Methodist Magazine,* New York, Volume IV, 1821, pp. 189–191.

49. Published in J. P. MacLean's article, "The Kentucky Revival and Its Influence on the Miami Valley," in *Ohio Archaeological and Historical Publications,* Volume XII, 1908, pp. 279–281.

50. T. Marshall Smith, *Legends*, cited previously.

51. Quoted in James Smith, *History of the Christian Church*, pp. 572–573.

52. Smith, *Legends*, p. 374.

53. McGready called it the "the great day of the feast" because the whole had been scheduled by him as a sacramental occasion. See his "Short Narrative," in the *New York Missionary Magazine*, p. 155.

54. Smith, *Legends*, p. 372.

55. *Ibid.*, pp. 372–373. The other accounts do not mention that McGee sang. The hymn itself, "Come, Holy Spirit, Heavenly Dove," was written by Isaac Watts and appears to have been first published in his 1709 edition of *Hymns and Spiritual Songs*. See Robert Guy McCutchan, *Our Hymnody*. New York: Abingdon, Press, 1977, p. 221. The hymn has a long tradition of Methodist usage, and appeared in the 1964 edition of *The Methodist Hymnal*.

56. The other accounts do not speak of two women who shouted, nor are they named. One account does say that the conversation of two women at Gasper River helped precipitate those revival services; see James Smith, *History of the Christian Church*, p. 574. However, the circumstances and descriptions are completely different, and it is obvious that each account is describing a different service and set of events.

57. See McGee, "Commencement of the Great Revival," in *Methodist Magazine*, p. 190.

58. See Smith, *Legends*, p. 373; see Rankin's account in MacLean, "Kentucky Revival," p. 280.

59. Rankin, *ibid*.

60. In his "Narrative" and "Short Narrative," McGready wrote that ten persons were converted. Smith, *Legends*, noted from thirty to forty converts, see p. 373. McGee wrote that four to five hundred people attended, see his October 27, 1800, letter. All accounts claim that a great number of persons left the services under a very heavy conviction for their sins.

These numbers must be interpreted properly to avoid misunderstanding. For example, it is said that as many as 25,000 persons attended Cane Ridge, but two different sources report only "828 communicants." See Oliver, *Guide to Cane Ridge*, pp. 38 and 41.

61. See McGready's "Short Narrative," p. 192.

62. Smith, *Legends*, p. 376.

63. Smith, *History of the Christian Church*, p. 573.

64. John McGee, letter dated October 27, 1800. Note the itinerary in this earliest source, and that its details agree with Smith, *Legends*.

65. Boles, *Great Revival*, p. 57.

66. Leonard I. Sweet, "Nineteenth Century Evangelicalism," in Charles H. Lippy and Peter W. Williams, eds., *Encyclopedia of the American Religious Experience*, 3 volumes. New York: Charles Scribners Sons, 1988, 2:888–890.

67. The physical exercises of these early camp meetings have become famous, especially the "jerks." They have been enumerated and studied by various sources; see Cleveland and Johnson, for example. Regarding the millennium, even Methodist Bishop Francis Asbury thought it had begun, see note 73. See Levi Purviance, *The Biography of Elder David Purviance*. Dayton: B. F. and G. W. Ellis, 1884, pp. 247–252.

68. For blacks at Cane Ridge, see letter in Oliver, *Guide to Cane Ridge*, p. 33, where the eyewitness claimed that the blacks met alone, hearing their own preachers. See also Johnson, *Frontier Camp Meeting*, pp. 46. Of his earlier services McGready wrote, "Some of the Negroes appeared to be powerfully seized with convictions." See "A Short Narrative," in the *New York Missionary Magazine*, p. 195. John Lyle wrote in his diary that the white ministers at Cane Ridge addressed the black assemblage out of due concern for their souls. Even so, the black Christians still had to sit in the balcony at Cane Ridge Meeting House! See Conkin, *Cane Ridge*, pp. 174–175. The Lyle manuscript diary covers June 1801 through July 1803, and is located at the Kentucky Historical Society, Frankfort, Ky.

69. Charles W. Ferguson, *Organizing to Beat the Devil, Methodists and the Making of America*. New York: Doubleday and Company, 1971, p. 119. See, too, Nathan O. Hatch, *The Democratization of American Christianity*. New Haven: Yale University Press, 1989, pp. 49–58.

70. Johnson claimed that "camp meeting revivalism" produced at least three schisms among the western Presbyterians, which ultimately led to the formation of three religious organizations in America: the Christian Church, the New Light Presbyterian Church, and the Cumberland Presbyterian Church. See Johnson, *Frontier Camp Meeting*, p. 71.

71. Hatch, *Democratization of American Christianity*, p. 49.

72. Asbury, *Journal and Letters*, p. 453.

73. Cullen T. Carter, *History of the Tennessee Conference and a Brief Summary of the General Conferences of the Methodist Church*. Nashville: Cullen T. Carter, 1948, p. 46.

74. In his September 2, 1811, letter to Thomas Coke, Asbury mentioned there were four to five hundred camp meetings held annually. See *Journal and*

*Letters*, 3:455. For his comment on the millennium, see 3:343. And to think it first appeared in Delaware!

75. Asbury, *Journal and Letters*, 3:436.

76. See Johnson, *Frontier Camp Meeting*, pp. 42–44, 47.

77. See Talbot Hamlin, *Benjamin Henry Latrobe*, New York: Oxford University Press, 1955, pp. 320–321. See also Edward C. Carter II, et al., *Latrobe's View of America*. New Haven: Yale University Press, 1985, pp. 276–277.

78. Jesse Lee, *A Short History of the Methodists in the United States of America*. Baltimore: Printed by Magill and Clime, 1810, pp. 360–362.

79. Ellen Weiss, *City in the Woods*, pp. xiii–xiv. For Copeland's work at Oak Bluffs see Weiss, pp. 79–80. For his work at Shelter Island, see correspondence between Ellen Weiss and the Society for the Preservation of Long Island Antiquities, April 24, 1980, in author's collection.

80. Kirk Mariner, "William Penn Chandler and Revivalism in the East," in *Methodist History*, April 1987, pp. 141–142. See also Kirk Mariner, *Revival's Children*, pp. 41–42.
Very little has been written about law enforcement on the camp grounds, or the camp meeting jails. An excellent jail has been preserved at Ball's Creek Camp Ground near Maiden, N.C. The Reverend J. E. Godbey tells of a Sabbath breaking whiskey seller who was brought to court at the Taylor Camp Meeting, where he was tried and convicted on three separate counts! See J. E. Godbey, *Lights and Shadows of Seventy Years*. St. Louis: Press of Nixon-Jones Printing Co., p. 136.

81. Mariner, "William Penn Chandler," in *Methodist History*, p. 142.

82. *Ibid.*, pp. 143, 145.

83. See Johnson, *Frontier Camp Meeting*, especially chapter 13, entitled "Decline of the Backwoods Revival." Here he speaks of the "camp meeting's rise and fall in popularity," p. 242. His argument about the camp meeting manual can easily be refuted, for this kind of material was available almost from the beginning. See *Observations on Camp Meetings*, published in *Minutes of a Camp Meeting Held by the Methodists*. New York: printed by John C. Totten, 1804. The original is at the Methodist Archives and History Center, Madison, N.J.

84. Strickland, *Autobiography of Cartwright*, p. 45.

85. Weiss, *City in the Woods*, p. 14.

86. *Ibid.*, pp. 14–15.

87. *Ibid.*

88. Russell E. Richey, "From Quarterly to Camp Meeting: A Reconsideration of Early American Methodism," in *Methodist History*, July 1985, p. 203.

89. The work of Lorenzo Dow is well known in scholarly circles. See John Kent, *Holding the Fort, Studies in Victorian Revivalism*. London: Epworth Press, 1978, pp. 48–59; and Richard Carwardine, *Transatlantic Revivalism, Popular Evangelicalism in Britain and America, 1790–1865*. Westport: Greenwood Press, 1978, pp. 106–107.

For the Millerite camp meetings see Isaac C. Wellcome, *History of the Second Advent Message and Mission, Doctrine and People*. Yarmouth: published by I. C. Wellcome, 1874, pp. 236–238; Francis D. Nichol, *The Midnight Cry*. Takoma Park: Review and Herald Publishing Association, 1944, pp. 104–113; and J. F. C. Harrison, *The Second Coming, Popular Millenarianism 1780–1850*. New Brunswick: Rutgers University Press, 1979, p. 193. For Apollos Hale, see Wellcome, *History of the Second Advent Message*, pp. 235–236; see also Don Neufield, editor, *Seventh Day Adventist Encyclopedia*, 10 volumes. Washington: Review and Herald Publishing Association, 1976, 10:553; and "Apollos Hale" file in author's collection.

For William B. Osborn see the author's study on "Ocean Grove," in the upcoming book to be published by the Wesleyan Holiness Project, Asbury Theological Seminary, Wilmore, Kentucky; and see "William B. Osborn" file in author's collection. Osborn established a camp meeting at Lanowli, India, in 1878. See William Taylor, *Ten Years of Self–Supporting Missions in India*. New York: Phillips and Hunt, 1882, pp. 350–354.

90. W. H. Boole, "The National Temperance Camp Meeting Association," in *The Christian Standard and Home Journal*, October 24, 1874, p. 4. Boole, a Methodist minister, member of the National Association for the Promotion of Holiness, outspoken temperance advocate, husband of woman's rights leader Ella Boole, was listed as the Corresponding Secretary of this new association. See "William H. Boole" file in author's collection.

91. See Mrs. Mary D. James, "Women's Gospel Temperance Camp Meeting at Ocean Grove," in the *Guide to Holiness*, September 1877, p. 91. Notices of this encampment also appeared in the annual *Reports* published by the Ocean Grove Association.

92. See "The Women's Holiness Camp Meeting" in the *Christian Witness*, July 4, 1885, p. 5, and August 7 and 14, 1885.

93. Charles Johnson based the major thesis of his book on this assumption, and so its title, *The Frontier Camp Meeting*. For an excellent brief critique see Richey, "From Quarterly to Camp Meeting," in *Methodist History*, July 1985.

94. Scholars have been patently wrong in the assumption that no permanent encampments were built before 1850 or even 1830. Charles Parker has said that permanent grounds began to appear in the 1830s, and suggested that the first in the East might have been Martha's Vineyard, founded in 1835. See Charles A. Parker, "The Camp Meeting on the Frontier and the Methodist Religious Resort in the East—Before 1900," in *Methodist History*, April 1980, p. 183. However, the Sing Camp Meeting at Ossining, New York (no longer a Methodist encampment), is much older and can probably qualify as the first permanent encampment in the northeast. See C. W. Christman, *Camp Meetings in the New York Annual Conference*. No publication date. See "Ossining Camp Meeting" file in author's collection. The early camp meeting structures were not all temporary, as Charles Johnson and others, have suggested. The fact that many of the early buildings, though rough and crude affairs, lasted two or three generations, is ample proof of their permanency.

The best study of the Georgia camps is Lawrence, *Feast of Tabernacles.*

95. See William Warren Sweet, *Methodism in American History*. Nashville: Abingdon Press, 1954, pp. 332–333. See, too, William Warren Sweet, *Religion on the Frontier, 1783–1840, Vol. IV, The Methodists, A Collection of Source Materials.* New York: Cooper Square Publishers, 1964, 4:68–69. See Johnson, *Frontier Camp Meeting*, pp. 242–250. See Richey's comments in "From Quarterly to Camp Meeting," *Methodist History*, July 1985, p. 202, note 5.

96. See George Hughes, *Days of Power in the Forest Temple, A Review of the Wonderful Work of God at Fourteen National Camp-Meetings, From 1867 to 1872.* Boston: John Bent and Co., 1874, pp. 26–28.

97. See Charles Parker, "The Camp Meeting on the Frontier," in *Methodist History*, April 1980, pp. 179–192. See also Stanford E. Demars, "Worship By-the-Sea; Seaside Resorts in 19th Century America," in *Focus*, Winter 1988, pp. 15–21.

98. See Parker, "The Camp Meeting on the Frontier," in *Methodist History*, April 1980, p. 184, and Demars, "Worship By-the-Sea," in *Focus*, Winter 1988, p. 16.

99. Martha's Vineyard, Ocean Grove, Pitman Grove, Mount Lebanon, Mountain Lake Park, and Lakeside still hold annual camp meetings. Moreover, these communities have become quite attractive to investors in real estate. It is increasingly difficult and expensive to buy a cottage on Martha's Vineyard, at Lakeside, or at Ocean Grove. See Jill Hand, "Quiet Corner Now Chic," in *Asbury Park Press*, August 3, 1986, p. 27.

For the lawsuit involving the Ocean Grove Camp Meeting Association see J. K. Towers, "Ocean Grove, N.J., Turmoil; the O.G.C.M.A., Citizens & Courts Speak Out," 1974-1975-1976-1977. This is a collection of letters and newspaper articles regarding the case, and is on file at the Ocean Grove

Historical Society. Ocean Grove had been granted a special state charter in 1870, and by it the Ocean Grove Camp Meeting Association operated the community much like any municipality. But the courts stripped the association of its legislative and municipal powers regarding such things as the ban for Sunday parking of automobiles and Sunday bathing at the beach. Ocean Grove was famous for these bans, but when they stopped the early Sunday morning delivery of newspapers, the courts agreed that this violated the constitutional rights of the businessman involved, and ordered the streets and beaches opened. In spite of public outrage and cries of protest, the law and charter were changed, the bans revoked, and the unique instance of living American religious history that had been preserved at Ocean Grove died. The association is still in control of the camp meeting and other religious functions, but it no longer acts as a municipality in any way.

Although the tabernacle still stands, and the homes around it can still be recognized as cottages, Pitman Grove Camp Meeting has all but disappeared. Some area churches still conduct summer evening services in the tabernacle, but the building is now owned and controlled by the borough. Its days are probably numbered.

Some of the later holiness associations reached far beyond the boundaries of their initial camp meeting work, and performed as if they were churches. The Iowa Holiness Association is one of the best examples, for it sponsored several camp meetings across the state, sent out evangelists, published a periodical, and opened a holiness college. See Kenneth O. Brown, "The Iowa Holiness Association and Its Relationship to the Camp Meeting Movement," an address read at the centennial celebration of the Iowa Holiness Association, July 3, 1978.

100. Much has been written about the Palmers and the history of the holiness movement. For the best work see John L. Peters, *Christian Perfection and American Methodism*. New York: Abingdon Press, 1956; Delbert R. Rose, *A Theology of Christian Experience*. Minneapolis: Bethany House, 1965; Charles E. Jones, *Perfectionist Persuasion*. Metuchen: Scarecrow Press, 1974; also Charles E. Jones, *A Guide to the Study of the Holiness Movement*. Metuchen: Scarecrow Press, 1974; Melvin E. Dieter, *The Holiness Revival in the Nineteenth Century*. Metuchen: Scarecrow Press, 1980; Kenneth O. Brown, "Leadership in the National Holiness Association, with Special Reference to Eschatology, 1867–1919," a Ph.D. dissertation submitted to Drew University, 1988. For the Palmers see George Hughes, *Fragrant Memories of the Tuesday Meeting and The Guide to Holiness*. Salem: Schmul Publishing Co., 1988 [reprint]; Harold E. Raser, *Phoebe Palmer Her Life and Thought*. Lewiston: The Edwin Mellen Press, 1987; Charles E. White, *The Beauty of Holiness*. Grand Rapids: Francis Asbury Press, 1986. See also the author's extensive Palmer files.

101. See Brown, "Leadership in the National Association," p. 46.

102. *Ibid.*, pp. 150–156, 167–178. See the "John Inskip" and "William McDonald" files in the author's collection.

103. Ocean Grove was founded specifically as a holiness camp meeting, and its founders and leaders were, for the most part, prominent members of the National Association for the Promotion of Holiness, such as founder William B. Osborn. Other leaders included John S. Inskip, Alfred Cookman, Elwood Stokes, Adam Wallace, and Dr. Aaron E. Ballard, often called "the grand old man of Ocean Grove." Ballard served as president from 1907 to 1919, dying in office at the age of 99. See files on each in the author's collection.

There is abundant material on Ocean Grove, and the serious researcher must visit the offices of the Ocean Grove Historical Society, which has a fine collection, including stereoscope views, periodicals, scrapbooks, etc. For history see the annual *Reports* published by the Association; Mrs. W. B. Osborn, *Pioneer Days of Ocean Grove*. New York: Methodist Book Concern, n.d.; Morris S. Daniels, *The Story of Ocean Grove Related in the Year of Its Golden Jubilee*. New York: The Methodist Book Concern, 1919; Mr. and Mrs. Richard F. Gibbons, *History of Ocean Grove, Compiled in the Year of Its Seventieth Anniversary*. Ocean Grove: *The Ocean Grove Times*, 1939; and Brenda Parnes, "Ocean Grove: A Planned Leisure Environment," in Paul A. Stellhorn, *Planned and Utopian Experiments*. Trenton: New Jersey Historical Commission, 1980.

104. Some encampments which are now holiness camp meetings are indeed older than Sychar, such as Hollow Rock, near Steubenville, Ohio, and Bentleyville Camp, Bentleyville, Pa. However, Sychar was founded as a holiness encampment, whereas the others were not. For the history of Camp Sychar see W. W. Cary, *Sychar, An Holiness Camp Meeting*. Louisville: Pentecostal Publishing Company, 1933.

105. Eleanor L. Smith, compiler and editor, *Hollow Rock: A History*. Columbus: The Watkins Printing Company, 1988.

The title page makes the claim for Hollow Rock, as does a huge sign on the campground. Nor does Hollow Rock stand alone in making such erroneous claims. The 1960 Program of the Brandywine Summit Camp Meeting in Delaware County, Pa., claimed it to be the "Oldest Continuous Camp Meeting in the East." Several eastern camps predate its 1866 founding year.

106. The best treatment to date is Dieter, *The Holiness Revival*; see chapter IV.

107. This criticism surfaced in both branches of Methodism. But see the episcopal address in *The Journal of the General Conference of the Methodist Episcopal Church (South) for 1894*. Nashville: Publishing House of the M. E. Church South, 1894, p. 25.

108. See the life and ministry of Smith in Rose, *A Theology of Christian Experience.* He had earned the right to appraise the ministry of the holiness camp meetings, for he spent nearly ten solid years of his life in ministry at such encampments. Smith's statement may be found in his article "Then and Now of the Holiness Camp Meetings," in the *Christian Witness and Advocate of Bible Holiness,* October 9, 1924, p. 2.

109. Smith, "Then and Now."

110. For Morrison's statements, see Henry Clay Morrison, "The Holiness Camp Meeting," in *The Herald,* July 5, 1967, p. 1. For saving the camp meeting, George Hughes hints strongly at this in *Days of Power,* pp. 26–29. See also Vinson Synan, *The Holiness Pentecostal Movement.* Grand Rapids: William B. Eerdman's Publishing Company, 1971, p. 41.

111. For the work of the Smiths and the European holiness revival see Dieter, *The Holiness Revival,* p. 156 ff. See also Michael P. Body, "The Hannah Whitall Smith Collection," in *The Asbury Seminarian,* Spring 1983, p. 3 ff., and Melvin E. Dieter, "The Smiths—A Biographical Sketch with Selected Items from the Collection," also in *The Asbury Seminarian,* Spring 1983, p. 7 ff. For the history of the Keswick Convention see Steven Barabas, *So Great Salvation; The History and Message of the Keswick Convention.* Westwood: Fleming H. Revell, 1952; Walter B. Sloan, *These Sixty Years; the Story of the Keswick Convention.* London: Pickering and Inglis, 1935.

112. For the story of the Prophecy Conference in America see Ernest R. Sandeen, *The Roots of Fundamentalism, British and American Millenarianism 1800–1930.* Chicago: The University of Chicago Press, 1970; George Marsden, *Fundamentalism and American Culture, The Shaping of Twentieth Century Evangelicalism 1870–1925.* New York: Oxford University Press, 1980; Timothy Weber, *Living in the Shadow of the Second Coming, American Premillennialism 1875–1982.* Grand Rapids: Academy Books, 1983; David O. Beale, *In Pursuit of Purity, American Fundamentalism Since 1850.* Greenville: Universal Publications, 1986.

Sandeen is wrong when he claims that "few Methodists were influenced by millenarianism and many of those that were seemed, inexplicably, to leave the denomination as their allegiance to millenarianism increased," p. 163. Marsden and Weber fare no better, while Beale ignores the issue completely. By 1900, several major holiness leaders, many of them Methodists (North and South), had become zealous advocates of premillennial dispensationalism. For a full critical treatment see Brown, "Leadership in the National Holiness Association," pp. 112–121.

113. Sandeen, Weber, and Beale offer a brief history of the Niagara Bible Conference, but see Larry Dean Pettegrew, "The Historical and Theological Contributions of the Niagara Bible Conference to American Fundamentalism," a doctoral dissertation submitted to Dallas Theological Seminary in 1976.

For Munhall, see the "L. W. Munhall" file in the author's collection; Paul C. Wilt, "Premillennialism in America, 1865–1918, With Special Reference to Attitudes towards Social Reform," a Ph.D. dissertation presented to the American University, Washington, D.C., 1970, p. 152; and Brown, "Leadership in the National Association," pp. 265–267. See the ads for the International Bible Conference in *Ocean Grove Record*, June 29, 1889, p. 1.

114. See Jill Torrey Renich, *The Montrose Bible Conference Story, A Dream That Refused to Fade*. Montrose: The Montrose Bible Conference, 1978. This work is an abbreviated edition of an unpublished history by Dr. Walter Vail Watson.

115. The Reverend L. L. Pickett, holiness evangelist and premillennial advocate in the Methodist Episcopal Church, South, made the complaint. See L. L. Pickett, *The Blessed Hope of His Glorious Appearing*. Louisville: Pentecostal Publishing Company, 1901, p. 335. But the leaders of the National Association, including the Reverend Charles J. Fowler, president, held firm on this issue. In 1897 the association passed its famous (or infamous) set of resolutions on the matter. See Brown, "Leadership in the National Association," pp. 214–215, 272–273.

116. Unfortunately, scholars have paid little attention to the eschatological battle that waged in the ranks of the holiness movement at the turn of the century. Some seem unaware that it even happened. For an extended treatment of it see Brown, "Leadership in the National Association," pp. 228–297. These issues spilled over into the new pentecostal movement as well and, interestingly, have been studied by various scholars. See Robert Mapes Anderson, *Vision of the Disinherited*. New York: Oxford University Press, 1979; Donald W. Dayton, *Theological Roots of Pentecostalism*. Grand Rapids: Francis Asbury Press, 1987; and D. William Faupel, "The Everlasting Gospel, The Significance of Eschatology in the Development of Pentecostal Thought," a Ph.D. dissertation submitted to the University of Birmingham, Birmingham, England, 1989.

117. For a history of Winona Lake see Vincent H. Gaddis and Jasper A. Huffman, *The Story of Winona Lake, A Memory and a Vision*. Winona Lake: published by Winona Lake Christian Assembly, 1960.

118. Theodore Morrison, *Chautauqua, A Center for Education, Religion, and the Arts in America*. Chicago: The University of Chicago Press, 1974, p. 31.

119. *Ibid.*, pp. 31–33; see also John H. Vincent, *The Chautauqua Movement*. Freeport: Books for Libraries Press, 1971, pp. 16–43. Vincent also provided a list of "other Chautauquas" and the year they started on pp. 41–42.

120. See Smith, "Then and Now," in the *Christian Witness*, October 9, 1924, p. 2. Such animosity, however, is a two-sided affair. Vincent made no bones about the fact that he did not like camp meetings, and other Chautauqua

writers shared his views. See Irene Briggs and Raymond F. DaBoll, *Recollections of the Lyceum & Chautauqua Circuits*. Freeport: The Bond Wheelwright Company, 1969. The authors claim that the founders of Chautauqua wanted something different than the "revival camp meeting style religion with its sapping emotional hysteria." Again they claimed that the grounds at Lake Chautauqua "had seen better days as the site of the tawdry sort of camp meeting that Vincent despised." See pp. 34–35. Their last remark about the condition of the grounds is false, for the camp meeting had only been there since 1869; see Vincent, *Chautauqua Movement*, pp. 16–17.

121. Morrison, *Chautauqua*, p. 35.

122. *Ibid.*, p. 69.

123. *Ibid.*, p. 182; see also Briggs and DaBoll, *Recollections*, pp. 50–90, for pictorial surveys. There is an excellent collection of Chautauqua memorabilia in the museum at the Chautauqua Institution, Chautauqua, New York.

124. Morrison, *Chautauqua*, p. 181.

125. *Ibid.*, p. 179; 1924 was the peak year for the circuits.

126. See W. W. Sweet, *Religion on the Frontier*, 4:69; Johnson makes this point, also, in *Frontier Camp Meeting*, pp. 6, 81.

127. Richey, "From Quarterly to Camp Meeting," in *Methodist History*, July 1985, p. 212.

128. The Churches of Christ in Christian Union have followed this practice for many years. See Kenneth O. Brown and P. Lewis Brevard, *History of the Churches of Christ in Christian Union*. Circleville: Circle Press, Inc., 1980, pp. 159–172.

129. One of the best examples, and largest of the holiness denominations, is the Church of the Nazarene. While some local churches sponsor a local camp, almost every district conducts official district camp meetings, and many of these grounds are now referred to as "District Centers." The national headquarters does not have a listing of these encampments; each district takes care of its own. Nor are they all advertised in the *Herald of Holiness*, the denominational periodical. See the "Denominational Camps" file in author's collection. As an observation, one wonders if this denomination is slowly moving from a point of ownership to a point of official adoption, similar to the position of the early Methodists. The best study of Nazarene encampments, though now dated, is Paul K. Moore, "History of the Camp Meeting in the Church of the Nazarene," a B.D. thesis submitted to the Nazarene Theological Seminary, Kansas City, Mo., 1951.

130. The black camp meetings are difficult to trace because, like many camps, most do not advertise outside their own community. Moreover, live

encampments are not mentioned in the black denominational histories. I have located several live black Methodist camps which predate the American Civil War, and some more modern ones are held by the Church of God (Anderson), the Church of the Nazarene, and the Seventh-day Adventist Church. See files in author's collection. A major reference tool is Charles E. Jones, *Black Holiness, A Guide to the Study of Black Participation in Wesleyan Perfectionist and Glossolalic Pentecostal Movements.* Metuchen and London: The American Theological Library Association and Scarecrow Press, Inc., 1987. As expected, it lists nothing on black camp meetings.

Anne Loveland suggests that Presbyterians in the South may have picked up the camp meeting again as early as the 1820s, and used them, sparingly, for the next thirty years or more. See Anne C. Loveland, "Presbyterians and Revivalism in the Old South," in *Journal of Presbyterian History*, Spring 1979, p. 39. However, it can be established that Presbyterians used the camp meeting idea much longer than that, for the Old Lebanon Camp Meeting in Ackerman, Mississippi, dates from 1840, and is still held each year. See "Old Lebanon Camp" file in author's collection.

The Millerite revival spawned camp meetings almost from its beginning. Isaac Wellcome claims the first one started on June 21, 1842, at Hadley, Canada. He said the first Millerite camp held in the United States started on June 29, 1842, in East Kingston, New Hampshire. See Wellcome, *History of Advent Message*, pp. 236–238. A few years later the famous American poet John Greenleaf Whittier visited the grounds, and penned a sketch of the services; see his *Prose Works*, 1:425–426. See also Francis D. Nichol, *The Midnight Cry*, pp. 104–113; he includes a picture on p. 113.

It has been commonly believed that the first Seventh-day Adventist camp meeting was held at Wright, Michigan, in September 1868. However, present research indicates that the first SDA encampment met at Johnstown Center, Wisconsin, in September 1867. See Adriel D. Chilson, "Don't Be Wrong about Wright," in the *Adventist Herald*, Winter 1987, pp. 3–8. For information on the Wright encampment see "Camp Meeting" in Don Neufield, editor, *Seventh-day Adventist Encyclopedia*, 10 volumes. Washington: Review and Herald Publishing Association, 1976, 10:223–225. For the earlier Millerite camps see Everett N. Dick, "Advent Camp Meetings," in *Adventist Heritage*, Winter 1977, pp. 3–10. Little scholarly work has been done on either the Universalist or Spiritualist camp meetings. Some postcard views of them have been found, and are available in the James Robertson collection.

131. The leaders of the Wesleyan Methodist Church held camp meetings before and after the formation of the denomination in 1844. See Lee M. Haines and Melvin E. Dieter, editors, *Conscience and Commitment, The History of the Wesleyan Methodist Church of America.* Marion: The Wesley Press, 1976, p. 45. The Wesleyan camp at West Chazy, New York, may date as early as 1842. See "West Chazy Camp" file in author's collection. The Free Methodists also conducted camp meetings before their church was founded in 1860; see Leslie

Ray Marston, *From Age to Age a Living Witness*. Winona Lake: Light and Life Press, 1960, p. 321. For a more detailed study of the problems surrounding the Bergen Camp Meeting and early Free Methodism see D. Gregory Van Dussen, "The Bergen Camp Meeting in the American Holiness Movement," in *Methodist History*, January 1983, pp. 69–89.

Many of the holiness and pentecostal organizations and associations conduct official encampments. I refer to these groups as "organizations and associations" because that is how they often refer to themselves, and I want to honor that self-acknowledgment. See Dillard L. Wood and William H. Preskitt, Jr., *Baptized with Fire, A History of the Pentecostal Fire-Baptized Holiness Church*. Franklin Springs: Advocate Press, 1982, pp. 65–76; Charles H. Moon, "A History of the Pilgrim Holiness Church, Incorporated (1967–1982)," a D.M. dissertation presented to the Anderson School of Theology, Anderson, Ind., 1982; John W. Zechman, general editor, *A History of God's Missionary Church, Penn's Creek, Pennsylvania, 1935–1985*. Penns Creek: God's Missionary Church, 1985.

132. For the story of the pentecostal revival see Synan, *The Holiness Pentecostal Movement*; Anderson, *Vision of the Disinherited*; Dayton, *Theological Roots of Pentecostalism*, and W. J. Hollenweger, *The Pentecostals, The Charismatic Movement in the Churches*. Minneapolis: Augsburg Publishing House, 1969. See reference tools, Charles E. Jones, *A Guide to the Study of the Pentecostal Movement*, 2 volumes. Metuchen and London: Scarecrow Press, Inc., and The American Theological Library Association, 1983; Watson E. Mills, *Charismatic Religion in Modern Research: A Bibliography*. Macon: Mercer University Press, 1985; Stanley M. Burgess and Gary B. McGee, editors, *Dictionary of Pentecostal and Charismatic Movements*. Grand Rapids: Regency Reference Library, Zondervan Publishing House, 1988.

133. For Charles Parham and the Columbus, Kansas, camp see Edith L. Blumhofer, *The Assemblies of God, A Chapter in the Story of American Pentecostalism*, 2 volumes. Springfield: Gospel Publishing House, 1:88–89; William W. Menzies, *Anointed to Serve, The Story of the Assemblies of God*. Springfield: Gospel Publishing House, 1971, pp. 46–47. For Synan see *Holiness Pentecostal Movement*, p. 95.

134. *A Historical Account of the Apostolic Faith, A Trinitarian-Fundamental Evangelistic Organization*. Portland: Apostolic Faith Publishing House, 1965, p. 73, and p. 124 ff.

135. Joseph E. Campbell, *The Pentecostal Holiness Church, 1898–1948*. Franklin Springs: Publishing House of the Pentecostal Holiness Church, 1951, pp. 399–404; Menzies, *Anointed to Serve*, p. 87.

136. For treatment of the Falcon Camp see Campbell, *Pentecostal Holiness Church*, pp. 362–366. For the Durant camp see Mayme E. Williams, *Memories of My Heart*. Honolulu: Orovan Books, 1988. The same logic must

apply to the Assemblies of God camp meeting at Charlton, Mass. It dates back to the Methodist campground at Montwait, but the leaders were not pentecostal at that time. A double schema must be used there, also. For a history of that camp see "Special Souvenir Issue" of *Word and Work*, May 1989.

137. See McGready, "Short Narrative," in *New York Missionary Magazine*, 1803, pp. 153, 193–195; McGready even thought a three-year-old child had been converted; see his letter to the *Western Missionary Magazine*, June 1803, pp. 176–177. Richard McNemar topped that, however, by claiming the Spirit's work on an eight-month-old child at the "general camp meeting" at Concord, Ky., in May 1801. See Richard McNemar, *The Kentucky Revival: A Short History of the Late Extraordinary Outpouring of the Spirit of God in the Western States of America*. New York: Reprinted by Edward O. Jenkins, 1846, p. 24.

138. For Martha Inskip see Kenneth O. Brown, "The World-Wide Evangelist—The Life and Work of Martha Inskip," in *Methodist History*, July 1983, pp. 179–191.

139. Clifford V. Anderson, "Camping History," in *An Introduction to Christian Camping*, Werner Graendorf and Lloyd D. Mattson, editors. Chicago: Moody Press, 1979, p. 33 ff. He offers a good bibliography on the history of the camping movement. See also Lloyd Mattson's new book, *Church in the Wilderness*, to be released in 1993 by Harold Shaw Publishers of Wheaton, Ill.

140. See Charles W. Maynard, *Where the Rhododendrons Grow, A History of Camping and Leisure Ministries in the Holston Conference*. Johnson City: The Overmountain Press, 1988. This is one of the few histories of conference or district camping published by any denomination.

141. See Clifford Anderson, "Camping History," p. 47. See "CCI Around the World," in *Christian Camping International/USA 1990–1991 Official Guide to Christian Camps and Conference Centers*, p. 11.

142. *Ibid.*, p. 12. The *Journal of Christian Camping* is a periodical devoted to Christian camping. It is filled with ads for materials camps would want or need, and has articles aimed at such needs as strategic planning, fund raising, marketing, and impacting lives for Christ.

143. Dr. Charles A. Parker, correspondence with author, October 9, 1987.

**Part Two
A Working Bibliography of
Materials Related to
Camp Meetings, Bible Conferences,
and Christian Retreats**

# A WORKING BIBLIOGRAPHY

This bibliography is fairly extensive, but it should be considered as an introductory working tool rather than an *exhaustive* treatment of the camp meeting, Bible conference, Chautauqua, and Christian retreat literature. Moreover, this volume has certain imposed limitations that must be acknowledged. It is not, nor does it pretend to be, a bibliography of revivalism, the Great Revival, the holiness movement, or the pentecostal charismatic movement. Such books and theses have already been written, and the best sources are cited in the notes.

Other exclusions also deserve mention. While some theses and books do cite individual camp meeting folders, brochures, programs, and booklets, the author's collection of these is so extensive that individual citation here is simply impossible. Moreover, the James Robertson collection of camp meeting pictures, stereoscope views, and postcards is so large that individual entry is impractical. This bibliography does not contain entries for taped sermons preached at camp meetings, published or unpublished. (Some denominationally related libraries have extensive holdings of this material, and should be consulted.) The subject of "camp meeting hymnals" is not treated separately here because it has been published elsewhere.

All the entries cited herein have been chosen with three basic criteria in mind: 1. importance to the founding of the camp meeting in general; 2. importance to the history of a specific encampment; 3. importance to the growth and/or development of the camp meeting movement.

*Unpublished Material*

## Collections

Archival Collections. Several of these deserve mention here, especially the United Methodist Archives and History Center in Madison, N.J., which has a fine collection of camp meeting materials, including a few early brochures and prints, and some very early published pamphlets. See the "Annotated Bibliography on Camp Meetings and Camp Grounds in the Drew University Library," on file. The archives at Duke University in Durham, N.C., contain several early Methodist diaries and many other resources relative to camp meeting history. The serious student must also consult the various denominational libraries and archives, as well as the independent archival collections at Asbury Theological Seminary, Wilmore, Kentucky; Oral Roberts University, Tulsa, Oklahoma; the Billy Graham Center on Evangelism, Wheaton, Ill.; and the Smith Library at Chautauqua Institution, Chautauqua, New York.

Brown, Kenneth O. and Charlotte E., extensive collection of camp meeting material, containing well over two thousand files on camp meetings, Bible conferences, and Christian retreats in the United States and Canada. The files include nearly three thousand folders, brochures, pamphlets, and broadsides, several pieces of unpublished historical material, over one hundred individual camp meeting histories, over one thousand items of correspondence and surveys, over two hundred post-cards, pictures, and stereoscope views, and a collection of camp meeting periodicals. This is the largest collection of camp meeting-related materials in the nation.

The Delbert R. Rose Papers at Asbury Theological Seminary, Wilmore, Kentucky. The collection includes brochures and other material, as well as the surveys of holiness camp meetings which Dr. Rose conducted as part of his research for the National Holiness Association.

McClarran, Harry, Chautauqua and Camp Meeting Files. Representative material gathered by Mr. McClarran over a period of many years, and used by him for articles and historical lectures.

Robertson, James, collection of several thousand postcard and stereoscope views of camp meetings, Bible conferences, and Christian retreat centers. This is the largest private collection of its kind in the nation.

Weiss, Ellen G., "Camp Meeting Research Files." These were compiled while conducting research for the excellent volume, *City in the Woods*.

## Theses

Beal, Ruth E., "History of Camp Meetings in America and Their Influence upon the Church," an M.A.R. thesis submitted to Chicago Evangelistic Institute, 1949.

Blanchard, Charles L., "The Modern Camp Meeting," a B.D. thesis submitted to the Louisville Presbyterian Seminary, 1962.

Boles, John B., "The Religious Mind of the Old South; the Era of the Great Revival, 1787–1805," a Ph.D. dissertation submitted to the University of Virginia, 1969.

Brown, Kenneth O., "Leadership in the National Holiness Association, With Special Reference to Eschatology," a Ph.D. dissertation submitted to Drew University, 1988.

Bruce, Dickson D., "And They All Sang Hallelujah; Plain-Folk Camp Meeting Religion 1800–1845," a Ph.D. dissertation submitted to the University of Pennsylvania, 1971.

Carter, Ernest L., "The Camp Meeting Movement in the Early Ohio Valley," an M.A. thesis submitted to Ohio Wesleyan University, 1922.

Crawther, Robert W., Jr., "Methodist Camp Meetings in Southern New Jersey," an M.A. thesis submitted to Princeton University, 1959.

Dalton, James S., "The Kentucky Camp Meeting Revivals of 1797–1805 as Rites of Initiation," a Ph.D. dissertation submitted to the University of Chicago, 1973.

Fankhauser, Craig C., "The Heritage of Faith: An Historical Evaluation of the Holiness Movement in America," an M.A. thesis submitted to Pittsburg State University, 1983.

Hearn, Anthony, "The Development of Camp-Meetings," a B.D. thesis submitted to the Candler School of Theology, Emory University, 1920.

Hough, Donald W., "A History of the Camp Meeting Movement From About 1800 to 1900," a B.D. thesis submitted to Nazarene Theological Seminary, 1951.

Howell, William E., "History of Camp Meetings," a B.D. thesis submitted to the School of Theology at Southern Methodist University, 1935.

Hughes, Howard R., "The History of Delanco Camp Meeting Association," a B.D. thesis submitted to Eastern Baptist Theological Seminary, 1961.

Hulan, Richard H., "Camp-Meeting Spiritual Folksongs: Legacy of the 'Great Revival in the West,'" a Ph.D. dissertation submitted to the University of Texas, 1978.

Johnson, Charles A., "The Frontier Camp Meeting, Methodist Harvest Time," a Ph.D. dissertation submitted to Northwestern University, 1951.

Johnson, David C., "The Importance of Doctrinal Teaching in Holiness Camp Meetings," an M.A.R. thesis submitted to Western Evangelical Seminary, 1976.

Kee, Francis J., "History of the Clear Lake, Iowa, Chautauqua," an M.A. thesis submitted the State University of Iowa, 1938.

Kewley, Arthur E., "Mass Evangelism in Upper Canada before 1830," a Th.D. dissertation submitted to Victoria University, 1960.

Kildall, Wayne F., "A History of the Northwest Washington Holiness Association and Camp Meeting, Ferndale, Washington, 1902–1952," a B.D. thesis submitted to Western Evangelical Seminary, 1952.

Kimbrell, Charles W., "The Camp Meeting as a Factor in the Growth of Early American Methodism, 1794–1844," a B.D. thesis submitted to the School or Religion, Duke University, 1937.

Moon, Charles R., "A History of the Pilgrim Holiness Church, Incorporated (1967–1982)," an M.A. thesis submitted the Anderson School of Theology, 1982.

Moore, Paul K., "History of the Camp Meeting in the Church of the Nazarene," a B.D. thesis submitted to Nazarene Theological Seminary, 1951.

Parker, Charles A., "A Study of the Preaching at the Ocean Grove, New Jersey, Camp Meeting, 1870–1900," a Ph.D. dissertation submitted to Louisiana State University, 1959.

Porter, Ellen Jane Lorenz, "A Treasury of Camp Meeting Spirituals," a Ph.D. dissertation submitted to the Union Graduate School, 1978.

Powell, John James, "The Origin and History of the Methodist Camp Meeting Movement in North Carolina," a B.D. thesis submitted to Duke Divinity School, 1944.

Russell, Emily W. B., "An Environmental History of Mt. Tabor, New Jersey," an M.A. thesis submitted to Rutgers University, 1974.

Sims, John N., "The Hymnody of the Campmeeting Tradition," an S.M.D. dissertation submitted to Union Theological Seminary, 1960.

Soderwall, Lorin Harris, "The Rhetoric of the Methodist Camp Meeting Movement: 1800–1850," a Ph.D. dissertation submitted to the University of Southern California, 1971.

Tremain, Lloyd Carlos, "An Evaluation of the Family Camp Program of the Pacific Northwest Conference of the Free Methodist Church," an M.Ed. thesis submitted to Seattle Pacific College, 1968.

Vesterfelt, Mark, "The Organization and History of the Church of Daniel's Band," an M.A. thesis submitted to Marion College, 1988.

Weinert, Leonard E., "A History of the Clark County Holiness Association, Vancouver, Washington," a B.D. thesis submitted to Western Evangelical Seminary, 1952.

Wesche, Percival A., "The Revival of the Camp Meeting by the Holiness Groups," an M.A. thesis submitted to the University of Chicago, 1945.

## Research Papers

Brown, Kenneth O., "The Development of Holiness Camp Meetings in Ohio," a research paper presented to Asbury Theological Seminary, 1975.

———, "From Seedtime to Harvest; The Great Awakening and the Founding of the American Camp Meeting," a research paper submitted to Drew University, 1979.

Bush, Albert W., Jr., "An Analysis of the Cain Ridge Meeting in Paris, Kentucky, 1801," a 1969 research paper on file at the Commission on Archives and History, Ohio West Conference, United Methodist Church, Delaware, Ohio.

Copeland, Jenny, "History of Rock Spring Camp Ground," a research paper submitted to Duke Divinity School, 1986.

Hinson, Edward T., "The Camp Meeting," a 1972 research paper on file at Sandor Tezsler Library, Wofford College, Spartanburg, S.C.

McKnight, Helen Bowling, "John McGee—Methodist Circuit Rider and Camp Meeting Evangelist," a research paper on file at the Tennessee State Library and Archives, Nashville, Tenn.

Mickel, Christopher A., "The Change in the Perspective on Camp Meetings, in the Methodist Magazine Between 1818 and 1826," a research paper submitted to Drew Theological Seminary, n.d.

Pierce, David W., "The History and Contemporary Significance of Camp Meetings in the Eastern Area of the Church of the United Brethren in Christ," a research paper submitted to United Theological Seminary, 1964.

Scott, Doug, "History of Indian Field Camp Meeting," a 1979 research paper on file with the Board of trustees, Indian Field Camp Meeting.

Strassburg, S. S., "A Study of the Psychological Factors in the American Camp Meetings during the Western Revival of 1800," an undated honors essay on file at Ohio Wesleyan University.

Winwright, Tobias, "Pilgrimage of Prayer and Praise: Antebellum Camp Meetings and Methodism," a research paper submitted to Duke Divinity School, 1989.

## Addresses

Brown, Kenneth O., "The Camp Meeting and the Holiness Movement," an address presented to the Ocean Grove Historical Society, August 10, 1989.

——, "Holy Ground, A Study on the Founding of the American Camp Meeting," an address presented to the Ocean Grove Historical Society, August 1, 1990.

——, "The Iowa Holiness Association and Its Relationship to the Camp Meeting Movement," a paper presented to the Iowa Holiness Association Camp Meeting on the observance of its centennial celebration, July 3, 1978.

"Cane Ridge," script of taped lecture given at the Cane Ridge Meeting House, n.d.

Grissom, W. L., "Some First Things in North Carolina Methodism," an address presented to the North Carolina Historical Society, 1908.

Jones, Dr. Willis R., "Journey into Union: Drama and Destiny," an address delivered at the Annual Cane Ridge Day, Cane Ridge, Kentucky, June 29, 1982.

McCurley, Edward B., "Our History through Music," an address delivered at the Annual Cane Ridge Day, Cane Ridge, Kentucky, June 19, 1984.

McLaughlin, George A., "For What Does the Iowa Holiness Association Stand," a paper read before the Iowa Holiness Association School of Evangelists, June 1, 1911.

Parker, Charles A., "Ocean Grove—Queen of Camp Meetings," a paper submitted to the Religious Speech Communication Association Convention, 1983.

Payne, Duke, "Cane Ridge Personalities," an address delivered at the Annual Cane Ridge Day, Cane Ridge, Kentucky, June 28, 1983.

Ridout, George W., "Some Aspects of the Camp Meeting," a paper presented to the Camden, N.J., preacher's meeting, 1913.

Short, Harry R., and D. Wayne Davis, "Peter Cartwright, A Legend in His Time," written to be read at the unveiling of a highway marker erected by the Kentucky Historical Society, September 13, 1970.

Stoddard, Paul W., "Pine Grove in Days Gone By," a revised transcript of a lecture delivered at Pine Grove, Canaan, Connecticut, September 2, 1951.

Stokes, E. C., "Ocean Grove, What It Was, Is and Hopes to Be," an address delivered on Founders' Day, July 31, 1914. No publishing data, n.d.

Stokes, Elwood H., "Ocean Grove: An Historical Address Delivered at Its Sixth Anniversary, July 31st, 1875," published in *The Ocean Grove Record*, August 14, 1875.

Warner, George R., "The Camp-Meeting Supporting Missions (Persons and Purses)," an address presented at the Campmeeting Seminar, 95th Annual Convention of the National Holiness Association, Chicago, Ill., April 16, 1963.

## Other Unpublished Papers and Works

"Annotated Bibliography on Camp Meetings and Camp Grounds in the Drew University Library," undated paper on file at the United Methodist Archives and History Center, Madison, N.J.

Byers, C. B., "Camp Meetings—Their Birth and Development in the Brethren in Christ Church," undated paper on file in the Brethren in Christ Church Archives, Myerstown, Pa.

Cheeck, Martha B., "A Resume of the History of the Old Red River Meeting House," a paper on file in the Manuscript Division of the Kentucky Library, Western Kentucky University, in Bowling Green, Ky.

"History of the Camp Meeting," undated typed paper on file in the Christian Holiness Association Collection, Asbury Theological Seminary, Wilmore, Ky.

Nelson, Duane, "The Frontier Campmeeting in the Evangelical Association," 1962, typed manuscript on file at the United Methodist Archives and History Center, Madison, N.J.

Thornton, Harrison John, "Chautauqua—Adventure in Popular Education," a two-volume unpublished typed manuscript on file at the University of Iowa.

## Minutes

"Minutes of the Central Michigan Holiness Association," 1909–1926; originals located in the B. L. Fisher Library, Asbury Theological Seminary, Wilmore, Ky.

"Minutes of the Detroit Holiness Association," 1923–1957; originals located in the B. L. Fisher Library, Asbury Theological Seminary, Wilmore, Ky.

"Minutes of the National Association for the Promotion of Holiness," 1907–1919; originals located in the B. L. Fisher Library, Asbury Theological Seminary, Wilmore, Ky.

"Proceedings of the South Carolina Holiness Association," 1914–1942; originals located in the B. L. Fisher Library, Asbury Theological Seminary, Wilmore, Ky.

*Published Material*

## General Literature on Camp Meetings

Adams, Doug. *Meeting House to Camp Meeting: Toward a History of American Free Church Worship from 1620 to 1835*. Saratoga: Modern Liturgy Resource Publications, 1981.

*An Apology for Camp-Meetings; Illustrative of Their Good Effects and Answering the Principal Objections Urged against Them*. New York: Printed by John C. Totten, 1810.

Ayars, John E. *The Holiness Revival of the Past Century, Commemorative of the National Holiness Camp Meeting Association, Its Work and the Philadelphia Friday Meeting*. Philadelphia: J. E. A., n.d.

Baugh, Stanley T. *Camp Grounds and Camp Meetings in South Arkansas*. Little Rock: Epworth Press, 1953.

Brown, Elizabeth, "Camps and Summer Conferences," in *Orientation in Religious Education*. Edited by Philip Henry Lotz. Nashville: Abingdon-Cokesbury Press, 1950.

Bruce, Dickson D. *And They All Sang Hallelujah: Plain-Folk Camp-meeting Religion, 1800–1845*. Knoxville: University of Tennessee Press, 1974.

Cain, J. B. *Tents and Tabernacles, Methodist Campmeetings in the Mississippi Conference, 1804–1856*. Published by the Methodist Conference Historical Society, 1956.

*The Camp Meeting Extra*. No publishing data, n.d. [Poem.]

*Camp Meeting Manual, Prepared by the National Holiness Association Camp Meeting Seminar, Bishop Henry Ginder, Director*. Marion: 196– .

*Camp Meeting Review; Containing the Proceedings of a Camp Meeting, and a Confutation of the Arguments Which are Produced in Favor of the Same, Also Showing that they are not for the Good of the Society, Written by a Visitor to one of the Meetings*. No publishing data, [1824].

*Camp Meetings, Described and Exposed; Strange Things Stated*. No publication data, [1820?].

*Cane Ridge Bicentennial Sampler; Commemorating the 200th Anniversary of the 1791 Construction of the Cane Ridge Meeting House*. Paris: Cane Ridge Preservation Project, 1991.

Cary, W. W. *On Going to Camp Meetings*. Wilmore: W. W. Cary, n.d.

Christman, C. W. *Camp Meetings in the New York Annual Conference*. No publication data, n.d.

Cleveland, Catherine. *The Great Revival in the West, 1797–1805*. Chicago: University of Chicago Press, 1916.

Conkin, Paul K. *Cane Ridge, America's Pentecost*. Madison: University of Wisconsin Press, 1990.

Cook, Silas Parsons. *After Twenty-Five Years, A Memorial of the Tent Meeting in Ludlow in 1875*. Ludlow: R. S. Warner, 1901.

*Cottage Dialogues: or Conversations on Camp Meetings and Other Subjects, between William James and Others*. New York: published by T. Mason and G. Lane, 1837.

Danford, S. A. *Spreading Scriptural Holiness, or The North Dakota Movement*. Chicago: The Christian Witness Co., 1913.

Dickinson, Hoke S. *The Cane Ridge Reader*. No publication data, 1972.

Dieter, Melvin E. *The Holiness Revival of the Nineteenth Century*. Metuchen: Scarecrow Press, 1980.

Doak, Ruth. *Cowboy Camp Meeting*. No publication data: by the author, n.d.

Duvall, George A. *A History of Methodist Camp Meetings*. No publishing data, 1931.

*An Essay on Camp Meetings. By the author of "The True Evangelist."* New York: Lane and Scott, 1849.

Evans, Joe M. *A Corral Full of Stories, Rounded Up by Joe M. Evans*. El Paso: The McMath Company, [1939].

*A Faithful Narrative on Transactions Noticed at the Camp Meeting in Goshen, Conn., Sept., 1808*. No publishing data, 1809.

Finlayson, Westbrook. *The Lure of the Camp Meeting*. Wilmore: The Herald Press, n.d.

Fitch, W. *The Encampment; A Record of Tuscarawas Valley Camp Meeting*. Canal Dover: n.d.

Gorham, Barlow W. *Camp Meeting Manual, A Practical Book for the Camp Ground*. Boston: published by H. V. Degen, 1854.

Graendorf, Werner, and Lloyd D. Mattson, eds. *An Introduction to Christian Camping*. Chicago: Moody Press, 1979.

Grimes, John F. *The Romance of the American Camp Meeting*. Cincinnati: The Caxton Press, 1922.

*A History of the Revival of Holiness in St. Paul's M. E. Church, Providence, R.I., 1880–1887; A Statement of the Circumstances which Led to the Formation of the South Providence Holiness Association and the People's Evangelical Church, Published by Order of the Association*. Providence: E. L. Freeman & Son, 1887.

Holmes, William. *The Camp Meeting; A Poem in Three Parts*. Boston: Printed by D. S. King, 1842.

Hughes, George. *Days of Power in the Forest Temple. A Review of the Wonderful Work of God at Fourteen National Camp-Meetings, from 1867 to 1872*. Boston: John Bent and Company, 1873.

Jackson, John B. *The Necessity for Ruins*. Published by John B. Jackson, 1980.

Jennings, S. K., "Defense of Camp Meetings," in Lorenzo Dow, ed. *The Dealings of God*. Cincinnati: Applegate & Company, 1869.

———. *Six Objections to Camp Meetings Stated and Answered*. No place of publication: Graniland Printers, 1806.

Jennings, Samuel K. *A Defense of the Camp Meetings in Six Objections: Stated and Answered*. Graniland: no publisher, 1806.

Jernigan, C. B. *Pioneer Days in the Holiness Movement in the Southwest*. Kansas City: Pentecostal Nazarene Publishing House, 1919.

Johnson, Charles A. *The Frontier Camp Meeting; Religion's Harvest Time*. Dallas: Southern Methodist University Press, 1955.

Johnson, Emily M., et al. *Heritage from the Lord, A History of Pitman United Methodist Church 1885–1985*. Printed by The Review Printing Company, 1985.

Jones, Charles E. *Guide to the Study of the Holiness Movement*. Metuchen: Scarecrow Press, 1974.

———. *Guide to the Study of the Pentecostal Movement*, 2 volumes. Metuchen: Scarecrow Press, 1983.

Kidder, Daniel. *The Grove Meeting*. New York: Lane and Scott, 1852.

Knapp, Martin Wells. *Electric Shocks from Pentecostal Batteries; or, Food and Fire from Salvation Park Campmeeting*. Cincinnati: M. W. Knapp, Revivalist Office, 1899.

————. *Electric Shocks no. II from Pentecostal Batteries; or, Pentecostal Glories from Salvation Park Campmeeting, 1900*. Cincinnati: M. W. Knapp, Revivalist Office, 1900.

————. *Electric Shocks no. III from Pentecostal Batteries; or, Salvation Park Campmeeting, 1901*. Cincinnati: M. W. Knapp, Salvationist Office, 1901.

Knapp, Minnie C. *Electric Shocks no. IV from Pentecostal Batteries*. Cincinnati: Mrs. M. W. Knapp, Revivalist Office, 1902.

Lawrence, Harold. *A Feast of Tabernacles, Georgia Campgrounds and Campmeetings*. Published by the author, 1990.

Long, Edwin M. *The Union Tabernacle; or Moveable Tent Church*. Philadelphia: Parry & McMillan, 1859.

McConnell, Lela G. *The Pauline Ministry in the Kentucky Mountains, or A Brief Account of the Kentucky Mountain Holiness Association*. Louisville: Pentecostal Publishing Company, [1942].

McLaughlin, G. A. *For What Does the Iowa Holiness Association Stand?* University Park: Printed by The College Press, n.d. (Reprint of a 1911 article published in *Christian Witness*.)

McLean, A., and J. W. Eaton. *Penuel; or Face to Face with God*. New York: W. C. Palmer, 1869.

McNemar, Richard. *The Kentucky Revival, or, A Short History of the Late Extraordinary Out-Pouring of the Spirit of God, in the Western States of America*. Cincinnati: 1807. (Also reprinted in 1846.)

Manship, Andrew. *History of Gospel Tents and Experience*. Philadelphia: Published by the author, 1884.

*A Manual for Leaders of Church Camps for Junior Boys and Girls*. Chicago: International Council of Religious Education, 1947.

Massebeau, W. A. *The Camp Meeting in South Carolina Methodism*. Published by order of the Upper South Carolina and South Carolina Conference Historical Societies, 1919.

Maynard, Charles W. *Where the Rhododendrons Grow, A History of Camping and Leisure Ministries in the Holston Conference*. Johnson City: The Overmountain Press, 1988.

Mead, A. P. *Manna in the Wilderness; or The Grove and Its Altar.* Philadelphia: Perkinpine & Higgins, 1859.

*Minutes of a Camp Meeting Held by the Methodists in the Town of Carmel, Dutchess County.* New York: Printed by John C. Totten, 1804.

*The Mow Cop Story 1807–1957; 150th Anniversary of the First Camp Meeting.* London: Epworth Press, 1957.

Nichols, Daisy Josephine. *Proceedings of Sychar Camp Meeting.* Cincinnati: God's Revivalist, 1903.

*Observations on Camp Meetings.* No place of publication, Hugh Bourne, 1807.

*Ocean Grove Auditorium.* No publishing data, 1949.

*Old Cane Ridge Meeting House; Bicentennial June 29, October 5, 1991.* No publishing data, n.d. [Pamphlet.]

Oliver, Lon D. *A Guide to the Cane Ridge Revival.* Lexington: Lexington Theological Seminary Library, 1988.

"Origin of Camp Meetings," in Thomas Mason, compiler. *Zion's Songster; or A Collection of Hymns and Spiritual Songs, Usually Sung at Camp-Meetings, and also in revivals of religion.* New York: Harper and Brothers, 1843.

Pearce, Joseph. *On the Holy Mount . . . A Remembrance of Mow Cop Primitive Methodist Camp Meetings.* London: Pickering and Inglis, 1937.

*A Poem Written on a Methodist Camp Meeting.* New York: [Rockwell and Churchill, printed for the purchaser, 1807.]

Pomeroy, B. M. *Visions from Modern Mounts.* Albany: VanBenthuysen Printing House, 1871.

*Primitive Methodist Church, 1807–1907, Mow Cop Centenary Celebration; Programme of Camp Meetings, Love Feasts, Public Meetings and Other Services.* No publication data, 1907.

Rees, Byron J. *Hallelujahs from Portsmouth, no. 2; or a Report of the Portsmouth Camp Meeting.* Springfield: Christian Unity Publishing Co., 1897.

———. *Hallelujahs from Portsmouth Campmeeting Number Three, a Report of the Camp Meeting held at Portsmouth Rhode Island, July 29th to August 8th, 1898.* Springfield: Christian Unity Publishing Co., 1898.

Rogers, James R. *The Cane Ridge Meeting House*. Cincinnati: Standard Publishing Company, 1910.

Sechler, R. *Camp Grounds in Missouri*. No publishing data, [1970].

Sharman, Edward. *The Christian World Unmasked; or an Enquiry into the Foundation of Methodist Camp Meetings*. Watertown: Sharman, 1819.

Spicer, Tobias. *Camp Meetings Defended*. New Haven: T. G. Woodward, 1828.

Stilgoe, John R. *Common Landscape of America 1580–1845*. New Haven: Yale University Press, 1982.

Stokes, Katy. *Paisano; Story of a Cowboy and a Camp Meeting*. Waco: Texian Press, 1980.

Sullivan, Charles L. *Gathering at the River: South Mississippi's Methodist Camp Meetings*. Perkinston: Mississippi Gulf Coast Community College Press, 1990.

Swallow, Silas. *Camp Meetings: Their Origin, History and Utility. Also, Their Perversion, and How to Correct it. Embracing a Careful Review of the Sabbath Question*. New York: Nelson and Phillips, 1879.

*"They Preach and Pray, and Sweetly Sing": Methodist Camp Meeting Hymns*. Madison: General Commission of Archives and History of the United Methodist Church, 1990.

Thompson, Rhodes, editor. *Cane Ridge Meeting-House, A Temple of Christian Unity*. No publication data, n.d.

————. *Voices from Cane Ridge*. St. Louis: The Bethany Press, 1954.

*A Treatise on the Proceedings of a Camp Meeting Held in Bern, N.Y., County of Albany*. Albany: Webster and Skinner, 1810.

Tuttle, J. H. *Description of a Methodist Camp Meeting. Held in Hannibal, Oswego County, N.Y., September, 1852*, Auburn: Henry M. Stone, Printer, 1852.

Voss, J. Ellis. *Summer Resort: An Ecological Analysis of a Satellite Community*. Philadelphia: University of Pennsylvania, 1941.

Wallace, Adam. *A Modern Pentecost*. Philadelphia: Methodist Home Journal Publishing House, 1873.

Ward, C. M. *Camp Meeting Religion*. Springfield: Gospel Publishing House, 1964.

Washburn, B. A. *Holiness Links. Contains Scripture Lessons for Morning and Evening Devotions, with Notes by the Author; also The*

*History of the Rise and Progress of the Holiness Movement in Southern California.* Los Angeles: published at Pentecost Office, 1887.

Wilkes, Arthur, and Joseph Lovatt. *Mow Cop and the Camp Meeting Movement; Sketches of Primitive Methodism.* Leominster: Orphans' Printing Press, Ltd., [1942].

Williams, Mrs. E. E. *Pentecostal Services at Mountain Lake Park ... 1896.* Philadelphia: published by Rev. John Thompson, 1896.

Woods, Gayle. *Kelly's Chapel: A Historical Survey.* No publication data, n.d.

Woodward, W. D. *Hallelujahs from Portsmouth; or, A Report of the Portsmouth Camp Meeting.* Springfield: Christian Unity Publishing House, 1896.

Yatman, C. H. *Young People's Meetings of Ocean Grove, Summer, 1887.* Newark: Wm. A. Baker Co., 1887.

## Periodical Articles

Adams, Doug, "Camp Meetings and Worship," in *Liturgy*, 1983, pp. 91–95.

Akers, Lewis R., "The Holiness Camp Meetings of America," in *The Herald*, May 21, 1958.

Albanese, Catherine, "Savage, Sinner and Saved: Davy Crockett, Camp Meetings and the Wild Frontier," in *American Quarterly*, Winter 1981, pp. 482–501.

Arminius, Theophilus, "The Origin of the Camp Meeting," in *Western Christian Advocate*, September 6, 1839, p. 77.

Balmer, Randall H., "From Frontier Phenomenon to Victorian Institution: The Methodist Camp Meeting in Ocean Grove, New Jersey," in *Methodist History*, April 1987, pp. 194–200.

Bennett, W. G., "The First American Camp Meeting," in *Pentecostal Herald*, May 31, 1950, p. 3.

Bittner, W. Sanford, "Camp Meeting Time," in *Ohio Historical Society Echoes*, July, 1965, p. 1.

Boehm, Henry, "Camp Meetings Eighty-Nine Years Ago," in *Christian Standard and International Holiness Journal*, November 7, 1895, p. 5.

Bowman, Tom, "Mount Gretna is Pennsylvania's Chautauqua," in *Pennsylvania Magazine*, August 1987, pp. 25–30.

Bradford, Richard S., "Take Me out to the Campgrounds!," article in file of Mr. Harry McClarran, no publishing data, n.d.

Brasher, J. L., "Some Samples of Camp Meeting History," in *The Herald*, May 13, 1953, p. 3.

Brown, Kenneth O., "Camp Meeting Evangelism—A Holiness Tradition," in *The Sounding Board*, Spring 1982, no pagination.

————, "Finding America's Oldest Camp Meeting," in *Methodist History*, July 1990, pp. 252–254.

————, "Holiness Camp Meetings in Ohio," in *The Advocate*, August 12, 1971, p. 5.

————, "UMs Should Be Proud of Camp Meeting Past," in *United Methodist Reporter*, June 9, 1989, p. 2.

Bryan, William Jennings, "The Nation-Wide Chautauqua," in *The Independent*, Volume 79, 1914, pp. 21–23.

Bugg, R., "Can We Let Ourselves Go?," in *Church School*, July 1969, p. 18.

————, "Ministry with Families, Christians Grow in Campfires' Glow," in *Adult Teacher*, Fall 1967, p. 11.

Burns, Gerald P., "A Short History of Camping," in *The Camping Magazine*, February 1949, p. 14.

Butler, C. W., "A Cross Section of Camp Meeting History," in *Christian Witness and Advocate of Bible Holiness*, September 22, 1938, p. 8.

Cain, J. B., "Methodist Camp Meetings in the Deep South, 1799–1859," in *World Parish*, August 1959, pp. 32–43.

Callaghan, A. A., "Camp Meetings in Maine," in *Journal of the Maine Annual Conference of the Methodist Episcopal Church*, 1951, pp. 59–67.

"Camp Meeting," no publisher, August 27, 1967, pp. 11–14. [Article on file at the United Methodist Archives and History Center, Madison, N.J.]

"Camp Meetings and a Great Revival," undated newspaper clippings about Red River Meeting House, on file at Manuscript Division, Kentucky Library, Western Kentucky University, Bowling Green, Ky.

"Camp Meetings and Campgrounds in South Georgia," in *Historical Highlights*, Spring 1990, pp. 42–50.

"Camp Meetings and Their Origin," in *Christian Advocate and Journal [New York Christian Advocate]*, August 26, 1831, p. 206.

"Camp Meeting of 1872" [reproduction of 1872 article in *Ours Illustrated*] in *Dukes County Intelligencer*, 1987 [29(2)], pp. 64–67.

Campbell, B. F., "Origin of Camp Meetings," in *Christian Witness and Advocate of Bible Holiness*, August 18, 1908, p. 11.

"Canadian Readers Take Notice," in *Christian Witness and Advocate of Bible Holiness*, December 8, 1910, p. 13.

Carradine, Beverly, "The Camp Meeting," in *Christian Witness and Advocate of Bible Holiness*, May 11, 1905, p. 4.

Carter, R. M., "Forum on the Bay," in *Methodist History*, January 1968, p. 50.

Cartwright, Charles, "Nipgen Camp," in *The Advocate*, July 15, 1977, pp. 8–9.

"Chautauqua and Its Founder," in *The Literary Digest*, Volume 65, 1920, pp. 43–44.

Chilson, Adriel D., "Don't Be Wrong about Wright," in *Adventist Heritage*, Winter 1987, pp. 3–8.

Clements, William M., "The Physical Layout of the Methodist Camp Meeting," in *Pioneer America*, January 1873, pp. 9–15.

Cochran, Charles B., "J. C. McPheeters and the Camp Meeting," in *The Herald*, June 7, 1967, pp. 3–4.

Cunningham, John T., "Ocean Grove Centennial: To These Shores," in *Newark Sunday News*, July 27, 1969, pp. 4–10.

Dahl, Curtis, "Mark Twain and Ben Ely; Two Missouri Boyhoods," in *Missouri Historical Review*, 1972 [66(4)], pp. 548–566.

Dalgety, George S. "Chautauqua's Contribution to America," in *Current History*, Volume 34, 1931, pp. 39–44.

Demers, Stamford E., "Worship-By-the-Sea: Camp Meetings and Seaside Resorts in 19th Century America," in *Focus*, Winter 1988, pp. 15–21.

Denman, Harry, "Arise and Go!," in *Standard of Holiness*, July–August 1951, p. 1.

Dick, Everett M., "Advent Camp Meetings of the 1840s," in *Adventist Heritage*, April 1977, pp. 3–10.

Dourte, Esther, "Roxbury Holiness Camp: Its History and Influence on the Brethren in Christ Church," in *Notes and Queries in Brethren in Christ History*, January 1970, pp. 8–9.

Dunlap, E. Dale, "Tuesday Meetings, Camp Meetings and Cabinet Meetings: A Perspective on the Holiness Movement in the Methodist Church in the United States in the Nineteenth Century," in *AME Zion Quarterly Review Methodist History News Bulletin*, April 1975, pp. 85–106.

Fielder, Boyd Ward, "Mission of the Early Camp Meetings in Virginia," in *Methodist Quarterly Review*, July–August 1896, pp. 473–475.

Flint, Micah P., "The Camp Meeting," in *Western Monthly Review*, May 1827, pp. 34–38. [Poem.]

Flood, R. G., "Old Fashioned Camp Meetings Live On," in *Christian Herald*, May 1984, p. 35.

Foster, Elizabeth P., "The Siloam Springs Camp Ground: Memoir of Elizabeth Pyburn Foster," in *North Louisiana Historical Association Journal*, 1977 [8(5)], pp. 203–206.

Foster, John O., "The First Des Plaines Camp Meeting, Des Plaines, Ill.: August, 1860," in *Journal of the Illinois State Historical Society*, January 1932.

Fowler, Charles J., "Report of the President," in *Christian Witness and Advocate of Bible Holiness*, July 11, 1907, p. 8.

———, "Report of the President," in *Christian Witness and Advocate of Bible Holiness*, July 7, 1910, p. 8.

———, "Report of the President," in *Christian Witness and Advocate of Bible Holiness*, July 6, 1911, pp. 2–4.

———, "Why Become Auxiliary?," in *Christian Witness and Advocate of Bible Holiness*, July 11, 1907, p. 8.

Fry, B. St. James, "The Early Camp-Meeting Song Writers," in *Methodist Quarterly Review*, July 1859, pp. 401–413.

Gage, Patricia A., "The Sawdust Trail Lives on at the Hudson Camp Meeting," in *North Louisiana Historical Association Journal*, 1979 [10(1)], pp. 23–25.

Geiger, Kenneth E., "Camp Meetings—Do They Have a Future?," in *Emphasis on Faith and Living*, July 15, 1980, p. 14.

Gewehr, W. M., "Some Factors in the Expansion of Frontier Methodism, 1800–1811," in *Journal of Religion*, January 1928, pp. 98–120.

Gibson, H. W., "The History of Organized Camping—Establishment of Institutional Camps," in *The Camping Magazine*, March 1936, p. 18.

———, "The History of Organized Camping, Leadership Training Conference and Course," in *The Camping Magazine*, November 1936.

———, "The History of Organized Camping—Spread of the American Camp to Other Lands," in The *Camping Magazine*, December 1936, p. 18.

———, "The History of Organized Camping—The Private Camps," in *The Camping Magazine*, April 1936, p. 18.

Gormally, Larry, "The Advent Campgrounds," in *Springfield Journal*, February 26, 1987, p. 1.

Harper, Vicki, "Camps Lure Vennard College Professor," in *Vennard Vision*, February 1977, p. 5.

Hartman, Mrs. Brigadier William, "Historical Hallmarks of Old Orchard Camp Meetings" [numbers 1–5] in *War Cry*, June and July 1985.

Hawbaker, John B., "Preaching Holiness at Roxbury Holiness Camp," in *Brethren in Christ History and Life*, April 1987, pp. 3–47.

Henricks, Sylvia C., "A Good and Profitable Occasion: The Story of Acton Camp Ground," in *Indiana Magazine of History*, December 1970, pp. 299–317.

Hill, J. W., Sr., "Camp Meeting Reforms," in the *Christian Witness and Advocate of Bible Holiness*, July 20, 1899, p. 3.

"History of Organization," in *Michigan Holiness Record*, January 1890, p. 23.

Hollabaugh, Martha, "Dedication of the Nipgen Tabernacle," in *The Advocate*, August 26, 1977, p. 8.

Holohan, Barry, "Camp Meetings: A Look Through the Years," in *Fundamentalist Journal*, June 1984, pp. 28–29.

Howells, W. C., "Camp Meetings in the West Fifty Years Ago," in *Lippincott's Magazine*, August 1872, p. 203.

Hudson, Winthrop, "Shouting Methodists," in *Encounter*, 1968 [29(1)], pp. 77–84.

Hughes, George, "The Key-Note is Sounded," in *Methodist Home Journal*, August 3, 1867, p. 1.

Hughes, H. Raymond, "The Purpose and a Brief History of Delanco Camp Meeting," in *The Historical Trail*, 1984, pp. 32–39.

Hutcherson, Faith Luce, "A Table in the Wilderness," in *Pentecostal Herald and Way of Faith*, August 6, 1947, p. 4.

"Interdenominational Bible Conference," in *Ocean Grove Record*, June 29, 1889.

Johnson, Charles A., "Early Ohio Camp Meetings, 1801–1816," in *Ohio State Archaeological and Historical Quarterly*, 1952, pp. 32–50.

———, "The Frontier Camp Meeting and Contemporary and Historical Appraisal 1805–1890," in *Mississippi Valley Historical Review*, June 1950, pp. 91–110.

Johnson, Guion Griffis, "The Camp Meeting in Ante-Bellum North Carolina," in *The North Carolina Historical Review*, April 1933, pp. 95–110.

Jorchow, Merrill E., "Red Rock: Frontier Methodist Camp Meeting," in *Minnesota History*, June 1950, pp. 79–92.

Kendall, W. S., "Present-Day Values of Camp Meetings," in *The Christian Minister*, July 1958, pp. 12–17.

Kewley, A. E., "Beginning of Camp Meetings in Canada," in *Canadian Journal of Theology*, October 1964, pp. 192–201.

Kiker, Ira, "The Camp Meeting: Its Origin and Early Methods," in *Christian Advocate* (Nashville), February 13, 1914, p. 205, and February 20, 1914, p. 237.

Kincheloe, Joe L., Jr., "Similarities in Crowd Control Techniques for the Camp Meeting and Political Rally: The Pioneer Role of Tennessee," in *Tennessee Historical Quarterly*, 1978 [37(2)], pp. 155–169.

———, "Transcending Role Restrictions: Women at Camp Meetings and Political Rallies," in *Tennessee Historical Quarterly*, 1981 [40(2)], pp. 158–169.

Kobielush, B., and J. Pearson, "Emerging Denominational Camping Trends," in *Journal of Christian Camping*, November 1984, pp. 12–14.

Kunz, George J., "Historical Sketch and Report of the President," in *The National Association for the Promotion of Holiness, 1924–1925*. No publishing data, n.d.

Laechel, David, "Sam P. Jones and Red Rock Camp," in *Heritage*, July 1985, pp. 18–26.

La Cossitt, Henry, "Yankee Camp Meeting," in *Saturday Evening Post*, August 20, 1955, p. 32.

Lord, Clyde W., "The Mineral Springs Holiness Camp Meeting," in *Louisiana History*, Summer 1975, pp. 257–277.

Love, N. C., "An Indian Camp Meeting," in *Ohio Archaeological and Historical Publication*, 1906, pp. 39–43.

Loveland, Anne C., "Presbyterians and Revivalism in the Old South," in *Journal of Presbyterian History*, Spring 1979, pp. 36–49.

Ludwig, C., "Those Wonderful Meetings," in *Vital Christianity*, June 13, 1976, p. 12.

Lynch, D., "Cowboy Camp Meeting; A Dying Symbol," in *Christian Century*, February 9, 1972, pp. 178–179.

McBath, James H., "The Emergence of Chautauqua as a Religious and Educational Institution, 1874–1900," in *Methodist History*, October 1981, pp. 3–12.

McCullough, B., "Alive and Well Under Spacious Western Skies," in *United Methodists Today*, August 1974, p. 28.

McDonald, William, "History of Camp Meetings," in *Advocate of Christian Holiness*, June 1879, p. 138. (This article was reprinted in the same periodical, October 9, 1924, p. 2.)

MacLaren, Gay, "Morally We Roll Along—To Chautauqua!," in *Atlantic Monthly*, April 1928, pp. 441–451.

MacLean, J.P., "The Kentucky Revival and Its Influence on the Miami Valley," in *Ohio Archaeological and Historical Publications*, 1908, pp. 242–286.

McLaughlin, George A., "For What Does the Iowa Holiness Association Stand," in *Christian Witness and Advocate of Bible Holiness*, June 22, 1911, pp. 2–3.

———, "The Origin of the Camp Meeting," in *Christian Witness and Advocate of Bible Holiness*, May 11, 1905, p. 1.

McPheeters, J. C., "At Ocean Grove," in *The Herald*, September 17, 1958, p. 8.

———, "The Camp Meeting," in *Pentecostal Herald and Way of Faith*, June 16, 1943, p. 1.

———, "Camp Meeting Days," in *The Herald*, May 21, 1958, p. 1.

————, "Camp Meeting Echoes," in *The Herald*, September 27, 1967, p. 3.

————, "Camp Meeting History," in *The Herald*, May 27, 1964, p. 1.

————, "Camp Meeting Revivals," in *The Herald*, May 20, 1959, p. 1.

————, "Camp Meeting Time," in *Pentecostal Herald*, May 31, 1950, p. 1.

————, "Campmeetings," in *Wesleyan Methodist*, June 16, 1965, p. 16.

————, "God and the Redwoods," in *The Herald*, August 27, 1958, p. 2.

————, "Little George Havens' Cowboy Camp Meeting," in *The Herald*, August 12, 1970, p. 3.

————, "New Life in Today's Camp," in *The Herald*, June 7, 1967, p. 3.

"The Making of a Summer Resort," in *Dukes County Intelligencer*, 1987 [29(2)], pp. 64–77.

Mariner, Kirk, "William Penn Chandler and Revivalism in the East," in *Methodist History*, April 1987, pp. 135–146.

Mattson, Lloyd, "Camping Pioneer: Charlie Ashmen," in *Journal of Christian Camping*, September 1986, pp. 22–23.

————, "Camping Pioneer: Richard W. Neale," in *Journal of Christian Camping*, November 1986, pp. 26–27.

Moore, Penny, "Reflections on One Hundred Twenty-five Years of Seaville Camp Meeting," in *The Historical Trail*, 1989, pp. 25–27.

————, "South Seaville Camp Meeting Ground Celebrates 125 Years," in *The Historical Trail*, 1988, pp. 12–17.

Moore, R., "Give Us that Old Time Religion," in *These Times*, March 1971, p. 6.

Morrison, H. C., "The Holiness Camp Meeting," in *The Herald*, July 5, 1967, p. 1.

————, "Holiness Camp Meetings," in *Pentecostal Herald and Way of Faith*, July 19, 1944, p. 9.

————, "The Ten Days Camp Meeting," in *Pentecostal Herald and Way of Faith*, June 16, 1943, p. 9.

Nall, T. Otto, "Lake Junaluska—Heir of Camp Meeting and Chautauqua," in *Methodist History*, October 1963, pp. 16–26.

"National Camp Meetings," in *Methodist Home Journal*, May 11, 1867, p. 5.

Nixon, Lloyd H., "The American Camp Meeting," in *Heart and Life*, June 1940, p. 10.

Odens, Donald L., "Frontier Camp Meetings," in *Central Bible Quarterly*, Winter 1969, pp. 16–22.

"Oh, To Be Young Again and at Wesleyan Grove . . . ," in *Yankee Magazine*, April 1990, pp. 116–121.

"Old Fashioned Camp Meetings Versus New Fashioned," in *Western Christian Advocate* (Cincinnati), September 17, 1873, p. 6.

Opie, John, Jr., "James McGready: Theologian of Frontier Revivalism," in *Church History*, December 1965, pp. 445–456.

Parker, Charles A., "The Camp Meeting on the Frontier the Methodist Religious Resort in the East—Before 1900," in *Methodist History*, April 1980, pp. 179–192.

———, "Ocean Grove, New Jersey: Queen of the Victorian Methodist Camp Meeting Resorts," in *Nineteenth Century Magazine*, Spring 1984, pp. 19–25.

Parkinson, George H., "Those Good Old Summer Camp Meetings," in *Christian Advocate*, July 10, 1947.

Parrish, Joseph, "Evolution of the Camp Meeting," in *Popular Science Monthly*, March 18, 1883, pp. 622–626.

Paul, John, "Scottsville Camp Meeting, A Historic Sketch," in *Texas Holiness Advocate*, July 26, 1906, p. 1.

———, "Some Camp Meetings of Yesterday," in *The Herald*, May 13, 1953, p. 5.

Pearson, F. Lamar, Jr., "Precursors to Epworth-By-the-Sea: The Spanish Missions in Georgia," in *Historical Highlights*, December 1978, pp. 6–19.

Pearson, Paul M., "The Chautauqua Movement," in *Lippincott's Magazine*, Volume 78, 1908, p. 190.

Plyler, Alva W., "The Early Circuit Riders of Western North Carolina," in *Historical Papers of the North Carolina Conference Historical Society and the Western North Carolina Conference Historical Society*, 1925, pp. 95–102.

"Points of Consideration in the Holiness Movement," in *Christian Witness and Advocate of Bible Holiness*, March 16, 1905, p. 5.

Purcell, Malcolm, "Why No More Shouting Methodists," in *Together*, June 1957, pp. 28–31.

Reed, Roy, "In Tennessee: A Family Goes to Camp Meeting," in *Time*, September 6, 1982, pp. 12–13.

Reid, Isaiah, "Iowa Holiness Association—President's Annual Address (25th Anniversary)," in *Christian Witness and Advocate of Bible Holiness*, July 7, 1901, p. 4.

———, "A Visit to Historic Ground," in *Christian Witness and Advocate of Bible Holiness*, July 7, 1901, p. 5.

"The Return of the Spirit, the Second Great Awakening," in *Christian History*, Issue 23, 1989, pp. 24–28.

Richey, Russell E., "From Quarterly to Camp Meeting: A Reconsideration of Early American Methodism," in *Methodist History*, July 1985, pp. 199–213.

"Ridge View Park Camp Meeting Recalled," in *Christian Witness*, July 18, 1889.

Ridout, George W., "The Revival and the Camp Meeting," in *Pentecostal Herald*, May 31, 1950, p. 2.

———, "Some Aspects of the Camp Meeting," in *Christian Witness and Advocate of Bible Holiness*, September 4, 1913, p. 2.

Rose, Delbert R., "Evangelism," in *Christian Life Supplement*, April 1965, pp. 42–44.

———, "John L. Brasher—Veteran Camp Meeting Preacher," in *The Herald*, June 7, 1967, pp. 5–6.

———, "Methodism's Harvest Time," in *The Herald*, February 15, 1967, p. 14.

Rothrock, Joseph T., "The History of Organized Camping—The Early Days," in *The Camping Magazine*, January 1936, p. 15.

Ryan, Calvin T., "I, Too, Went to the Camp Meeting," in *Crozer Quarterly*, January 1950, pp. 240–243.

Ryan, John H., "Old Time Camp Meetings in Central Illinois," in *Transactions of the Illinois State Historical Society*, 1924, pp. 64–69.

Savage, J. E., "Do We Need the Old-Time Camp Meeting Today?," in *Pentecostal Herald*, June 11, 1952, p. 3.

Sharp, Lloyd B., "The Role of Camping and Our American Heritage," in *The Camping Magazine*, February 1942, p. 11.

Sherk, Morris N., "Tent Evangelism among the Brethren in Christ," in *Brethren in Christ History and Life*, August 1988, pp. 157–204.

Shipps, Howard F., "The Camp Meeting, Its Development and Influence upon the People of the U.S.," in *The Herald*, May 20, 1959, p. 3.

Shurter, Robert L., "The Camp Meeting in the Early Life and Literature of the Mid-West," in *The East Tennessee Historical Society Publications*, January 1933, pp. 142–149.

"Sketches of Round Lake National Camp Meeting," in *Harper's Weekly*, July 31, 1869.

Smith, James, "Camp Meeting Origins," in *Western Christian Advocate*, September 23, 1839, p. 81.

Smith, Joseph H., "Then and Now of the Holiness Camp Meeting," in *Christian Witness and Advocate of Bible Holiness*, October 9, 1924, p. 2.

Smith, Zane F., "The Great Revival of 1800, the First Camp Meeting," in *Kentucky Historical Society Register*, 1909, pp. 19–23.

Smucker, Isaac, "The Cane Ridge Camp Meeting: An Unique Page of Early-Time Kentucky History," in *Magazine of Western History*, 1889 [11], pp. 134–143.

Stokes, Elwood H., "Ocean Grove: An Historical Address Delivered at Its Sixth Anniversary, July 31st, 1875," in *Ocean Grove Record*, August 14, 1875.

Sunderman, E. F., "Washington Irving's Comment on an Early New York Camp Meeting," in *Methodist History*, January 1968, pp. 47–49.

"'Tabernacle': A Memory, An Event," in *United Methodist Reporter*, August 10, 1979.

"The Third National Camp Meeting," in *Methodist Home Journal*, July 24, 1869.

"Urbana National Camp Meeting Recalled," in *Christian Witness*, April 15, 1886.

Van Dusen, D. Gregory, "The Bergen Camp Meeting in the American Holiness Movement," in *Methodist History*, January 1983, pp. 69–89.

"Vineland Camp Meeting," in *Methodist Home Journal*, July 20, 1867, and July 27, 1867.

Wakefield, Dana, "Camp Meetings," no publishing data, n.d.

Wallace, Robert, "The Rugged Basis of American Protestantism," in *Life*, December 26, 1955, pp. 71–75.

Wandersee, Delores, "Red Rock Camp," in *Heritage*, July 1985, pp. 7–17.

Ward, C., "The Camp Meeting Idea," in *Pentecostal Evangel*, May 18, 1975, p. 14.

Weisberger, Bernard A., "Pentecost in the Backwoods," in *American Heritage Magazine*, June 1959, pp. 26–81.

West, J., "Camp Meeting—Alive and Well," in *Pentecostal Testimony*, July 1983, p. 8.

Whaley, Howard A., "The Second Great Awakening," in *Moody Monthly*, January 1976, pp. 40–43.

Windell, Marie G., "The Camp Meeting in Missouri," in *Missouri Historical Review*, April 1943, pp. 253–270.

Witherington, Ben, "Circuit Riders and Camp Meetings," in *Ashland Theological Journal*, Spring 1987, pp. 38–47.

Wittlinger, Carlton O., "The Advance of Wesleyan Holiness among the Brethren in Christ since 1910," in *Mennonite Quarterly Review*, January 1976, pp. 21–36.

Wright, M. Emory, "Is the Modern Camp Meeting a Failure?," in *Methodist Review*, October 1861, pp. 582–604.

Wright, Susan Ramey, "It's August, and the Taylors are Coming Home to Tennessee," in *Progressive Farmer*, August 1988.

Zook, A. C., "The Brethren in Christ Holiness Camp Meeting at Roxbury, Penna.," in *Visitor*, September 22, 1941, p. 297.

## Camp Meeting Movies

"Come Hungry, Come Thirsty: The Frontier Camp Meeting." Produced by Melvin R. Mason. Huntsville, Tex.: Sam Houston State University, 1990.

"Gathering at the River." Produced by Charles L. Sullivan. Perkinston, Miss.: Mississippi Gulf Coast Community College, Magnolia Series. No. 2, 1990.

"Last of the Great Camp Meetings—Ocean Grove, New Jersey." Produced by Jennifer Boyd and John Sosenko. Ocean Grove, N.J.: Community Heritage Film Group, n.d.

"Sing Glory Hallelujah." Produced by Family Films. Panorama City: Panorama Films, 1976.

## Biography Related to Camp Meetings

Allen, Stephen. *The Life of Rev. John Allen, Better Known as "Camp-Meeting John."* Boston: B. B. Russell, 1888.

Carr, John. *Early Times in Middle Tennessee*. Nashville: The Parthenon Press, 1958. (Reprint of original 1857 edition.)

Cartwright, Peter. *Autobiography of Peter Cartwright, The Backwoods Preacher*. Edited by W. P. Strickland. New York: The Methodist Book Concern, n.d.

Clark, Elmer T., editor. *The Journal and Letters of Francis Asbury*, 3 volumes. Nashville: Abingdon Press, 1958.

Cossitt, Franceway R. *The Life and Times of Rev. Fenis Ewing, One of the Fathers and Founders of the Cumberland Presbyterian Church. To Which is Added Remarks on Davidson's History, or, a Review of His Chapters on the Revival of 1800*. Louisville: Rev. Lee Roy Woods, 1853.

Duryea, Jennie Sworn. *John A. Duryea, Spirit-Filled Evangel*. Wilmore: The Herald Press, n.d.

Findlay, James F. *Dwight L. Moody*. Chicago: University of Chicago Press, 1969.

Finley, James B. *Autobiography of Rev. James B. Finley; or, Pioneer Life in the West*. Edited by W. P. Strickland. Cincinnati: printed at the Methodist Book Concern, 1857.

Garbutt, Mrs. J. William. *Rev. W. A. Dodge as We Knew Him*. Atlanta: The Franklin Printing and Publishing Company, 1906.

Graw, A. C. *Forty Six Years in the Methodist Ministry: Life of Rev. J. B. Graw, D.D.* Published by A. C. Graw, 1903.

Haney, Milton L. *Pentecostal Possibilities, or Story of My Life*. Chicago: The Christian Witness Company, 1906.

Hills, Aaron M. *A Hero of Faith and Prayer; or Life of Rev. Martin Wells Knapp.* Cincinnati: Mrs. M. W. Knapp, 1902.

Hughes, John Wesley. *The Autobiography of John Wesley Hughes, D.D.* Louisville: Pentecostal Publishing Company, 1923.

McConnell, Lela G. *Faith Victorious in the Kentucky Mountains; the Story of Twenty-two Years of Spirit-Filled Ministry.* Winona Lake: Light and Life Press, 1946.

McDonald, William, and John E. Searles. *The Life of the Rev. John S. Inskip.* Chicago: The Christian Witness Co., 1885. (Also issued in a reprint edition by Garland Publishing, 1985.)

McGready, James. *The Posthumous Works of the Reverend James McGready,* 2 volumes. Edited by James Smith. Louisville: W. W. Worsley, 1831–1833.

McKnight, Helen Bowling, "John McGee—Methodist Circuit Rider and Camp Meeting Evangelist," a research paper on file at the Tennessee State Library and Archives, Nashville, Tenn.

————. *My McGee and Joyner Families, Pioneers, Patriots and Preachers.* Huntsville: Helen Bowling McKnight, 1983.

McPheeters, Chilton C. *Pardon Me, Sir . . . Your Halo's Showing; the Story of J. C. McPheeters.* Wilmore: Francis Asbury Society, 1984.

Matthews, Annie MacDonell. *Memorial Stones; Spiritual Epochs in the Lives of George and Annie Matthews.* Louisville: Pentecostal Publishing Company, n.d.

Moody, William R. *The Life of Dwight L. Moody.* No place of publication: Fleming H. Revell Company, 1900.

Morrison, H. C. *Some Chapters of My Life Story.* Louisville: Pentecostal Publishing Company, 1941.

Northcott, H. C. *Biography of Rev. Benjamin Northcott, A Pioneer Local Preacher in the Methodist Episcopal Church in Kentucky, and for more than Sixty-three Years in the Ministry.* Cincinnati: printed at the Western Methodist Book Concern, 1875.

Opie, John M., "James McGready: Theologian of Frontier Revivalism," in *Church History,* December 1965, pp. 445–456.

Osborn, Lucy Reed Drake. *Heavenly Pearls Set in a Life; A Record of Experiences and Labors in America, India and Australia.* New York: Revell, 1894.

Purviance, Levi. *The Biography of Elder David Purviance . . . Together with a Historical Sketch of the Great Kentucky Revival.* Dayton: B. F. & G. W. Ellis, 1884.

Rees, Paul S. *Seth Cook Rees, the Warrior Saint.* Indianapolis: Pilgrim Book Room, 1934.

Rogers, John R. *The Biography of Eld. Barton Warren Stone.* Cincinnati: J. A. and U. P. James, 1847.

Rose, Delbert R., "John L. Brasher—Veteran Camp Meeting Preacher," in *The Herald,* June 7, 1967, pp. 5–6.

Short, Harry R., and D. Wayne Davis, "Peter Cartwright, A Legend in His Time," written to be read at the unveiling of a highway marker erected by the Kentucky Historical Society, September 13, 1970.

Wesche, Percival A. *Henry Clay Morrison: Crusader Saint.* Berne: Herald Press, 1963.

## Denominational History Related to Camp Meetings

Albright, Raymond W. *A History of the Evangelical Church.* Harrisburg: The Evangelical Press, 1956.

Anderson, James A. *Centennial History of Arkansas Methodism, Illustrated.* Benton: printed by L. B. White Printing Company, 1935.

Armstrong, C. A., editor. *History of the Methodist Church in North Dakota and Dakota Territory.* Nashville: printed by the Parthenon Press, 1960.

Arnold, William E. *A History of Methodism in Kentucky,* 2 volumes. Louisville: The Herald Press,

Barrus, Ben M., et al. *A People Called Cumberland Presbyterians.* Memphis: Frontier Press, 1978.

Baumgartner, S. H. *Historical Data and Life Sketches of the Deceased Ministers of the Indiana Conference of the Evangelical Association, 1835–1915,* 2 volumes. Cleveland: Publishing House of the Evangelical Association, 1915.

Bennett, William W. *Memorials of Methodism in Virginia, From its Introduction into the State, in the year 1772, to the year 1829.* Richmond: published by the author, 1871.

Betts, Albert Deems. *History of South Carolina Methodism*. Columbia: The Advocate Press, 1952.

Blake, William. *Cross and Flame in Wisconsin, the Story of United Methodism in the Badger State*. Stevenspoint: Warzalla Publishing Company, 1973.

Brooks, William E., editor. *From Saddlebags to Satellites, A History of Florida Methodism*. Nashville: The Parthenon Press, 1969.

Brown, Charles Ewing. *When the Trumpet Sounded, A History of the Church of God Reformation Movement*. Anderson: Warner Press, 1951.

Brown, Kenneth O., and P. Lewis Brevard. *History of the Churches of Christ in Christian Union*. Circleville: The Circle Press, 1980.

Brown, Kenneth O., and J. Lawrence Rhoads. *The History of the Christian Union Church*. Excelsior Springs: published by the General Council of the Christian Union, n.d.

Bucke, Emory Stevens, editor. *The History of American Methodism*, 3 volumes. New York: Abingdon Press, 1964.

Bugbee, Leroy E. *He Holds the Stars in His Hands, The Centennial History of the Wyoming Annual Conference of the Methodist Church*. Scranton: The Haddon Craftsmen, Inc., 1952.

Burrows, Carl E. *Melting Times, A History of West Virginia United Methodism*. Marceline: Walsworth, 1984.

Buzzard, Theodore R. *Lest We Forget, A History of the Evangelical United Brethren Church in the Pacific Northwest*. Portland: Theodore R. Buzzard, 1988.

Campbell, Joseph E. *The Pentecostal Holiness Church 1898–1948, Its Background and History*. Franklin Springs: The Publishing House of the Pentecostal Holiness Church, 1951.

*Celebrating the 75th Anniversary of the Holiness Christian Conference 1894–1969*. Gibralter: Holiness Christian Church of the USA, 1969.

Chaffee, A. F. *History of the Wyoming Conference of the Methodist Episcopal Church*. New York: Eaton and Mains, 1904.

Chreitzberg, A. M. *Early Methodism in the Carolinas*. Nashville: Publishing House of the Methodist Episcopal Church, South, 1897.

Clark, Elmer T. *Methodism in Western North Carolina*. Nashville: The Parthenon Press, 1966.

Clegg, Leland, and William B. Oden. *Oklahoma Methodism in the Twentieth Century*, Nashville: The Parthenon Press, 1968.

Cole, Otis, and Oliver S. Baketel. *History of the New Hampshire Conference of the Methodist Episcopal Church*. New York: The Methodist Book Concern, n.d.

Crawford, R. R., et al. *A Historical Account of the Apostolic Faith, A Trinitarian Fundamental Evangelistic Organization*. Portland: The Apostolic Faith Mission, 1965.

Davidson, Robert. *History of the Presbyterian Church in the State of Kentucky: with a Preliminary Sketch of the Churches in the Valley of Virginia*. New York: Robert Carter, 1847.

Douglass, Paul F. *The Story of German Methodism*. Cincinnati: The Methodist Book Concern, 1939.

Evers, Joseph C. *The History of the Southern Illinois Conference of the Methodist Church*. Nashville: The Parthenon Press, 1964.

Finley, James B. *Sketches of Western Methodism, Biographical, Historical and Miscellaneous, Illustrative of Pioneer Life*. Edited by W. P. Strickland. Cincinnati: 1854.

Garrison, Winfred Ernest, and Alfred T. DeGroot. *The Disciples of Christ: A History*. St. Louis: The Bethany Press, 1948.

Gibble, Phares B. *History of the East Pennsylvania Conference of the United Brethren in Christ*. Dayton: The Otterbein Press, 1951.

Grissom, W. L. *History of Methodism in North Carolina, from 1772 to the Present Time*. Nashville: Publishing House of the M. E. Church, South, 1905.

Haines, Lee M., and Melvin E. Dieter, editors. *Conscience and Commitment, The History of the Wesleyan Methodist Church of America*. Marion: The Wesley Press, 1976.

Harmon, Nolan B., general editor. *Encyclopedia of World Methodism*, 2 volumes. Nashville: Abingdon Press, 1974.

Harrell, David E., Jr. *Quest for a Christian America: The Disciples of Christ and American Society to 1866*. Nashville: Disciples of Christ Historical Society, 1966.

Heller, Herbert L. *Indiana Conference of the Methodist Church 1832–1956*. Published by the Historical Society of the Indiana Conference, 1956.

Hillman, Joseph. *The History of Methodism in Troy, N.Y.* Troy: published by Joseph Hillman, 1888.

Hilson, James B. *History of the South Carolina Conference of the Wesleyan Methodist Church of America: 55 Years of Wesleyan Methodism in South Carolina.* Winona Lake: Light and Life Press, 1950.

Hobart, Chauncey. *History of Methodism in Minnesota.* Red Wing: Red Wing Printing Company, 1887.

Hyde, A. B. *The Story of Methodism Throughout the World.* Toronto: William Briggs, Publisher, 1894.

Kerr, Charles W. *God, Grace and Granite, the History of Methodism in New Hampshire 1768–1988.* Canaan: Phoenix Publishing Company, 1988.

Kulbeck, Georgia G. *What God Hath Wrought, A History of the Pentecostal Assemblies of Canada.* Toronto: The Pentecostal Assemblies of Canada, 1958.

Lamos, Aldis M., editor. *One Hundred and Twenty-five Years for Christ, 1843–1968; History of the Champlain Conference of the Wesleyan Methodist Church of America.* Published by the Conference Historical Committee, 1968.

Lazenby, Marion E. *History of Methodism in Alabama and West Florida.* Published by the North Alabama Conference and Alabama–West Florida Conference of the Methodist Church, 1960.

Leaton, James. *History of Methodism in Illinois from 1793 to 1832.* Cincinnati: printed by Walden and Stowe, 1883.

Lee, Jesse. *A Short History of the Methodists, in the United States of America; Beginning in 1766, and Continued till 1809.* Baltimore: printed by Magill and Clime, 1810.

Leedy, Roy B. *The Evangelical Church in Ohio.* Published by the Ohio Conference of the Evangelical United Brethren Church, 1959.

McDonnold, B. W. *History of the Cumberland Presbyterian Church.* Nashville: Board of Publication of Cumberland Presbyterian Church, 1888.

McFerrin, John B. *History of Methodism in Tennessee*, 3 volumes. Nashville: Publishing House of the M. E. Church, South, 1888.

McKinley, William. *A Story of Minnesota Methodism.* Cincinnati: Jennings and Graham, 1911.

McLeister, Ira F., and Roy S. Nicholson. *History of the Wesleyan Methodist Church of America*. Marion: Wesley Press, 1959.

MacMillan, Margaret B. *The Methodist Church in Michigan: The Nineteenth Century*. Grand Rapids: William B. Eerdmans Publishing Company, 1967.

Marston, L. R. *From Age to Age a Living Witness: An Historical Interpretation of Free Methodism's First Century*. Winona Lake: Light and Life Press, 1960.

Maser, Frederick E. *Methodism in Central Pennsylvania*. Lebanon: Sowers Printing Company, 1971.

Miller, Charles R., and William L. Raker. *The Histories of the Pennsylvania and Central Pennsylvania Conferences of the Evangelical United Brethren Church*. No publishing data, 1968.

Miller, Gene Ramsey. *A History of North Mississippi Methodism 1820–1900*. Nashville: The Parthenon Press, 1966.

Miller, Rennets C., editor. *Souvenir History of the New England Southern Conference*, 3 volumes. Nantasket: Rennets C. Miller, 1897.

Mudge, James. *History of the New England Conference of the Methodist Episcopal Church 1796–1910*. Boston: published by the Conference, 1910.

Nail, Olin W., editor-in-chief. *Texas Methodist Centennial Yearbook*. Elgin: published by Olin W. Nail, 1934.

Nall, T. Otto. *Forever Beginning, A History of the United Methodist Church and her Antecedents in Minnesota to 1969*. Nashville: The Parthenon Press, 1973.

Niklaus, Robert, et al. *All for Jesus, God at Work in the Christian and Missionary Alliance Over One Hundred Years*. Camp Hill: Christian Publications, Inc., 1986.

Nuefeld, Don F., editor. *Seventh Day Adventist Encyclopedia*, 10 volumes. Washington: Review and Herald Publishing Association, 1968.

Nye, John A. *Between the Rivers, A History of Iowa United Methodism*. Lake Mills: Graphic Printing Company, 1986.

Olsen, M. Ellsworth. *A History of the Origin and Progress of Seventh Day Adventists*. New York: AMS Press, 1972. (Reprint of 1925 edition.)

Pierce, Alfred M. *A History of Methodism in Georgia.* Published by the North Georgia Conference Historical Society, 1956.

Pike, John M. *Preachers of Salvation, the History of the Evangelical Church.* Milwaukee: Evangelical Church of N. A., 1984.

Pilcher, Elijah. *Protestantism in Michigan: Being a Special History of the Methodist Episcopal Church and Incidentally of Other Denominations.* Detroit: R. P. S. Tyler & Company, 1878.

Price, R. N. *Holston Methodism from Its Origin to the Present Time,* 5 volumes. Nashville: Publishing House of the M. E. Church, South, 1906.

Ratzlaff, Nina, editor. *A Heritage that Challenges—The First Hundred Years of the Church of God in Colorado, 1888–1898.* No publishing data, n.d.

Redford, A. H. *Methodism in Kentucky,* 3 volumes. Nashville: Southern Methodist Publishing House, 1869.

Schwartz, Charles D., and Ouida Davis Schwartz. *A Flame of Fire, the Story of the Troy Annual Conference.* Rutland: Academy Books, 1982.

Semple, Robert Baylor. *History of the Baptists in Virginia.* Revised and Extended by G. W. Beale. Lafayette: Church History Research and Archives,1976.

Shipp, Albert M. *The History of Methodism in South Carolina.* Nashville: Southern Methodist Publishing House, 1884. (Reprinted in 1972.)

Short, Roy H. *Methodism in Kentucky.* Rutland: Academy Books, 1979.

Simpson, Matthew. *A Cyclopedia of Methodism.* Philadelphia: Everts and Stewart, 1878.

Singsworth, John W. *The Battle Was the Lord's; A History of the Free Methodist Church in Canada.* Oshawa: Sage Publishers, 1960.

Smeltzer, Wallace Guy. *The History of United Methodism in Western Pennsylvania.* Nashville: Printed by the Parthenon Press, 1975.

——. *Methodism on the Headwaters of the Ohio, The History of the Pittsburgh Conference of the Methodist Church.* Nashville: The Parthenon Press, 1951.

Smith, James. *History of the Christian Church from Its Origin to the Present Time; Compiled from Various Authors, Including a History of the Cumberland Presbyterian Church.* Nashville: Cumberland Presbyterian Office, 1835.

Smith, John Abernathy. *Cross and Flame, Two Centuries of United Methodism in Middle Tennessee*. Nashville: The Parthenon Press, 1984.

Spencer, J. H. *A History of the Kentucky Baptists, from 1798 to 1885*, 2 volumes. Cincinnati: J. R. Baumes, 1885. (Reprinted in 1976.)

Stanger, Frank Bateman, editor. *The Methodist Trail in New Jersey*. Camden: I. F. Huntzinger Company, 1961.

Steelman, Robert B. *What God Has Wrought, A History of the Southern New Jersey Conference of the United Methodist Church*. Rutland: Academy Books, 1986.

Tees, Francis H., et al. *Pioneering in Penn's Woods, Philadelphia Methodist Episcopal Annual Conference through One Hundred Fifty Years*. Published by the Philadelphia Conference Tract Society of the Methodist Episcopal Church, 1937.

Thompson, Ernest Trice. *Presbyterians in the South, Volume One: 1607–1861*. Richmond: John Knox Press, 1963.

Thurston, William Albert. *Souvenir History of the East District New England Conference*. Boston: Press of Lounsbery, Nichols & Worth, 1896.

Tucker, Frank C. *The Methodist Church in Missouri 1798–1939, A Brief History*. Nashville: The Parthenon Press, 1966.

Tucker, William E., and Lester G. McAllister. *Journey in Faith: A History of the Christian Church Disciples of Christ*. St. Louis: The Bethany Press, 1975.

Vernon, Walter N. *Methodism Moves across North Texas*. Nashville: The Parthenon Press, 1967.

Vernon, Walter, et al. *The Methodist Excitement in Texas, A History*. Nashville: The Parthenon Press, 1984.

Versteeg, John M., editor. *Methodism: Ohio Area 1812–1962*. Published by the Ohio Area Sesquicentennial Committee, 1962.

Voist, M. *History of the East Michigan Conference of the Free Methodist Church*. Owosso: Times Printing Company, 1925.

Ward, William Ralph, Jr. *Faith in Action, A History of Methodism in the Empire State 1784–1984*. Rutland: Academy Books, 1986.

Waring, Edmund H. *History of the Iowa Annual Conference of the Methodist Episcopal Church*. No publishing data, n.d.

Washburn, Josephine F. *History and Reminiscences of Holiness Church Work in Southern California and Arizona.* South Pasadena: Record Press, [1912].

Wellcome, Isaac. *History of the Second Advent Message.* Yarmouth: I. C. Wellcome, 1874.

Whitlock, Elias D., et al. *History of the Central Ohio Conference of the Methodist Episcopal Church, Illustrated, 1856–1913.* Cincinnati: Press of the Methodist Book Concern, n.d.

Wittlinger, Carlton O. *Quest for Piety and Obedience, The Story of the Brethren in Christ.* Nappanee: Evangel Press, 1978.

Wood, Dillard, and William H. Preskitt, Jr. *Baptized with Fire, A History of the Pentecostal Fire Baptized Holiness Church.* Franklin Springs: Advocate Press, 1983.

Woods, Dale A. *East Michigan's Great Adventure, A History of the East Michigan Conference of the Free Methodist Church 1884–1984.* Winona Lake: Light and Life Press, 1984.

Woods, Gayle. *Kelly's Chapel: A Historical Survey.* No publishing data, n.d.

Worcester, Paul W. *The Master Key, The Story of the Hephzibah Faith Missionary Association.* Kansas City: Nazarene Publishing House, 1966.

Yeakel, R. *History of the Evangelical Association,* 2 volumes. Cleveland: J. H. Lamb, 1902.

Zahniser, Arthur D., and John B. Easton. *History of the Pittsburgh Conference of the Free Methodist Church.* Chicago: Free Methodist Publishing House, 1932.

Zechman, John W., et al. *A History of God's Missionary Church, Penns Creek, Pennsylvania, 1935–1985.* No publication data, 1985.

## Sermons and Addresses

Baker, Sheridan. *Living Waters; Being Bible Expositions and Addresses Given at Different Camp Meetings and to Ministers and Christian Workers on Various Other Occasions.* New York: Phillips and Hunt, 1888.

*Camp Meeting Sermons: Sermons Preached at the General Annual Camp-Meeting of the Church of God Held at Anderson,* Indiana, June 6–15, 1913. Anderson: Gospel Trumpet Co., 1913.

Chapman, James B. *Camp Meeting Sermons.* Kansas City: Nazarene Publishing House, 1935.

————. *With Chapman at Camp Meeting.* Kansas City: Beacon Hill Press, 1961.

Church, John R. *Nine Scriptural Reasons for Holiness.* [*"Sermon preached in July, 1968, at Central Holiness Camp Meeting, Wilmore, Ky."*] No publishing data, 1979.

*The Double Cure; Echoes from the National Camp Meetings.* Boston: The Christian Witness, 1887.

*The Double Cure; Sermons from National Camp Meetings.* Salem: Schmul Publishing Company, 1965.

*The Philosophy of Methodism: An Address Delivered at Crystal Springs Camp Meeting, Mississippi.* No publishing data, 1880.

Sanderson, J. E. *Sufferings and Glory; A Sermon Preached at the Oakville Camp Meeting, October 5, 1857.* Toronto: No publishing data, [1857].

*Select Camp-meeting Sermons, Preached at the International Camp Meeting of the Church of God.* Anderson: Gospel Trumpet Company, [1928].

*Sermons by the Sea.* New York: The Abingdon Press, 1938.

*Sermons by the Sea (Third Series): Selected Sermons Preached at Ocean Grove 1941 Season.* Ocean Grove: published by the Association, 1941.

Smith, William M. *The Two-fold Purpose of the Baptism of the Holy Ghost.* [*"A Sermon preached . . . at a meeting of the Hamilton County, Indiana, Holiness Association."*] Westfield: Union Bible Seminary, 1950.

Stauffer, Joshua. *Living under the Weight of the Cross.* [*"Sermon . . . preached at God's Bible School Camp Meeting, Cincinnati, Ohio, June 12, 1960."*] Owosso: Joshua Stauffer, n.d.

Stevenson, Herbert F., editor. *Keswick's Authentic Voice, Sixty-five Dynamic Addresses Delivered at the Keswick Convention 1875–1957.* Grand Rapids: Zondervan Publishing House, 1959.

————. *Keswick's Triumphant Voice; Forty-eight Outstanding Addresses Delivered at the Keswick Convention, 1882–1962.* Grand Rapids: Zondervan Publishing House, 1963.

Stiles, S. M., and J. G. Patterson. *Fraternal Camp Meeting Sermons, Preached by Ministers of the Various Branches of Methodism at the Round Lake Camp-Meeting, New York, July, 1874.* New York: Phillips and Hunt, 1875.

## Camp Meeting Constitutions, By-Laws, Charters, Rules

Articles of Agreement Governing the Scottsville Holiness Camp Ground. Marshall: Southern Methodist Print, 1900.

Articles of Faith, Georgia Holiness Association Organized for the Promotion of Scriptural Holiness. No publishing data, n.d.

Articles of Incorporation and By-Laws of the Lake Bluff Camp Meeting Association, Lake Bluff, Illinois. Chicago: J. A. Van Fleet, [1875?].

Articles of Incorporation, Asbury Camp Meeting Association. No publishing data, 1926.

Articles of Organization of Central Holiness Association. No publishing data: [H. C. Morrison, 1919.]

By-Laws of the American Holiness Campmeeting Association. No publishing data, 1960.

By-Laws of the Bald Eagle Valley Holiness Association, Inc. Port Matilda: Bald Eagle Valley Holiness Association, 1978.

By-Laws of the Jamestown Holiness Camp Meeting Association. No publishing data, n.d.

By-Laws of the Ranchmen's Camp Meeting Association of the Southwest. No publishing data, n.d.

By-Laws of the Rhodes Grove United Brethren Campmeeting Association. No publishing data, 1980.

"By-Laws of the Smith Mills Camp Meeting Association", in *Smith Mills Camp Meeting, History, Echoes and By-Laws.* North Dartmouth: The Vining Press, 1930.

Charter, Constitution, By-Laws, Rules and Regulations of the Camp Meeting Association. Mount Tabor: published by the Board of Trustees, Camp Meeting Association, 1969.

Charter of the Brandywine Summit Camp Meeting Association. No publishing data, 1884.

Church Discipline of the Reese Holiness Association, Interdenominational. No publishing data, 1942.

Constitution and By-Laws, Chesapeake Interdenominational Holiness Association, Matthews, Virginia. No publishing data, 1968.

Constitution and By-Laws, Mt. Lookout Camp Meeting Association. Waynesfield: Mt. Lookout Camp Meeting Association, 1946.

Constitution and By-Laws of the Detroit Holiness Association. No publishing data, 1923.

Constitution and By-Laws of the Foothill Association for the Promotion of Holiness. No publishing data, n.d.

Constitution and By-Laws of the Indiana Holiness Association. No publishing data, n.d.

Constitution and By-Laws of the Interdenominational Holiness Association of Ashley, Ohio. No publishing data, n.d.

Constitution and By-Laws of the Ithiel Falls Camp Meeting Association, Johnson, Vermont. Johnson: 1980.

"Constitution and By-laws of the Kansas State Holiness Association," in *Year Book of the Fifty-Ninth Annual Camp Meeting of the Kansas State Holiness Association, Incorporated, Interdenominational.* No publishing data, 1947.

Constitution and By-Laws of the King County Holiness Association. No publishing data, n.d.

Constitution and By-Laws of the Michigan State Holiness Camp Meeting Association. Eaton Rapids: published by the Michigan State Holiness Camp Meeting Association, 1963.

Constitution and By-Laws of the Missouri Association for the Promotion of Holiness. No publishing data, n.d.

"Constitution and By-Laws of the National Association for the Promotion of Holiness, 1930," in *The National Association for the Promotion of Holiness, 1932–1936.* Chicago: Christian Witness, n.d.

Constitution and By-Laws of the New York State Holiness Association. No publishing data, n.d.

Constitution and By-Laws of the North Dakota Methodist Camp Meeting Association. No publishing data, 1907.

Constitution and By-Laws of the Peniel Holiness Camp Meeting Association, Bucyrus, Ohio. No publishing data, 1962.

Constitution and By-Laws of the West Jersey Grove Association. No publishing data, n.d.

Constitution and By-Laws That Shall Govern the Hancock County Camp Meeting Association. Findlay: The Carey Times Printers, 1968.

Constitution of Stoutsville Camp Meeting Association. Stoutsville: published by the association. 1954.

Constitution of the Central Holiness Camp Meeting Association. No publishing data, n.d.

Constitution of the Elkland Holiness Camp Meeting Association. No publishing data, 1973.

Constitution of the Hardin County Camp Meeting Association. Dunkirk: Hardin County Camp Meeting Association, 1970.

Constitution of the Iowa Holiness Association, Auxiliary to the National Association for the Promotion of Holiness. No publishing data, n.d.

Constitution of the John Wesley Camp Meeting Association of High Point, North Carolina. High Point: 1967.

Constitution of the Lake Creek Camp Meeting Association. No publishing data, n.d.

"Constitution of the Missouri Association for the Promotion of Holiness," in *Yearbook and Minutes of the Twelfth Annual Encampment of the Missouri Association for the Promotion of Holiness*. Hannibal: Missouri Association for the Promotion of Holiness, 1916.

"Constitution of the National Association for the Promotion of Holiness," in *The National Association for the Promotion of Holiness, 1924–1925*. No publishing data, n.d.

Constitution of the Ohio State Camp Meeting Association. No publishing data, 1907.

Constitution of the Southern California Pentecostal Association. No publishing data, 1908.

Constitution of the Western Pennsylvania Holiness Association. Pittsburgh: Light and Truth Press, n.d.

County and Band Constitution and By-Laws of the County Holiness Association Auxiliary to the Iowa and National Holiness Associations. No publishing data, n.d.

Digest of Rules and Regulations and Charter and By Laws. Mt. Gretna: Mt. Gretna Campmeeting Association, 1972.

"Guidebook of Our Association Including a Sketch of Organization and Work, Constitution and By-Laws, Statement of Doctrine, Object and Mission, Reception of Members, Rules for Organizing Auxiliary Associations and Bands," in *Michigan Holiness Record*, January to March 1885.

"Incorporate Articles, By-Laws and Statement of Doctrine of the Indiana Holiness Association," in *Year Book of the Indiana Holiness Association*. Wabash: Wildoner Press, 1911.

An Ordinance Relating to the Parking of Automobiles or Vehicles and of the Building of Structures for the Placing or Storing of Automobiles or Vehicles There in, in Ocean Grove. Published by the Ocean Grove Camp Meeting Association, 1923.

Ordinances of the Ocean Grove Camp Meeting Association of the Methodist Episcopal Church, Together with the Sanitary Code of the Board of Health. Ocean Grove: Times Record Print, 1896.

Regulations and By-Laws of the Adams County Holiness Association. No publishing data, n.d.

Revised Constitution of the Kentucky Mountain Holiness Association. Vancleve: Kentucky Mountain Holiness Association, 1976.

Rules and Regulations of the Hedding Camp Meeting Association. Hedding: published by the association, 1961.

"Texas State Holiness Association: Statement of Doctrine; Form of Government," in *Texas Holiness Banner*, May 1900, p. 5.

## Camp Meeting Lists

"The Camp Meeting Challenge," published biannually since 1977 by Asbury College, Wilmore, Ky.

"The Holiness Camp Calendar," published annually since 1946 by the New York State Holiness Association, Corinth, N.Y.

## Camp Meeting Yearbooks and Minutes

*Christian Holiness Almanac and Yearbook*, 4 volumes. Edited by George Hughes. New York: Palmer and Hughes, 1884–1887.

*Holiness Association of Oklahoma; Yearbook, 1906–1907*. Oklahoma City: 1906.

*The National Association for the Promotion of Holiness*. Chicago: The Christian Witness Co., [1908].

*The National Association for the Promotion of Holiness, 1913–1914*. No publishing data, 1913.

*The National Association for the Promotion of Holiness, 1924–1925*. Chicago: Christian Witness, n.d.

*The National Association for the Promotion of Holiness, 1932–1936*. No publishing data, n.d.

*Official Record, Year Book and Minutes of the South Dakota Holiness Association*. Mitchell: published by the Committee of Publication, booklets for 1929 and 1940.

*Year Book and Minutes of the Iowa Holiness Association*. No publishing data, separate booklets for 1900–1928.

*Year Book and Minutes of the Twelfth Annual Encampment of the Missouri Association for the Promotion of Holiness*. No publishing data, n.d.

*Year Book, Indiana Holiness Association*. Wabash: Wildoner Press, 1911.

*Year Book of the Fifty-ninth Annual Camp Meeting of the Kansas State Holiness Association, Incorporated, Interdenominational*. No publishing data, separate booklets for 1943–1948.

## Chautauqua History

Bestor, Arthur Eugene, Jr. *Chautauqua Publications: An Historical and Bibliographical Guide*. Chautauqua: Chautauqua Press, 1934.

Case, Victoria, and Robert Ormond. *We Called It Culture*. New York: Doubleday, 1948.

Galey, Mary. *The Grand Assembly, the Story of Life at the Colorado Chautauqua.* No publication data, n.d.

Gould, Joseph E. *The Chautauqua Movement.* Albany: State University of New York, 1961.

Harrison, Harry P., and Karl Datzer. *Culture under Canvas.* New York: Hastings House, 1958.

Hurlbut, Jesse Lyman. *The Story of Chautauqua.* New York: G. P. Putnam's Sons, 1921.

Irwin, Alfreda. *Three Taps of the Gavel: The Chautauqua Story.* Westfield: The Westfield Republican, 1970.

Morrison, Theodore. *Chautauqua. A Center for Education, Religion, and the Arts in America.* Chicago: University of Chicago Press, 1974.

Orchard, Hugh A. *Fifty Years of Chautauqua.* Cedar Rapids: The Torch Press, 1923.

Richmond, Rebecca. *Chautauqua, An American Place.* New York: Duell, Sloan and Pearce, 1943.

Scott, Marian. *Chautauqua Caravan.* New York: D. Appleton-Century, 1939.

Vincent, John H. *The Chautauqua Movement.* Boston: Chautauqua, 1886.

Wells, L. Jeanette. *A History of the Music Festival at Chautauqua Institution, 1847–1957.* Washington: The Catholic University of America Press, 1958.

# Camp Meeting Histories

Agrafiotis, Sandy, "Bayside, Maine," in *Yankee Magazine,* June 1987, pp. 58–69.

*Alabama Bible Methodist Camp, 1938–1988, Golden Anniversary.* Pell City: Bible Methodist Camp Association, 1988.

Allison, G. M. *John Wesley Camp 20th Anniversary.* High Point: John Wesley Camp Meeting Association, 1962.

Appleby, J. Gavin. *History of Indian Field Campground.* St. George: Indian Field Camp Meeting, 1980.

Autry, Bernice, and Hassie Hancock. *History of Union Camp Ground.* Jake: Union Camp Meeting, 1976.

Baker, Emma Lamb. *Stories of Bay View*. Bay View: The Caxton Press, 1925.

Balsbaugh, Susan J. *History of the Mt. Lebanon Campmeeting Association: 1892–1954*. Lebanon: Mt. Lebanon Campmeeting Association, 1954.

Banks, Charles Edward. *The History of Martha's Vineyard*. Boston: George H. Dean, Publisher, 1911.

Barrett, H. D., and A. W. McCoy. *Cassadaga, Its History and Teachings with Histories of Spiritualist Meetings*. Meadville: Gazette Printing Co., 1891.

Barrett, Rev. J. Norman. *Hedding Camp Ground Centennial, 1862–1962*. Epping: Hedding Camp Meeting Association, 1962.

Bickford, C. A. *At Ocean Park, Old Orchard, Me*. Published by C. A. Bickford, Morning Star Publishing House, 1893.

Blackburn, Venola Cook. *Historical Story Alabama Conference Annual Camp Meeting of the Wesleyan Methodist Church*. No publishing data, n.d.

Blackford, Rev. John C. *Historic Red Rock Camp Meeting, Centennial Celebration, 1968*. Paynesville: Red Rock Camp Meeting, 1968.

Blow, Mrs. Dorance. *Brushton Camp Meeting, 1934–1984*. No publishing data, 1989.

Boas, Karen and Ray. *Through These Gates: Linwood Park*. Linwood Press, 1984.

Bouton, Rev. Leon Webster. *One Hundred Years of Dimock Camp Meeting*. Dimock: Dimock Camp Meeting Association, 1976.

Bowman, Tom, "Mount Gretna Is Pennsylvania's Chautauqua," in *Pennsylvania Magazine*, August 1987, pp. 25–30.

Bradley, James A. *A Story of Ocean Grove*. No publishing data, 1874.

Brasher, J. L. *Brasher. Springs Camp Meeting*. No publishing data, 1947.

———. "History of Hartselle Holiness Camp Meeting," manuscript history in the "John Lakin Brasher Papers" at Duke University Archives, Durham, N.C.

Brewer, Mrs. Bruce. *A Synopsis of the Absaraka Methodist Episcopal Camp Meeting Association*. No publishing data, 1967.

Brewer, Richard E. *Perspectives on Ocean Grove*. Ocean Grove: Ocean Grove Historical Society, 1976.

*A Brief History of Frost Bridge Holiness Campmeeting*. Unpublished, undated typed manuscript.

*A Brief History of Mooers Camp Meeting*. Mooers: Mooers Holiness Camp Meeting Association, 1952.

*Brief History of Salem Campground*. No publishing data, n.d.

"Brief History of the American Holiness Campmeeting," in *The American Holiness Campmeeting Association*. No publishing data, 1960.

*A Brief History of the Founding and Development of the Camping Program through Fifty Years at Waldheim Park and Twin Pines Camp*. No publishing data, 1970.

Brooks, F. L. *Yarmouth Camp Meeting, Its History and Its Leaders*. Published by the Board of Managers, 1910.

Brooks, Paul Q. *Yesteryear at Empire Grove*. South Yarmouth: Paul Q. Brooks, 1985.

Brown, Kenneth O., "Hollow Rock History," in *The Herald*, May 16, 1973, p. 3.

Bruell, William H. *Ocean City: Its Authentic Early History Graphically Told by One of Its Founders*. Camden: no publisher, 1899.

*Building the Church, Pocono Mountain Primitive Methodist Bible Conference*. No publishing data, 1966.

Burton, Rush. *History of Poplar Springs Campground, Centennial Celebration*. Lavonia: The Lavonia Times, 1935.

Byers, C. B., "Camp Meetings—Their Birth and Development in the Brethren in Christ Church," an unpublished paper on file in the Brethren in Christ Church Archives, Myerstown, Pa.

Caldwell, Nathan S. *The Balls Creek Campmeeting*. Jenkins Printing, Inc., 1986.

"Camp Sychar," in *Standard of Holiness*, July–August 1951, p. 7.

"Camping on the Old Camp Grounds; Frost Bridge, Mississippi," unpublished, undated typed manuscript.

*A Capsule History of Ocean Grove*. Published by the Department of Public Information, Township of Neptune, N.J., n.d.

Carruth, Beth Nixon. *Retrospect and Prospect, History of Eaton Rapids Holiness Camp Meeting*. Eaton Rapids: Eaton Rapids Holiness Camp Meeting, [1982].

Cartwright, Charles, "A Brief History of Nipgen Camp," in *The Advocate*, August 26, 1977, pp. 8–9.

————, "Nipgen Camp," in *The Advocate*, July 15, 1977, pp. 8–9.

Cary, W. W., and Kathleen Cary. *Sychar, An Holiness Camp Meeting*. Mt. Vernon: Ohio State Camp Meeting Association, 1933.

*Celebrating Our 125th Annual United Methodist Summer Assembly; The United Methodist Camp Ground, Des Plaines, Illinois*. No publication data, 1984.

*Celebrating the Harvest, The Gladstone Era, 1930–1987*. Clackamas: Oregon Conference of Seventh Day Adventists, 1987.

Chamberlain, J. N. *Cottage City Illustrated*. Woonsocket: no publishing data, 1888.

Chappell, Lodge, Harry Daniels, and John P. Campbell. *Camp Meeting Memories*. Sunbury: Sunbury Daily Item, 1951.

*Chautauqua Hall, Hedding Camp Meeting*. Epping: Published by Hedding Camp Meeting Association, 1987.

*Cherry Run Camp, 1862–1987, 125th Anniversary*. Rimersburg: Cherry Run Camp Meeting, 1987.

"Chesapeake—Preface History," in Constitution and By-Laws, *Chesapeake Interdenominational Holiness Association*. No publishing data, 1968.

"Chicago District Camp Ground Association," in the *Journal of the Rock River Conference of the Methodist Episcopal Church*, 1966, pp. 107–109.

"A Chronology of Buildings at Epworth by the Sea," in *Historical Highlights*, June 1986, pp. 18–19.

Clapp, Dr. Helen. *The Miracle of Jennings Lodge Assembly Grounds of the Evangelical United Brethren Church, 50 Years a Center of Biblical Evangelism*. Portland: Garcia Printing Co., 1954.

Cobb, Dee W., ed. *Simpson Park Camp Grounds, Centennial Souvenir History*. Romeo: Simpson Park Camp Meeting, 1964.

Coe, Erwin, Irene Hutchinson, George Wiltse, Alberta and Reatha Rowe. *Dempster Grove, 1875–1975*. New Haven: published by the Historical Committee of Dempster Grove, 1975.

Cogar, Edith. *Coolville Camp, 1880–1980, Coolville, Ohio*. No publishing data, [1980].

Conner, J. H., "Silver Heights," in the *Christian Witness and Advocate of Bible Holiness*, April 30, 1891, p. 5.

Cook, Jacquelyn. *A Tabernacle of Living Water*. Vienna: Dooly Campground Trustees, n.d.

Copeland, Jenny, "History of Rock Springs Camp Ground," a research paper submitted to Duke Divinity School, 1986.

Crum, Mason. *The Story of Lake Junaluska*. Greensboro: The Piedmont Press, 1950.

Cunningham, John T., "Ocean Grove Centennial: To These Shores," in *Newark Sunday News*, July 27, 1969, pp. 4–10.

Dagnall, Sally W. *Martha's Vineyard Camp Meeting Association, 1835–1985*. Oak Bluffs: Martha's Vineyard Camp Meeting Association, 1985.

Daniels, Morris. *The Story of Ocean Grove Related in the Year of Its Golden Jubilee*. New York: The Methodist Book Concern, 1919.

Daniels, N. B. *History of Mount Moriah Camp Ground*. No publishing data, n.d.

Davies, Rev. Edward. *History of Silver Lake Camp Meeting*. Reading: Holiness Book Concern, 1887.

————. *Illustrated History of Douglas Camp Meeting*. Boston: McDonald, Gill & Co., 1890.

Deal, William S., "100 Years of Continuous Camp Meeting," in *The Herald*, May 25, 1966.

Dornbierer, Chris, and Margaret Dornbierer. *The Story of Blue Mountain Christian Retreat*. No publication data, n.d.

Douds, Mary S. *The History of Hollow Rock Camp Grounds*. No publishing data, 1935.

"Douglas Camp Meeting," in the *Christian Witness and Advocate of Bible Holiness*, August 4, 1904, p. 1.

Dourte, Esther, "Roxbury Holiness Camp: Its History and Influence on the Brethren in Christ Church," in *Notes and Queries in Brethren in Christ History*, January 1970.

Drury, Clifford M., "The Beginning of Talmaks: 'Galloping Over the Butte': the Introduction of the Fourth of July Address at the Talmaks Camp Meeting." Craigmont: no publishing data, 1958.

Durr, Eleanor. *Lakeside, Ohio: First 100 Years*. New York: Carlton Press, Inc., 1973.

Durrence, George T. *Tatnall Camp Ground, 100th Anniversary*. Reidsville: Tatnall County Camp Meeting, 1967.

Eaton, Walter Prichard. *Martha's Vineyard, A Pleasant Island in a Summer Sea*. New York: New Haven and Hartford Railroad and New England Steamship Co., 1923.

*Echoes from Bentleyville*. No publishing data, 1944.

*1875–1950, Seventy-fifth Anniversary, Douglas Camp Meeting*. Douglas: Douglas Camp Meeting Association, 1950.

*1869–1959, Malaga Camp Meeting, West Jersey Grove Association, 90th Anniversary*. Newfield: West Jersey Grove Camp Meeting Association, 1959.

*1869–1949, West Jersey Grove Camp Meeting Association, 80th Anniversary*. Newfield: West Jersey Grove Camp Meeting Association, 1949.

"80 Years at Riverside Camp, South Dakota Holiness Association," Mitchell, S.D. No publishing data, 1974.

Eisenlohr, Gail A. *From Vision to Reality, A History of Malaga Camp Meeting*. Malaga: West Jersey Grove Camp Meeting Association, 1969.

Erwin, William I., "The Early Days of Epworth by the Sea," in *Historical Highlights*, June 1986, pp. 31–36.

Evans, Emma Mae, and Reverend David Charles, "West Jersey Grove History," in *West Jersey Grove Camp Association 80th Anniversary*. Malaga: published by the association, 1949.

Evans, William F. *Border Skylines*. Dallas: C. Baugh, [1940].

———. "Border Skylines; Fifty Years of 'Tallying Out' on the Bloys Roundup Ground." Dallas: C. Baugh, [1940].

*Events and Dates in the History of Mission Farms and the Founding of the Bible Conference and Camp Grounds.* No publishing data, n.d.

Farmer, Rev. R. G. *Jonesville Camp Ground.* Jonesville: Camp Ground Preservation Fund Committee, 1931.

Fennimore, Keith J. *The Heritage of Bay View, 1875–1975, A Centennial History.* Grand Rapids: William B. Eerdman's Publishing Company, 1975.

*Fiftieth Anniversary of the Crystal Springs Camp Meeting, 1936.* No publishing data, 1936.

Flood, Rev. Ernest C. *Empire Grove, the First 150 Years.* Empire Grove: Poppenburg's Press, 1983.

Foster, John O. *The First Des Plaines Camp Meeting, Des Plaines, Ill., August, 1860.* Springfield: Schnepp & Barnes, 1932.

————, "The First Des Plaines Camp Meeting, Des Plaines, Ill., August, 1860," in *Journal of the Illinois State Historical Society,* January 1932.

Fradenburgh, Rev. F. L. *The Golden Anniversary of the Oylen Camp and Church.* Oylen: Rev. F. L. Fradenburgh, [1965].

Freeberg, Virginia M., "History of Des Plaines Methodist Camp Ground 1860–1940," in Almer M. Pennewell. *The Methodist Movement in Northern Illinois.* Sycamore: The Sycamore Tribune, 1982.

Frey, Howard J. *Fiftieth Anniversary of God's Holiness Grove Camp Meeting Association.* No publishing data, 1969.

Friedlin, Joan B. *Pitman: A Town for all Occasions.* Dallas: Taylor Publishing Company, 1979.

Gabrielson, John. *The Story of Methodism in Pacific Palisades.* No publishing data, n.d.

Gaddis, Vincent H., and Jasper A. Huffman. *The Story of Winona Lake, A Memory and A Vision.* Winona Lake: Winona Lake Christian Assembly, 1960.

Gage, Patricia A., "The Sawdust Trail Lives On at the Hudson Camp Meeting," in *North Louisiana Historical Association Journal,* 1979 [10(1)], pp. 23–25.

Galey, Mary. *The Grand Assembly, The Story of Life at the Colorado Chautauqua.* No publishing data, n.d.

Gibbons, Mr. and Mrs. Richard F. *History of Ocean Grove 1869–1939*. Ocean Grove: Ocean Grove Times, 1939.

"God's Square Mile," in *Grit*, June 2, 1968, p. 9.

Good, Harold M. *History of the Indiana State Holiness Association*. No publishing data, n.d.

Goodgion, Mary H. S. *Recollections of Mt. Bethel Camp Meeting*. No publishing data, n.d.

Gracey, Rev. Frank. *A History of the Willimantic Camp Meeting Association, 1860–1960*. Willimantic: Willimantic Camp Meeting Association, 1960.

Graves, William P. E., "Martha's Vineyard," in *National Geographic*, June 1961, pp. 778–807.

Grimes, John Franklin. *The Romance of the American Camp Meeting*. Cincinnati: The Caxton Press, 1912.

Groce, Rev. John W. *Brief History of John Wesley Camp Meeting*. High Point: John Wesley Camp Meeting, 1985.

Hartman, Mrs. Brigadier William, "Historical Hallmarks of Old Orchard Camp Meetings, A Great Tradition: 'The Trees Sing Out,'" in the *War Cry*, July 6, 1985, p. 17.

————, "Historical Hallmarks of Old Orchard Camp Meetings, A Mecca for Salvationists," in the *War Cry*, June 29, 1985, pp. 18–21.

————, "Historical Hallmarks of Old Orchard Camp Meetings, Milestones of Sacred History," in the *War Cry*, June 15, 1985, pp. 18–19.

————, "Historical Hallmarks of Old Orchard Camp Meetings, The First Camp Meetings," in the *War Cry*, June 15, 1985, pp. 16–20.

————, "Historical Hallmarks of Old Orchard Camp Meetings, The Salvation Army Acquires the Camp Grounds," in the *War Cry*, July 13, 1985, pp. 6–7.

————. "Historical Hallmarks of Old Orchard Camp Meetings, Warriors of the Cross," in the *War Cry*, June 22, 1985, p. 18.

————, "A Hundred Years Ago . . .," in *A Centennial Celebration, Old Orchard Beach Camp Meetings, 1885–1985*. No publisher, 1985.

————, "A Hundred Years Ago . . . And More," in *Holiness Our Heritage, Old Orchard Beach Camp Meeting, 1885–1989*. No publisher, 1989.

Hartoog, Vera. *Simpson Park Camp Grounds, Our One Hundred and Twentieth Year*. Romeo: Simpson Park Camp Meeting, 1984.

Hearn, Anthony, "Epworth by the Sea, The Early Years," in *Historical Highlights*, June 1986, pp. 21–28.

*Hedding Camp Ground Centennial, 1862–1962*. No publishing data, 1962.

Heiges, George L., "The National Camp Meeting at Manheim in 1868," in *Papers of the Lancaster County Historical Society*, 1943, No. 1, pp. 13–22.

Henricks, Sylvia. *A Good and Profitable Occasion, the Story of Acton Camp Ground*. Bloomington: no publisher, 1970.

Hilbert, Norman. *Harvest Time Camp*. Elizabethville: published by Harvest Time Camp, n.d.

Hine, C. J. *The Story of Martha's Vineyard*. New York: Hine Bros., 1908.

Hirsch, Gordon, "Ole-Time Religion Lives In Dorchester Campground," in *The State*, November 22, 1983, p. 3B.

"Historical Items," in *Year Book and Minutes of the Forty-first Annual Meeting, Iowa Holiness Association*. No publishing data, 1919.

*An Historical Review of the Old Methodist Camp-Meeting Grounds Located on Cherokee Creek in Chappel Community*. No publishing data, n.d.

"Historical Sketch," in *Manual of Denville Camp Ground of the Newark Conference Camp Meeting Association*. Denville: no publishing data, 1874.

"History," *Year Book and Minutes of the Twelfth Annual Encampment of the Missouri Association for the Promotion of Holiness*. Hannibal: Freeman Printing Co., 1916.

*The History of Asbury Camp from 1925 to 1975, A Dream Come True*. No publishing data, [1975].

"History of Nebraska State Holiness Association," in the *Christian Witness and Advocate of Bible Holiness*, July 2, 1908, p. 9.

"History of Northern Indiana Holiness Association," in the *Christian Witness and Advocate of Bible Holiness*, August 1, 1907, pp. 4–5.

"History of Perkasie Park," in *Perkasie Park Handbook*. Perkasie: The Perkasie Park Association, 1987.

*History of Shiloh Church and Camp Meeting*. No publishing data, n.d.

*History of the Green Mountain Camp Ground Association.* Camas: Lacamas Camp Ground Association, n.d.

"History of the Long Island Holiness Camp Meeting Association, Inc.," in *Thirtieth Anniversary Brochure and Program.* Freeport: published by the association, 1940.

"A History of the Pittsburgh-Tarentum Campgrounds," in *Tarentum Times,* 1988, pp. 69–88.

*A History of the Round Lake Association, 1868–1968.* Round Lake: Woman's Round Lake Improvement Society, 1968.

*History of the Southern Illinois Holiness Association.* No publishing data, n.d.

*History of the United Methodist Assembly, Beersheba Springs, Tennessee.* No publishing data, n.d.

*History of Wakefield, Virginia, Camp Meeting.* No publishing data, n.d.

"History, Ohio State Holiness Association," in the *Christian Witness and Advocate of Bible Holiness,* September 14, 1905, p. 5.

Hodges, Dr. J. E. *A History of Balls Creek Camp Ground, 1853–1929.* No publishing data, 1929.

Hoffman, Rev. Harley. *40th Anniversary of God's Holiness Grove Camp Meeting Association.* Hummel's Wharf: God's Holiness Grove Camp Meeting Association, 1960.

Hogle, Charles P. *A Half Century of Saving Grace, 1903–1952.* Mooers: Mooers Camp Meeting Association, 1952.

Hollis, William C. *Memories of Beulah Park Holiness Camp Meeting, 70th Anniversary.* Richland: Richland Holiness Camp Meeting Association, 1972.

Holm, Fleming. *Berwick Camp Meeting.* Antigonish, Nova Scotia: Casket Printing and Publishing Co., Ltd., 1972.

Hord, Harry. *Ruggles Campground, 1873–1973, Centennial Celebration.* Flemingsburg: Ruggles Camp Meeting Association, 1973.

Horst, Elmer H. *History of Mt. Lebanon Campmeeting: 1892 to 1966.* Lebanon: Mt. Lebanon Campmeeting Association, 1966.

Hough, Henry Beetle. *Martha's Vineyard, Summer Resort.* Rutland: The Tuttle Publishing Co., 1936.

————. *Summer Resort after 100 Years.* Rutland: Academy Books, 1966.

Hoyt, Harold B., "History of the Kansas State Holiness Camp Meeting," in *Year Book of the Eightieth Annual Camp Meeting of the Kansas State Holiness Association*. Wichita: Kansas State Holiness Association, 1967.

Hughes, H. Raymond, "The Purpose and a Brief History of Delanco Camp Meeting," in *The Historical Trail*, 1984, pp. 32–39.

Hughes, Howard R., "The History of Delanco Camp Meeting Association," a B.D. thesis submitted to Eastern Baptist Theological Seminary, 1961.

*Hughesville Holiness Camp Meeting*. Hughesville: Hughesville Holiness Camp Meeting Association, 1954.

*Hughesville Holiness Camp Meeting Jubilee 1904–1954*. Hughesville: Hughesville Holiness Camp Meeting Association, 1954.

Hunton, Gail, and Jenifer Boyd. *A Home Renovator's Guide for Historic Ocean Grove*. Ocean Grove: Ocean Grove Home Owners Association, 1989.

*Hurricane Camp Meeting, Centennial Celebration, 1889–1988*. Tolu: Hurricane Camp Meeting, 1988.

*Island Heights, N.J.* Published by the Monmouth County Historical Society, n.d.

*Jacksonville Campmeeting, One Hundred Years, 1865–1965*. No publishing data, [1965].

Jacox, Helen P., and Eugene B. Kleinhans, Jr. *Thousand Island Park: One Hundred Years, and Then Some, A Centennial History*. Thousand Island Park: Valhalla Printing Co., 1975.

Jakeman, Albert M. *The Story of Ocean Park*. Ocean Park: Ocean Park Association, 1956.

Jennings, Thomas F. *Marthaville Holiness Campmeetings, Marthaville, La., 1895–1981*. Marthaville: Thomas F. Jennings, 1981.

Johnson, Emily M., editor. *Heritage from the Lord, A History of Pitman United Methodist Church 1885–1985*. Printed by the Review Printing Company, 1985.

Johnson, Frank A. *History of White Pine Holiness Association Camp Meeting*. No publishing data, n.d.

Johnson, Z. T. *The Story of Indian Springs Holiness Camp Meeting*. Wilmore: Asbury College, 1965.

Jorchow, Merrill E., "Red Rock: Frontier Methodist Camp Meeting," in *Minnesota History*, June 1950, pp. 79–92.

*Jubilee Year for Gladwin Camp.* No publishing data, n.d.

Karls, Sandra. *75 Years by the Bay; A History of Bay Shore Evangelical Camp, 1911–1986.* Sebewaing: Bay Shore Camp Association, 1986.

Kealiher, Grace, and Marilyn Johnson. *Carmel Campmeeting History.* No publishing data, n.d.

Keen, S. A. *Forest Chronicles; A History of the Origin, Progress and Achievements of the Ohio Conference Camp Meeting.* Columbus: A. C. Berlin & Co., 1887.

Keller, Mavis. *Seventy-five Years of Campmeeting, 1906–1981.* Forest Junction: Forest Assembly Grounds, Inc., 1981.

Kestle, James Allen. *This Is Lakeside, the Centennial History, 1873–1973.* Lakeside: Lakeside Association, 1973.

Kildall, Wayne F., "A History of Northwest Washington Holiness Association and Camp Meeting, Ferndale, Washington, 1902–1952," a B.D. thesis submitted to Western Evangelical Seminary, 1952.

Laechel, David F., "Sam P. Jones and Red Rock Camp," in *Heritage*, July 1985, pp. 18–26.

Lake, William, "History of Ocean City," undated manuscript history on file at Free Public Library, Ocean City, N.J.

*Lakeside Centennial Celebration, 1873–1973, 100th Anniversary Season.* Lakeside: published by the Lakeside Association Board of Trustees, 1973.

Lance, Rev. Lyman F. *Brief History of Shady Grove Campground.* Colfax: Shady Grove Campmeeting, 1962.

LeBaron, Ira W. *The Camp Meeting at Martha's Vineyard.* Nashville: The Parthenon Press, 1958.

Lee, Harold. *A History of Ocean City, New Jersey.* Ocean City: Ocean City Historical Museum, 1965.

Lewis, Jim L., "'Beautiful Bismark—Bismark Grove, Lawrence, 1878–1900," in *The Kansas Historical Quarterly*, Autumn 1969, pp. 225–256.

Lippincott, Herbert, and David Weaver, eds. *100th Anniversary, Mt. Tabor, New Jersey, 1869–1969.* Mt. Tabor: Mt. Tabor Camp Meeting Association, 1969.

Lipscomb, H. C. *Forty Years of Camp Meetings at Old Bluff Creek*. No publishing data, 1933.

Lobeck, A. K. *Brief History of Martha's Vineyard Camp Meeting Association*. Oak Bluffs: Martha's Vineyard Camp Meeting Association, 1956.

Longenecker, C. R. *History of the Mount Lebanon Camp Meeting Association, 1892–1954*. Lebanon: no publishing data, n.d.

Lord, Clyde W., "The Mineral Springs Holiness Camp Meeting," in *Louisiana History*, Summer 1975, pp. 257–277.

Love, Mary I., "'The Mountain Chautauqua'—Mountain Lake Park 1881–1941," in *The Glades Star*, March 1982.

Lovell, Irving W. *The Story of the Yarmouth Camp Ground and the Methodist Camp Meetings on Cape Cod*. Yarmouth: Irving W. Lovell, 1985.

Lowery, Kevin T., "An Overview of the History of Bentleyville Camp Meeting," a research paper submitted to Wesley Biblical Seminary, 1991.

McCollough, Almeda, editor. *The Battle Ground Story*. Lafayette: Morehouse Printing, n.d.

McCulloch, Maude. *Junaluska*. Atlanta: Byrd Printing Co., n.d.

McCullough, David, "Oak Bluffs," in *American Heritage*, 1961, pp. 39–46.

McGarvey, Joel W. *Summit Grove, 100th Anniversary*. New Freedom: no publishing data, 1973.

McPheeters, Julian C., "At Ocean Grove," in *The Herald*, September 17, 1958, p. 8.

———, "The Beulah Camp Meeting," in *The Pentecostal Herald*, August 23, 1950, p. 8.

———, "The Brandywine Camp Meeting," in *The Herald*, September 9, 1953, p. 8.

———, "God and the Redwoods," in *The Herald*, August 27, 1958, pp. 1–2.

———, "Little George Havens' Cowboy Camp Meeting," in *The Herald*, August 12, 1970, p. 3.

"Malaga Camp." Unpublished typed manuscript history, September 2, 1966.

Martin, Emory S. *History of Taylor's Creek Camp Meeting, Liberty County, Georgia.* No publishing data, 1933.

Martin, Ina Hixon. *History of Imperial Valley Holiness Association, Inc.* Imperial: Imperial Valley Holiness Association, 1956.

Marton, Emory S. *History of Taylor's Creek Camp Meeting, Liberty County, Georgia.* No publishing data, 1933.

Massey, Walter, "Camp Meeting," no publishing data, August 27, 1967, pp. 11–14. [Article is on file at the United Methodist Archives in Madison, N.J.]

Mathis, Vance B., "Indian Springs Campmeeting and Georgia Methodism, Perspectives on Holiness," in *Historical Highlights,* Spring 1990, p. 76.

Matthews, Clifton T. *Brief History of the Freeport Camp Meeting.* No publishing data, 1968.

Mayhew, Eleanor R., ed. *Martha's Vineyard: A Short History and Guide.* New Bedford: Reynolds Printing, Inc., 1956.

*Memorial Holiness Camp, 25th. Anniversary, 1943–1968.* West Milton: Anniversary Committee of the Central Conference, Brethren in Christ Church, 1968.

*The Methodist Camp Grounds, Sabina, Ohio.* Sabina: Sabina News Record, 1959.

Miller, Rebecca W., ed. *The 100th Session of Rawlinsville Camp Meeting, 1886–1985.* Rawlinsville: Rawlinsville Camp Meeting Association, 1985.

*The Miracle of the Evangelical Center, 75 Years a Center of Biblical Evangelism, 1905–1980.* Pacific Conference of the Evangelical Church of North America, 1980.

Moore, Penny, "Reflections on One Hundred Twenty-five Years of Seaville Camp Meetings," in *The Historical Trail,* 1989, pp. 25–27.

————, "South Seaville Camp Meeting Ground Celebrates 125 Years," in *The Historical Trail,* 1988, pp. 12–17.

Moore, Taylor. *History of Carthage Holiness Camp Meeting.* No publishing data, 1967.

Moore, Rev. William L. *New Jersey Conference Camp Meeting Association 100 Year Anniversary.* Pitman: New Jersey Conference Camp Meeting Association, 1970.

Morris, W. Eddie. *Falcon Camp Meeting, Fiftieth Anniversary, 1900–1949.* Franklin Springs: Publishing House Pentecostal Holiness Church, 1949.

Morrison, Rev. W. W. *Martha's Vineyard Campmeeting (Souvenir History).* Oak Bluffs: Martha's Vineyard Camp Meeting Association, 1897.

Morrow, Florence Marion. *History of Sterling Camp Ground, Sterling Junction Massachusetts, 1852–1942.* No publishing data, 1942.

*Mountain Lake Park, The Christian Summer Resort of the Alleghenies, Fourth Season, 1885.* Harrisburg: Central Pennsylvania M. E. Book Room Print, 1885.

Mudge, James. *Fifty Years at Sterling.* No publishing data, 1902.

Nelson, Grace B., "Davidson Camp Ground and Camp Meeting," in *Clark County Historical Journal,* Spring 1981.

Neville, G. D. *History of Discovery Bay Camp Meeting.* No publishing data, n.d.

Norris, Mary Hariett. *Camp Tabor: A Study of Life in the Woods.* Cincinnati: Hitchcock and Walden, 1874.

Norton, Henry Franklin. *Martha's Vineyard.* No publishing data, 1923.

*The Observance of the One Hundredth Anniversary of the Hedding Camp Meeting, 1862–1962.* No publishing data, 1962

*Observing 100 Years, 1867–1967, Bentleyville Union Holiness Association.* Bentleyville: Bentleyville Union Holiness Association, 1967.

*Ocean Grove Auditorium, Ocean Grove, New Jersey.* Ocean Grove: 1949.

"Ocean Grove Files re: transfer of government to Neptune Township," located in the Asbury Park Public Library, Asbury Park, N.J.

*Ocean Park, Chautauqua-By-the-Sea.* Ocean Park: Ocean Park Association, 1991.

*Official Record, 1929 Year Book and Minutes of the South Dakota Holiness Association, Thirty-Sixth Annual Meeting held at Mitchell, S.D.* Mitchell: Published by the Committee of Publication, 1929.

*Official Record, 1940 Year Book and Minutes of the South Dakota Holiness Association.* Mitchell: Published by the Committee of Publication, 1940.

*Old Des Plaines.* No publication data, 1984.

*Old Orchard Then and Now.* Old Orchard Beach: published by Old Orchard Beach Historical Society, n.d.

*100th Anniversary, Camp Meeting Sunday.* Brochure published by First United Methodist Church, Island Heights, N.J., 1990.

*100th Anniversary of the Bowman Park Camp Meeting, 1891–1991.* No publishing data, 1991.

*100th Anniversary, Stoverdale Memorial Camp Meeting, 1872–1972.* Stoverdale: Stoverdale Camp Meeting, 1972.

*125th Anniversary History of Willimantic Camp Meeting Association.* Willimantic: Willimantic Camp Meeting Association, 1985.

"The Origin of the Hedding Camp Meeting Association," in *The Hedding News*, August 1917, p. 1.

Osborn, Mrs. William B. *In the Beginning God; Pioneer Days at Ocean Grove.* New York: Methodist Book Concern, n.d.

*Paisano 50th Anniversary.* Supplement to *The Alpine Avalanche*, July 21, 1966.

Parker, Charles A., "The Camp Meeting on the Frontier and the Methodist Religious Resort in the East—Before 1900," in *Methodist History*, April 1980, pp. 179–192.

———, "Ocean Grove, New Jersey: Queen of the Victorian Methodist Camp Meeting Resorts," in *Nineteenth Century Magazine*, Spring 1984, pp. 19–25.

———, "Ocean Grove—Queen of the Camp Meetings," a paper presented to the Religious Speech Communication Association Convention, 1983.

———. *Pitman Grove, New Jersey, 1870–1900, Through a Tiffany Window.* Woodbury: Gloucester County Historical Society, 1984.

Parker, Charlotte Goodrich. *Before '07 through '70.* No publishing data, 1974.

Paterson, Mrs. Mildred, "History of Brandywine Summit Camp, One Hundredth Year," in *Program, One Hundredth Year, Brandywine Summit Camp Meeting.* West Chester: published by the association, 1965.

Patterson, Richard S., ed. *Patterson Grove Centennial, 1868–1968.* Huntington Mills: Patterson Grove Camp Meeting Association, 1968.

Paul, John, "Scottsville Camp Meeting, A Historic Sketch," in *Texas Holiness Advocate*, July 26, 1906, p. 1.

Pearson, F. Lamar, Jr., "Precursors to Epworth-by-the-Sea: the Spanish Missions in Georgia," in *Historical Highlights*, December 1978, pp. 6–19.

Pease, Richard L., and Sumner Myrick. *A Guide to Martha's Vineyard and Nantucket with a Directory of the Campground*. Boston: Rockwell and Churchill, 1876.

Perry, W. E. *Origin and History of the New Jersey Camp Meeting Association*. Barclay & Cheesman, Printers, n.d.

Phinney, William R. *The Hunter Camp Meeting*. Rye: Commission on Archives and History, New York Annual Conference, United Methodist Church, 1971.

Reed, Roy, "In Tennessee: A Family Goes to Camp Meeting," in *Time*, September 6, 1982, pp. 12–13.

Rees, James A., Jr. *Dwelling in Beulah Land, Davidson Camp Meeting, 1884–1984*. Hollywood: Davidson Camp Meeting Centennial Committee, 1984.

Reid, Isaiah, "'Grand Depositum' of the I.H.A.," in the *Christian Witness and Advocate of Bible Holiness*, May 9, 1907, p. 4.

————, "Iowa Holiness Association—President's Annual Address" (25th anniversary), in the *Christian Witness and Advocate of Bible Holiness*, July 7, 1901, p. 4.

————, "A Visit to Historic Ground," in the *Christian Witness and Advocate of Bible Holiness*, July 7, 1901, p. 5.

Renich, Jill Torrey. *The Montrose Bible Conference Story*. Montrose: The Montrose Bible Conference, 1978.

*Retrospect and Prospect, The First Eighty-Five Years, Eaton Rapids Camp*. Eaton Rapids: Michigan State Holiness Association, [1970].

Ridout, Rev. G. W. *"Remember the Days of Old," Anniversary Sermon Preached on the Fiftieth Anniversary of Douglas Camp Meeting, July 24, 1924*. Douglas: Douglas Camp Meeting Association, 1924.

*Riverside Camp Meeting under the Auspices of the Illinois State Holiness Association*. No publishing data, 1912.

Robinson, Dorothy. *A Brief History of the Tremont Advent Christian Campmeeting Association*. Attleboro: Tremont Advent Christian Campmeeting Association, 1985.

Rose, Delbert R., "An Anniversary Day at Douglas," in *The Herald*, October 22, 1969, p. 7.

————, "Camp Sychar," in *The Herald*, May 20, 1970, p. 4.

————, "A Century of Blessing at Bentleyville," in *The Herald*, September 27, 1967, p. 5.

*Rosedale Grove Association, Inc., 50th Anniversary 1924–1973*. No publishing data, 1973.

*Round Lake Year Book for the Year 1891*. Chatham: Courier Printing House, 1891.

Sailor, Daniel R. *The Des Plaines Camp Ground, 125 Years of Methodist History*. No publication data, n.d.

*Salem Campground, 1826–1976*. No publishing data, 1976.

Sayre, Harry E., "Historical Sketch of Bentleyville Camp," in the *Standard of Holiness*, July–August 1951, p. 6.

————, "Some Typical Camp Meeting History," in *The Herald*, June 8, 1955, p. 2.

Schenk, David J. *Mt. Lebanon Campmeeting: 1892–1976; A Walk through Mt. Lebanon*. Lebanon: Mt. Lebanon Campmeeting Association, 1976.

Schleicher, Pauline. *A History of Camp Hedding*. Epping: no publishing data, 1949.

Scott, Doug, "Indian Fields Camp Meeting," a research paper on file with the Trustees of Indian Field Camp Meeting, 1979.

Seckinger, Ernest W., "Effingham Camp Ground: Then and Now, A History," in *Historical Highlights*, Spring 1990, pp. 54–67.

*75th Anniversary, Landisville Camp Meeting*. Landisville: Landisville Camp Meeting Association, 1945.

Shaver, Helen Putnam. *Steps to the Heights*. Tucson: Pima Printing Co., 1957.

Sheffield, Rev. Wayne. *History of Joyner's Camp Ground*. No publishing data, n.d.

Shepard, O. L. *The Story of Lakeside, Golden Anniversary Booklet*. Lakeside: Lakeside Association, 1923.

*Short History of New Prospect Camp Grounds*. No publishing data, 1953.

Sider, E. Morris. *Beyond Our Dreams, The Story of Kenbrook Bible Camp on Its Fortieth Anniversary*. Lebanon: Kenbrook Bible Camp, 1990.

————. *Holiness unto the Lord, The Story of Roxbury Holiness Camp.* Napanee: The Evangel Press, 1985.

Sigmon, Mrs. Gabriel, "History and Traditions of Rock Springs Camp Ground," in *Rock Springs Camp Meeting, 142nd Annual Session Booklet.* Denver: Rock Springs Camp Meeting, 1971.

Sigmon, Lilly Estelle. *Rock Springs Camp Meeting, 158th Annual Session.* Denver: Rock Springs Camp Meeting, 1987.

*Simpson Park Camp Grounds Souvenir History.* Simpson Park Camp Meeting Association, 1946.

*Sixtieth Anniversary, 1891–1951, Evangelical United Brethren Camp Meeting, Bowman Park, Bowmanstown, Pa.* Bowmanstown: No publishing data, 1951.

*Sixtieth Anniversary, God's Holiness Grove Camp Meeting Association.* Hummel's Wharf: God's Holiness Grove Camp Meeting Association, 1979.

*69 Years on the Grounds.* Chambersburg: Rhodes Grove Camp Association, 1967.

Smith, Eleanor L., ed. *Hollow Rock: A History.* Columbus: The Watkins Printing Company, 1988.

Smith, Ethel Stebbins. *Washington Advent Christian Campground, 1886–1986, The First 100 Years.* No publishing data, 1986.

Smith, Francis Samuel. *History of the Camp Meeting and Chautauqua Movement at Bethesda, Ohio.* No publishing data, [1983].

Smith, Harry A. *Apart with Him—Fifty Years of the Mount Hermon Conference.* Oakland: Western Book and Tract, 1956.

Smith, Janet Schoen. *100th Encampment; Silver Heights Camp, 1888–1987.* New Albany: Silver Heights Camp Meeting, 1987.

Smith, Jeanne Jacoby. *An Altar in the Forest; A History of Mount Lebanon Campmeeting 1892–1992.* Lebanon: Mt. Lebanon Campmeeting Association, 1990.

Smith, Rose Marie, "'Tabernacle': A Memory, An Event," in the *United Methodist Reporter*, August 10, 1979.

Smith, Vagie D. *A Brief History of Ball's Creek Camp Meeting.* No publishing data, [1989].

————. *A Brief History of Rock Springs Camp Meeting.* No publishing data, 1988.

Smith, Zane F., "The Great Revival of 1800, the First Camp Meeting," in *Kentucky Historical Society Register*, 1909.

*Smith Mills Camp Meeting, History, Echoes and By-Laws*. New Bedford: The Vining Press, 1930.

*Some Past History of the Vilonia Camp*. No publishing data, 1965.

Souders, Rev. Bruce C. *A Brief History of the Mount Gretna Campmeeting Association*. Mt. Gretna: Rev. Bruce C. Souders, 1959.

*Souvenir, Detroit Holiness Association, Dedication of the Tabernacle*. Detroit: Detroit Holiness Association, 1919.

Springsteen, Fanny, "The First One Hundred Years of Crystal Springs," typed manuscript, 1956.

Stoddard, Chris. *A Centennial History of Cottage City*. Oak Bluffs: Oak Bluffs Historical Commission, 1981.

Stoddard, Paul W., "Pine View Grove in Days Gone By," a revised transcript of a lecture delivered at Pine Grove, Canaan, Connecticut, September 2, 1951.

Stokes, E. C. *Ocean Grove, What It Was, Is and Hopes to Be; Address of Hon. E. C. Stokes on the Occasion of Founders Day, July 31, 1914*. No publishing data, 1914.

Stokes, Kitty. *Paisano: Story of a Cowboy and a Camp Meeting*. Waco: Texian Press, 1980.

*The Story of Ocean Park, First Fifty Years*. Ocean Park: Ocean Park Association, 1931.

Sullivan, Audrey G. *Nineteenth Century South Jersey Camp Meeting, South Seaville, N.J.* Fort Lauderdale: Audrey G. Sullivan, 1980.

Sullivan, Audrey, and Doris Young. *A Time to Remember; A History of New Jersey Methodist's First Camp Meeting, South Seaville, New Jersey*. South Seaville: The South Seaville Camp Meeting Association, 1988.

Sutton, Katherine Augusta, and Robert Francis Needham. *Universalists at Ferry Beach*. Boston: Universalist Publishing House, 1948.

Teeter, Herman B., "Lakeside Ohio: 'A Place Like the Whole World Ought to Be,'" in *United Methodists Today*, June 1974, pp. 36–42.

Terrill, Joseph Goodwin. *The St. Charles Camp Meeting*. Chicago: T. B. Arnold, 1883.

*This Is Bethel, Its 50th Year.* Paynesville: Holiness Methodist Publishing Company, 1968.

"Thornley Chapel . . . 100 Years Ministering to the Children of Ocean Grove," in *The Journal Update*, August 1989, pp. 1–3.

Towers, J. K., "Ocean Grove, N.J., Turmoil; The O. G. C. M. A., Citizens & Courts Speak Out; 1974-1975-1976-1977," a collection of letters and newspaper clippings on file at the Ocean Grove Historical Society.

Uhrig, Robert E. *One Man's Dream; History Ohio Council of Christian Union Campgrounds.* Greenfield: Ohio Council of the Christian Union, 1988.

*Unto the Lord, Seventy-fifth Anniversary, Douglas Camp Meeting.* No publishing data, 1950.

Valade, C. C., "Historical Sketch" in *Tabernacle Tidings*, The Detroit Holiness Association, January–November 1953.

Valentine, Emma L. *Peniel Holiness Association, Conneautville Camp, 1896–1946.* Conneautville: Peniel Holiness Association, 1946.

VanGilder, Charles W. *Bentleyville Camp Meeting 100 Years Old.* No publishing data, 1967.

*Victory Camp Jubilee, 1926–1976, 50 Years of Service.* No publishing data, 1976.

Vincent, Hebron. *The Vineyard as It Was, Is, and Is to Be, By an Observer.* New Bedford: No publishing data, 1872.

Vincent, Rev. Hebron. *History of the Camp Meeting and Grounds at Wesleyan Grove, Martha's Vineyard, for the Eleven Years ending with the Meeting of 1869.* Boston: Lee and Shepard, 1870.

————. *A History of the Wesleyan Grove Camp Meeting from the First Meeting Held There in 1835 to That of 1858.* Boston: George C. Rand and Avery, 1858.

"The Virginia State Holiness Association," in *The Virginia State Holiness Association Roanoke Area Rally.* Roanoke: published by First Wesleyan Methodist Church, 1956. [Leaflet.]

Vollmeke, Alfred. *Story of the Campground.* Boston: Warren Press, 1942.

Vuilleumier, Marion. *Craigville on Old Cape Cod.* Taunton: William S. Sullwald Publishing, 1972.

Waite, Mary Abbott, "Epworth's Beginnings and the Legacy of History," in *Historical Highlights*, June 1986, pp. 11–17.

*Waldheim, 75th Anniversary, 1904–1979.* No publishing data, 1979.

Wandersee, Delores, "Red Rock Camp," in *Heritage*, July 1985, pp. 7–17.

Watson, Dr. Walter V. *History of Montrose Bible Conference.* No publishing data, 1974.

Weinert, Leonard E., "A History of the Clark County Holiness Association, Vancouver, Washington," a B.D. thesis submitted to Western Evangelical Seminary, 1952.

Weise, Arthur James. *History of Round Lake.* Troy: Douglas Taylor, 1887.

Weiss, Ellen B. *City in the Woods; The Life and Design of an American Camp Meeting on Martha's Vineyard.* New York: Oxford University Press, 1987.

White, Fairy Mapp. *Turlington Camp Meetings.* No publishing data, 1957.

Williams, Ben-Eva Grimes. *Pioneering in Faith, 100 Years at Lancaster United Methodist Campground.* Lancaster: Lancaster Camp Meeting Association, 1972.

Willowby, Richard L. *Family Reunion; A Century of Camp Meetings.* Anderson: Warner Press, 1986.

Wilson, Harold F. *Cottages and Commuters, A History of Pitman New Jersey.* Pitman: Pitman Borough, 1955.

Woodward, W. D., "Douglas" (25th Anniversary), in the *Christian Witness and Advocate of Bible Holiness*, August 3, 1899, p. 1.

Wright, Susan Ramey, "It's August, and the Taylors are Coming Home to Tennessee," in *Progressive Farmer*, August 1988.

Wrightsel, Kenneth E. *The History of Stoutsville Camp.* Stoutsville: Stoutsville Camp Meeting Association, 1985.

*Yarmouth Camp Meeting.* Yarmouth: Yarmouth Camp Meeting Association, 1910.

Young, Jared W., "Mt. Lake Park," unpublished typed manuscript, February 24, 1951.

Zerby, Ida M. *A Brief History of the Herndon Camp Meeting.* Herndon: Herndon Camp Grove, 1972.

Zitek, Sylvia. *Except as We Forget, 1878–1978*. Gresham: Three Cedars Publishing Association, 1978.

Zook, A. C., "The Brethren in Christ Holiness Camp Meeting at Roxbury, Penna.," in the *Visitor*, September 22, 1941, p. 297.

# Part Three

## A Working List of Camp Meetings, Bible Conferences, Chautauquas, Assembly Grounds, and Christian Retreat Centers

# A WORKING LIST

The following is a table of nearly two thousand camp meetings, Bible conferences, and assembly grounds, Chautauquas and Christian retreat centers which exist in the United States and several foreign countries. There are perhaps as many as six thousand such sites around the world, but much of the information was not available to me at the time of this writing. I am very conscious of the gaps in this list, and consequently ask the reader to regard this table as an introductory working tool. The list is arranged alphabetically by unit name. It begins with the United States, then proceeds to Canada and a few other countries. The material is arranged in columns for easy reference. The "affiliation" column tells at a glance whether the unit is denominational (D;), associational (A;), or interdenominational (I), and provides the name of the sponsor when possible. The "O/R" column tells if the unit is owned or rented, the "year" column provides the founding year, if known, and the "founder" column provides the name(s) of the key person(s) responsible for the founding of the particular unit.

Again it must be stressed that this is a working list. If you find an error in the data, if you can upgrade the material, or if you can provide any information on a unit or units not listed, *please* contact the author. (See author's address at end of the introduction.)

## Alabama

| Name | City | Affiliation | O/R | Year | Founder |
|---|---|---|---|---|---|
| Alabama Bible Methodist Camp | Pell City | D; Bible Methodist Church | O | 1938 | |
| Alabama Camp | Birmingham | D; Church of God of Prophecy | | | |
| Alabama Camp | Clanton | D; Church of God (Anderson) | O | 1895 | |
| Alabama Camp | Floralla | D; Congregational Methodist Church | | | |
| Alabama Camp | Grier | D; Pentecostal Fire Baptized Holiness Church | O | 1950 | Rev. W. H. Preskitt, Sr., et al. |
| Alabama Conference Camp | River Springs | D; International Pentecostal Holiness Church | O | 1932 | |
| Alabama District Camp | | D; United Pentecostal Church | | | |
| Alabama District Camp | Calera | D; Church of the Nazarene | O | | |
| Autanga County Camp | Prattville | D; Congregational Holiness Church | O | 1970 | |
| Beulah Camp Meeting | Excel | I . . . | O | 1942 | Rev. Henry A. Screws, Jr. |
| Birmingham Baptist Camp | Cooks Springs | D; Baptist Church | | | |
| Blue Lake Assembly Grounds | Covington County | D; United Methodist Church | O | 1951 | |
| Brasher Springs Camp | Atalla | I . . . | O | 1940 | Dr. John L. Brasher |
| Camp Alamisco | Montgomery | I . . . | | | |
| Camp Challenge | Palmer | D; Church of God (Anderson) | | 1970 | |
| Camp Chula Vista | Birmingham | D; Church of God (Anderson) | O | 1895 | |
| Camp Desoto | Mentone | I . . . | | | |

| Name | Location | Affiliation | O/R | Year | Notes |
|---|---|---|---|---|---|
| Camp Ground Mission Camp | Jasper | D; Bible Methodist Church | O | 1953 | |
| Camp Maxwell | Haleyville | I . . . | O | 1967 | Rev. Gus Buttram |
| Camp Victory | Samson | A; CBM Ministries | O | | |
| Camp Victory | Samson | I . . . | O | | |
| Christian Life Center Camp | Florala | D; Bible Methodist Connection of Churches | O | 1970 | |
| Church of God Camp | Sylacauga | D; New Testament Church of God | R | | |
| Cullman Camp | Cullman | I . . . | O | | Rev. George Creel |
| Frost Bridge Camp | Silas | I; Frost Bridge Holiness Camp Meeting Association | O | 1896 | |
| Hartselle Camp | Hartselle | I . . . | O | 1898 | Rev. B. W. Huckabee et al. |
| King's Vineyard Conference Center | Ariton | I . . . | | | |
| La Grange Tabernacle Camp | Leighton | I . . . | O | 1870 | |
| Little Texas Camp Meeting | Tuskegee (12 mi. E.) | D; United Methodist Church | O | 1828 | |
| Mid-Gulf District Camp | Calera | D; Wesleyan Church | O | | |
| Millport Camp | Millport | D; Church of the Nazarene | O | 1900 | |
| Mobile Baptist Assembly | Citronelle | D; Baptist Church | O | | |
| Piedmont Springs Camp | Piedmont | D; Congregational Holiness Church, Inc. | O | 1935 | |
| Shocco Springs | Talladega | D; Baptist Church | O | 1948 | |
| Society Hill Camp | Society Hill | D; United Methodist Church | O | | |
| South Central Conference Camp | Huntsville | D; Seventh Day Adventist Church | O | | |
| South-East District Camp | Jasper | D; Bible Missionary Church | O | 1957 | |

| Name | City | Affiliation | O/R | Year | Founder |
|---|---|---|---|---|---|
| Southern Annual Camp | Cuba | D; Church of God (Anderson) | O | 1970 | |
| Southern Camp | Sylacauga | D; New Testament Church of God | R | | |
| Tabernacle Camp Meeting | Columbus | D; United Methodist Church | O | 1828 | Ancestors of Dr. W. G. Henry |
| Trinity Bible Camp | Eight Mile | D; Trinity Bible Church | O | 1959 | |
| Unity Grove Camp | Reform | D; United Methodist Church | O | 1842 | Sheltons, Whites, et al. |
| White Water Camp | Prattville | I . . . | O | 1956 | Mrs. Jodie L. Faulk |

## Alaska

| Name | City | Affiliation | O/R | Year | Founder |
|---|---|---|---|---|---|
| Alaska Conference Camp | Palmer | D; Seventh Day Adventist Church | | | |
| Alaska District Camp | Anchorage | D; Church of the Nazarene | | 1970 | |
| Alaska District Camp | Sterling | D; United Pentecostal Church | | | |
| Alaska District Camp | Wasilla | D; Assembly of God Church | | | |
| Camp Li-Wa | Fairbanks | I . . . | O | | |
| Coal Bay Camp | Ketchikan | I . . . | | | |
| Laverne Griffin Baptist Assembly | Anchorage | D; Baptist Church | | | |
| Solid Rock Bible Camp | Soldotna | | | | |

## Arizona

| Name | City | Affiliation | O/R | Year | Founder |
|---|---|---|---|---|---|
| Arizona Camp | Phoenix | D; Church of God of Prophecy | R | | |

| Name | Location | Affiliation | | Year | Notes |
|---|---|---|---|---|---|
| Arizona Conference Camp | Phoenix | D; International Pentecostal Holiness Church | R | 1946 | |
| Arizona Conference Camp | Prescott | D; Seventh Day Adventist Church | O | | |
| Arizona District Camp | Prescott | D; Assembly of God Church | | | |
| Arizona Regional Indoor Camp | Tucson | D; Churches of Christ in Christian Union | R | 1970 | |
| Camp Good News | Prescott | D; Wesleyan Church | | 1970 | |
| Camp Grace | Lakeside | | | | |
| Camp Pinerock | Prescott | D; Church of the Nazarene | O | 1939 | |
| Church of God Camp | Middle Verde | D; Church of God (Trumpet) | | 1970 | |
| Church of God Camp | Phoenix | D; New Testament Church of God | | | |
| Community of Living Water, Inc., The | Cornville | | | | |
| Emmanuel Pines Camp | Prescott | | R | | |
| Emmanuel Pines Camp | Prescott | D; Free Methodist Church | O | | |
| Gospel Center Camp Meeting | Phoenix | A; Faith Missionary Association | | 1960 | |
| Huachuca Oaks Baptist Camp | Sierra Vista | D; Baptist Church | | | |
| Indian Campmeeting | Glendale | A; World Gospel Mission | O | 1954 | Rev. Kenneth Mendenhall |
| Indian Holiness Mission Camp | Chambers | I . . . | | 1970 | |
| Indian Winter Camp | Mesa | D; Fire Baptized Holiness Church | | 1959 | |
| Mount Elden Christian Conference Center | Flagstaff | | | | |

| Name | City | Affiliation | O/R | Year | Founder |
|---|---|---|---|---|---|
| Mountain View Camp | Prescott | D; United Pentecostal Church | | | |
| Navajo Trails Camp | Flagstaff | D; Church of God (Holiness) | | | |
| Pine Canyon Camp | Tucson | D; United Methodist Church | O | | |
| Pine Summit Bible Camp and Conference | Prescott | | | | |
| Prescott Pines Baptist Camp and Conference Center | Prescott | D; Baptist Church | | | |
| Prescott Pines Camp | Prescott | D; Church of God (Anderson) | | 1950 | |
| Southwest Camp Meeting | Surprise | I . . . | O | 1961 | Rev. H. P. Morgan et al. |
| Tonto Rim American Baptist Camp | Payson | D; American Baptist | | | |
| Western Spanish Camp | Glendale | D; Church of God of Prophecy | | | |

## Arkansas

| Name | City | Affiliation | O/R | Year | Founder |
|---|---|---|---|---|---|
| Aldersgate Camp | Little Rock | D; Church of God (Anderson) | O | 1910 | Rev. Johnson |
| Arkansas Baptist Assembly | Siloam Springs | D; Baptist Church | | | |
| Arkansas Camp | Forrest City | D; Church of God of Prophecy | R | | |
| Arkansas District Camp | Cabot | D; Bible Missionary Church | O | 1950 | Rev. L. G. Milbum |
| Arkansas District Camp | Redfield | D; United Pentecostal Church | | | |
| Arkansas Nazarene Camp | Vilonia | D; Church of Nazarene | O | 1899 | Local Holiness People |
| Arkansas-Louisiana Conference Camp | Gentry | D; Seventh Day Adventist Church | O | | |
| Beebe Camp | Beebe | I . . . | O | 1900 | |
| Ben Few Camp | Princeton | I . . . | O | 1898 | Rev. B. A. Few |

| Name | Location | Affiliation | | Year | Notes |
|---|---|---|---|---|---|
| Camp Aldersgate | Little Rock | D; United Methodist Church | O | 1946 | |
| Camp Ozark | Gentry | D; Free Methodist Church | O | | |
| Camp Tanako | Malvern | D; United Methodist Church | O | 1945 | Conference leaders |
| Chiricahua Ranchmen's Camp | Willcox | A; Ranchmen's Camp Meeting of the Southwest | O | 1945 | |
| Davidson Camp Meeting | Hollywood | D; United Methodist Church | O | 1884 | |
| Ebenezer Camp | Center Point | D; United Methodist Church | O | 1822 | |
| Iron Mountain Christian Camp | Mountain View | | | | |
| Nawake Conference Center | Prim | D; United Methodist Church | O | 1968 | Conference leaders |
| Nondenominational Church Camp | Cabot | I; . . . | O | 1900 | |
| North Arkansas District Camp | Greenbrier | D; Church of the Nazarene | | | |
| Northwest Arkansas Camp | Gravette | D; Church of God (Holiness) | O | 1925 | |
| Ozark Conferences, Inc. | Little Rock | I; . . . | | | |
| Salem Camp | Benton | D; United Methodist Church | O | 1838 | |
| Snow Springs Camp | Hot Springs | D; Church of God (Anderson) | | | |
| Southwest Arkansas State Camp | Hope | D; Church of God (Anderson) | | | |
| Wayland Springs Camp | Alicia | D; United Methodist Church | O | 1960 | |
| Western Methodist Assembly | Fayetteville | D; United Methodist Church | O | | |

### California

| Name | Location | Affiliation | | Year | Notes |
|---|---|---|---|---|---|
| Agape Retreat & Conference | Perris | I; . . . | | | |
| Alliance Redwoods Conference Grounds | Occidental | D; Christian Missionary Alliance Church | O | | |

| Name | City | Affiliation | O/R | Year | Founder |
|---|---|---|---|---|---|
| Alpine Covenant Conference Center | Blue Jay | I . . . | | | |
| Angeles Crest Camp | Fullerton | I . . . | | | |
| Beulah Park Camp | Santa Cruz | D; Church of the Nazarene | O | 1920 | |
| Bible Missionary Camp | Cucamonga | D; Bible Missionary Church | O | 1970 | |
| California Camp | Fresno | D; Church of God (Independent Holiness People) | | 1965 | |
| California Camp Meeting | Bakersfield | D; Church of God (Servant) | | 1970 | |
| California Conference Camp | Azusa | D; Wesleyan Church | R | 1970 | |
| California Conference Camp | Boulder Creek | D; Free Methodist Church | R | | |
| California Conference Camp | Madera | D; International Pentecostal Holiness Church | O | 1936 | |
| California Conference Camp | Modesto | D; Free Methodist Church | O | | |
| California State Camp | Pacoima | D; Church of God (Servant) | O | 1960 | |
| California-Nevada Camp | Garden Grove | D; Church of God of Prophecy | R | | |
| Calistoga Camp | Calistoga | D; Seventh Day Adventist Church | R | | |
| Camp Lassen Pines | Redding | | O | | |
| Camp Maranatha | Idyllwild | I . . . | | | |
| Camp May-Mac Conference Grounds | Felton | I; City Team Ministries | | | |
| Camp Pinebrook | Pinecrest | I; Sierra Christian Camping | | | |
| Camp Sugar Pine | Oakhurst | I . . . | | | |
| Campus By The Sea | Avalon | A; InterVarsity Christian Fellowship | O | 1951 | |

| | | | |
|---|---|---|---|
| Family Camp | Boise | D; Church of God (Anderson) | O |
| Hi-Way Chapel Camp | McCall | D; Church of God (Holiness) | O 1965 |
| Idaho Conference Camp | Caldwell | D; Seventh Day Adventist Church | O |
| Idaho District Camp | McCall | D; United Pentecostal Church | |
| Inter-Mountain District Camp | Nampa | D; Church of the Nazarene | O 1920 |
| Lake Pend Oreille Retreat | Coeur d'Alene Center | | |
| Northwest District Camp | Nampa | D; Bible Missionary Church | O |
| Quaker Hill Conference Center, Inc. | McCall | D; Friends Church | |
| Ross Point Conference Center | Post Falls | | |
| Southern Idaho District Camp | Bellevue | D; Assembly of God Church | |
| Southern Idaho District Camp | Boise | D; Assembly of God Church | |
| Star Camp | Star | I; Idaho State Holiness Association | O 1934 |

## Illinois

| | | | |
|---|---|---|---|
| Benton Church of God Camp | Benton | D; Church of God of Prophecy | O |
| Beulah Holiness Camp | Eldorado | I; Beulah Holiness Campmeeting Association | O 1903 |
| Bonnie Holiness Camp | Bonnie | I; Southern Illinois Holiness Association | O 1890 |

| Name | City | Affiliation | O/R | Year | Founder |
|---|---|---|---|---|---|
| Camp Canaan | Rushville | D; Evangelical Church of North America | R | 1975 | |
| Camp Epworth | Belvidere | D; Wesleyan Church | O | | |
| Camp Kearney | Peoria | | | | |
| Camp Manitoqua | Frankfort | | | 1990 | |
| Camp Maranatha | Ramsey | I . . . | | | |
| Camp Warren | Decatur | D; Church of God (Anderson) | O | | |
| Central Illinois Holiness Camp | Normal | I; Central Illinois Holiness Association | O | 1884 | |
| Charleston Camp | Charleston | D; Wesleyan Church | O | 1920 | |
| Chicago Area Indoor Camp | Chicago | D; Wesleyan Missionary Church | O | 1972 | Rev. Thomas Reed |
| Chicago Camp | Chicago | D; Church of God of Prophecy | | | |
| Chicago Central Camp | Aroma Park | D; Church of the Nazarene | O | 1960 | |
| Clay County Camp | Louisville | I; Clay County Interdenominational Holiness Association | O | 1930 | |
| Cowden District Camp | Cowden | D; Free Methodist Church | O | 1915 | |
| Des Plaines Camp | Des Plaines | D; United Methodist Church | O | 1859 | Rev. Arlo Brown et al. |
| Des Plaines Chautauqua, The | Des Plaines | D; United Methodist Church | R | | |
| Dickson Valley Camp and Conference | Newark | | | | |
| Durley Camp | Greenville | D; Free Methodist Church | O | 1870 | |
| Faith Mission Camp | Springfield | A; Faith Mission Acreage | O | 1959 | Grace Pourchot |
| Flora Camp | Flora | I . . . | O | 1933 | |

| Name | Location | Affiliation | | Year | |
|---|---|---|---|---|---|
| Green Valley Camp | Grand Detour | D; Holiness Methodist Church | R | 1962 | Rev. W. H. Bast et al. |
| Hertz Grove Camp | Bonfield | D; United Methodist Church | O | 1853 | |
| Hillcrest Holiness Camp | Kempsville | I . . . | | | |
| Illiana Camp | Danville | I . . . | | | |
| Illinois Camp | Murphysboro | D; Apostolic Faith | O | 1890 | |
| Illinois Camp | Quincy | D; Church of God (Independent Holiness People) | O | 1970 | |
| Illinois Conference Camp | LaFox | D; Seventh Day Adventist Church | O | | |
| Illinois District Camp | Carlinville | D; Assembly of God Church | O | | |
| Illinois District Camp | Wapella | D; United Pentecostal Church | O | | |
| Illinois Southern Camp | West Frankfort | D; Church of God (Anderson) | O | 1919 | |
| Iowa–Illinois District Camp | Rock Island | D; Bible Missionary Church | O | 1966 | |
| Jacob's Camp | Springerton | I . . . | O | 1910 | Jacob Fleck |
| Lake Williamson Christian Center | Carlinville | | | | |
| Lena Camp | Lena | D; United Methodist Church | O | 1870 | Rev. F. A. Reade et al. |
| Little Galilee Christian Assembly | Clinton | | | | |
| Menno Haven Camp and Retreat Center | Tiskilwa | D; Mennonite Church | O | | |
| Methodist Men's Camp | Salem | I . . . | O | 1943 | |
| Midwest Allegheny Wesleyan Methodist Camp | Oblong | D; Allegheny Wesleyan Methodist Connection | O | 1935 | |
| Milan Camp | Milan | D; United Methodist Church | O | 1900 | |
| Nazarene Acres | Mechanicsburg | D; Church of the Nazarene | O | 1946 | |
| New Plasa Chautauqua | Plasa | I . . . | O | | |

| Name | City | Affiliation | O/R | Year | Founder |
|------|------|-------------|-----|------|---------|
| North Central Spanish Camp | Chicago | D; Church of God of Prophecy | O | | |
| Northwest Illinois District Camp | Manville | D; Church of the Nazarene | O | 1915 | Rev. Harry W. Morrow |
| Olivet Camp | Olivet | I . . . | O | 1915 | |
| Reynoldswood Retreat Center | Dixon | | | | |
| Riverwoods Christian Center | St. Charles | | | | |
| Romanian Camp | Chicago | D; Church of God of Prophecy | | | |
| Shelby County Camp | Mode | I . . . | O | 1943 | |
| Sherman's Camp | Sherman | I; Illinois Holiness Association | O | 1871 | |
| Springfield Camp | Springfield | D; Wesleyan Holiness Church | R | 1980 | |
| Springfiled District Camp | Rushville | D; Free Methodist Church | O | 1900 | |
| Tabernacle Camp | Marquette Heights | I . . . | O | 1852 | |
| Tilden Holiness Camp | Tilden | I; Tilden Holiness Campmeeting Association | O | | |
| Wesleyan Christian Camp | Chauncey | I . . . | | | |
| Zion's Hill Camp | Fairfield | I . . . | O | 1944 | Rev. Garrett H. Phillips |

### Indiana

| Name | City | Affiliation | O/R | Year | Founder |
|------|------|-------------|-----|------|---------|
| Adams County Camp | Monroe | I . . . | O | 1918 | |
| Back Woods Camp | Veedersburg | I . . . | O | 1964 | Rev. Delbert Lighty |
| Battle Ground Camp | Battle Ground | D; United Methodist Church | O | 1870 | |
| Bethel Camp | Richmond | I; Wayne County Holiness Association | O | | |

| Camp | Location | Affiliation | | Year | Leader |
|---|---|---|---|---|---|
| Bible Covenant Camp | Alexandria | D; Bible Covenant Church | R | 1975 | |
| Bible Holiness Camp | Anderson | D; Bible Holiness Church | R | 1980 | |
| Bobo Camp | Bobo | I; . . . | | 1952 | |
| Brethren Retreat Center | Shipshewana | D; Church of the Brethren | | | |
| Brown County Holiness Camp | Gnawbone | I; . . . | O | 1919 | Rev. Garnett Jewell, Rev. Charles Galbraith |
| Bryantsburg Camp | Bryantsburg | I; . . . | O | 1902 | Rev. James W. Codrey |
| Camp 56 | Madison | I; . . . | | | |
| Camp Alexander Conference Center | Milford | | | | |
| Camp Reveal | Evansville | I; . . . | O | | |
| Canaan Valley Camp | Peru | A; National Association of Holiness Churches | O | 1950 | |
| Cedar Lake Bible Conference | Cedar Lake | I; . . . | | | |
| Central State Camp | Brooklyn | D; Church of God (Anderson) | O | | |
| Central Yearly Meeting Camp | Muncie | D; Central Yearly Meeting of Friends | R | 1952 | |
| Chandler Holiness Camp | Chandler | I; . . . | O | 1941 | |
| Cherry Grove Camp | Lynn | I; . . . | O | 1914 | |
| Christian Pilgrim Camp | Montpelier | D; Christian Pilgrim Church | O | 1962 | |
| Church of God Camp | Muncie | D; New Testament Church of God | O | | |
| Craigville Holiness Camp | Craigville | I; . . . | O | 1954 | Rev. Walter Leimenstoll |
| Crossroads of America Camp | Indianapolis | I; . . . | O | 1950 | Mr. Qualls |
| Crystal Lake Baptist Camp | Warsaw | D; Baptist Church | | | |

| Name | City | Affiliation | O/R | Year | Founder |
|---|---|---|---|---|---|
| Delaware County Camp | Muncie | I . . . | O | 1955 | Lou Standley |
| East Enterprise Camp | East Enterprise | I . . . | O | 1906 | Rev. C. Eskew |
| Eckerty Camp | Eckerty | I . . . | O | 1908 | |
| Epworth Forest Conference Center | North Webster | D; United Methodist Church | O | | |
| Fairmount Camp | Fairmount | D; Wesleyan Church | O | 1895 | |
| First United Methodist Church Camp | Fowler | D; United Methodist Church | | | |
| Fountain Park Chautauqua | Remington | O | | | |
| Global Conference Camp | South Bend | I . . . | R | | Dr. Lester Sumrall |
| Guiding Light Camp | South Whitley | I . . . | | | |
| Hamilton County Camp | Westfield | I . . . | | | |
| Higher Ground Retreat | West Harrison | D; Church of the Nazarene | O | | |
| Higher Ground Retreat Center West | Harrison | | O | 1950 | |
| Hilltop Tabernacle Camp | Connersville | I . . . | O | 1960 | Rev. Elwood Lucas et al. |
| Holiness League Camp | Terre Haute | A; Holiness League | R | 1985 | |
| Illiana Camp | West Terre Haute | I . . . | O | 1946 | Rev. E. O. Hobbs |
| Indiana Camp | Greenwood | D; Church of God of Prophecy | R | | |
| Indiana Camp | Muncie | D; Christian Church | R | 1965 | |
| Indiana Central Camp | Frankfort | D; Wesleyan Church | O | | |
| Indiana Conference Camp | Cicero | D; Seventh Day Adventist Church | O | 1896 | |
| Indiana District Camp | Fortville | D; United Pentecostal Church | | | |

| Name | Location | | Status | Year | Notes |
|---|---|---|---|---|---|
| Indiana District Camp | Hartford City | D; Assembly of God Church | | | |
| Indiana District Conference Center | Lafayette | D; Pentecostal Church of God | O | | |
| Indiana Southern District Camp | Orleans | D; Wesleyan Church | O | 1952 | Pilgrim Holiness Church |
| Indiana State Camp | Portland | I . . . | O | 1951 | Mr. & Mrs. Harrison Horn |
| Indianapolis District Camp | Camby | D; Church of the Nazarene | O | 1946 | |
| International Convention Grounds | Anderson | D; Church of God (Anderson) | O | 1907 | |
| John T. Hatfield Camp | Cleveland | I . . . | O | 1901 | Rev. John T. Hatfield |
| Lake James Christian Assembly | Angola | | | | |
| Lake Placid Conference Center | Hartford City | | | | |
| Lake Region Christian Assembly | Crown Point | | | | |
| Letts Camp | Letts | I . . . | O | 1923 | |
| Martin County Salvation Camp | Dover Hill | I . . . | O | 1968 | |
| Midwest Conference Camp | West Terre Haute | D; Pilgrim Holiness Church of New York | R | 1966 | |
| Midwest District Camp | Clear Lake | D; Christian Missionary Alliance | O | | |
| Missionary Boot Camp | Anderson | A; Friends of Missions | R | 1987 | |
| Mizpah Camp | Wabash | I . . . | | | |
| National Camp | Vincennes | A; National Association of Holiness Churches | O | 1966 | |

| Name | City | Affiliation | O/R | Year | Founder |
|---|---|---|---|---|---|
| National Hispanic Family Camp | Lafayette | D; Pentecostal Church of God | R | | |
| North Central District Camp | Muncie | D; Bible Missionary Church | R | 1960 | |
| Northeast Indiana District Camp | Marion | D; Church of the Nazarene | O | 1943 | |
| Northwest Indiana District Camp | San Pierre | D; Church of the Nazarene | R | 1947 | |
| Nottingham Holiness Camp | Nottingham | I . . . | R | 1960 | Rev. Armor Brown |
| Odon Camp | Odon | I . . . | R | 1966 | Rev. John Ricks et al. |
| Prairie Camp | Elkhart | D; The Missionary Church | O | 1880 | Rev. Daniel Brenneman et al. |
| Quaker Haven Camp | Syracuse | D; Friends Church | | | |
| Ramsey Camp | Ramsey | I; Harrison County Holiness Association | O | 1904 | |
| Randolph County Holiness Camp | Winchester | I . . . | O | 1915 | |
| Rector Memorial Camp | Muncie | D; United Brethren in Christ Church | O | | |
| Redkey Holiness Camp | Redkey | I . . . | R | 1973 | Rev. Phil Jellison |
| Santa Claus Camp | Santa Claus | D; United Methodist Church | O | 1849 | L. H. Luckemeyer |
| Silver Heights Camp | New Albany | I; Ohio Falls Holiness Association | O | 1887 | Rev. Conner |
| Singing Hills Camp | Shoals | D; Immanuel Missionary Church | O | 1954 | |
| Southeastern Indiana Camp | Scottsburg | D; Church of God (Anderson) | | | |

| Camp | Location | Affiliation | Status | Year | Leader |
|---|---|---|---|---|---|
| Southern Indiana Holiness Camp | Oakland City | I; Southern Indiana Holiness Association | O | 1895 | Rev. C. W. Ruth et al. |
| Sullivan County Camp | Sullivan | I; Sullivan County Holiness Association | R | 1965 | |
| Tabernacle Holiness Camp | Washington | I... | O | 1950 | Rev. Rybum Ray |
| Tennyson Camp | Tennyson | I... | O | 1940 | |
| Tri-County Camp | Columbus | I... | O | 1930 | Rev. M. H Reynolds |
| Tri-County Camp | Hartford City | I; Tri-County Holiness Association | O | 1944 | Rev. H. Jennings, Rev. George Cochard |
| True Holiness Camp | Geneva | D; True Holiness Church | O | 1952 | Rev. Burley Huff |
| United Holiness Camp | Milan | D; United Holiness Churches | O | 1946 | Rev. Leonard Bennett et al. |
| Upland Community Camp | Upland | I; Upland Evangelistic Association | R | 1960 | |
| Vigo County Camp | Terre Haute | I... | R | 1935 | Raymond Halt |
| Wabash Park Camp | Clay City | D; Free Methodist Church | O | 1918 | |
| Wayside Holiness Camp | Roann | I; Wayside Holiness Association | O | 1968 | |
| Wheeling Holiness Camp | Francisco | I; Union Holiness Association | O | 1890 | |
| Winona Lake Assembly [Chautauqua] | Winona Lake | I... | R | | |
| Winona Lake Christian Assembly | Winona Lake | I; Winona Lake Christian Assembly, Inc. | O | 1895 | Dr. Solomon Dickey et al. |
| Yellow Lake Camp | Claypool | D; Church of God (Anderson) | O | 1887 | |

## Iowa

| Name | City | Affiliation | O/R | Year | Founder |
|------|------|-------------|-----|------|---------|
| Boone-Story Camp | Boone | I; Boone-Story Holiness Association | O | 1920 | |
| Camp Inspiration Acres | Madrid | D; Church of God (Anderson) | O | | |
| Camp Pine Lake | Eldora | D; Friends Church | | | |
| Camp Quaker Heights | Eldora | D; Friends Church | | | |
| Central Baptist Camp | Lansing | D; Baptist Church | | | |
| Chariton Bible Camp | Chariton | I . . . | | 1920 | |
| Clear Lake Camp | Clear Lake | D; United Methodist Church | O | 1875 | |
| Dayton Oaks Camp | Dayton | D; Baptist Church | | | |
| Episcopal Center of Camps and Conferences | Boone | D; Episcopal Church | | | |
| Ewalu Retreat Center | Strawberry Point | | | | |
| Forest Lake Camp | Bloomfield | D; Baptist Church | | | |
| Four-County Holiness Camp | Coon Rapids | I . . . | | 1913 | |
| Inspiration Hills Camp | Inwood | D; Reformed Church | | | |
| Iowa Camp | Arnold Park | D; Christian Missionary Alliance | R | 1970 | |
| Iowa Camp | Des Moines | D; Church of God of Prophecy | | | |
| Iowa Conference Camp | Birmingham | D; Free Methodist Church | O | 1874 | |
| Iowa Conference Camp | Cedar Falls | D; United Methodist Church | O | 1897 | |
| Iowa Conference Camp | Cedar Springs | D; Wesleyan Church | O | 1853 | |
| Iowa District Camp | Ogden | D; Assembly of God Church | | | |
| Iowa District Camp | West Des Moines | D; Church of the Nazarene | O | 1912 | |

## Kansas

| Camp | Location | Church/Association | | Year | Founder |
|---|---|---|---|---|---|
| Iowa Holiness Camp | University Park | I; Iowa Holiness Association | O | 1878 | Rev. Isaiah Reid et al. |
| Jeffers Memorial Camp | Sioux City | I; Sioux City Holiness Mission | O | 1914 | Rev. William Jeffers |
| North Central District Camp | Denmark | D; Wesleyan Holiness Church | | | |
| North Central District Camp | University Park | D; Wesleyan Holiness Association of Churches | R | 1975 | |
| North Missouri–South Iowa Camp | Moulton | D; Church of God (Holiness) | O | 1950 | |
| Okoboji Lakes Camp | Arnold's Park | D; United Methodist Church | O | 1934 | |
| Tabor Nazarene Camp Association | Tabor | D; Church of Nazarene | O | 1892 | Hepzibah Faith Association |
| **Kansas** | | | | | |
| Beulah Park Camp | Miltonvale | I; Kansas State Holiness Association | R | 1888 | Rev. Ira Putney et al. |
| Camp Daniel | Bonner Springs | | | | |
| Camp Fellowship | Goddard | D; Church of God (Anderson) | O | | |
| Camp Quaker Haven | Arkansas City | D; Friends Church | | | |
| Community Holiness Camp | Haviland | I; Kiowana County Holiness Association | O | 1914 | Scott Clark |
| Eastern Kansas Camp | Ft. Scott | D; Church of God (Holiness) | | | |
| Family Camp | McPherson | D; Free Methodist Church | R | | |
| General Camp | Independence | D; Fire Baptized Holiness Church | O | 1897 | |
| General Camp | Overland Park | D; Church of God (Holiness) | O | 1930 | |
| Hill City Camp | Hill City | D; Church of God (Anderson) | | | |

| Name | City | Affiliation | O/R | Year | Founder |
|---|---|---|---|---|---|
| Hutchinson Camp | Hutchinson | D; Wesleyan Church | O | 1903 | |
| Indoor Camp | Kansas City | D; Church of God (Holiness) | R | 1970 | |
| Indoor Camp | Wichita | D; Church of the Nazarene | | 1975 | |
| Interstate Camp | Topeka | D; Church of God (Anderson) | | | |
| Kansas Camp | Parsons | D; Church of God of Prophecy | R | | |
| Kansas Camp | Wichita | D; Church of God (Anderson) | | | |
| Kansas City District Camp | Overland Park | D; Church of the Nazarene | O | 1944 | |
| Kansas Conference Camp | Macksville | D; Wesleyan Holiness Church | O | 1926 | Free Methodist Conference |
| Kansas Conference Camp | Wichita | D; International Pentecostal Holiness Church | O | 1926 | |
| Kansas District Camp | Augusta | D; Assembly of God Church | R | | |
| Kansas District Camp | Miltonvale | D; Wesleyan Church | O | 1909 | |
| Kansas District Camp | Woodston | D; Assembly of God Church | O | | |
| King Solomon Camp | Solomon | D; Brethren in Christ | O | 1900 | |
| Lake Webster Camp | Stockton | D; United Methodist Church | O | | |
| Liberal Camp | Liberal | D; Church of God (Anderson) | | | |
| Lundy Memorial Camp | Natoma | D; Church of God (Holiness) | O | | |
| Mt. Ayr Camp | Alton | I . . . | O | 1904 | |
| Oak Grove Camp | Fulton | D; Church of God (Independent Holiness People) | O | 1950 | Mrs. Feemster |
| Rock Creek Holiness Camp | Lawrence | D; Church of God (Holiness) | O | 1975 | |
| Shepherd's Staff Conference Center | Rexford | I . . . | | | |

| Camp | Location | Denomination | O/R | Year | Founder/Notes |
|---|---|---|---|---|---|
| West Kansas Conference Camp | Macksville | D; Free Methodist Church | O | 1890 | |
| Wheat State Camp | Augusta | D; United Pentecostal Church | | | |
| Wichita Camp | Wichita | D; Seventh Day Adventist Church | | | |

## Kentucky

| Camp | Location | Denomination | O/R | Year | Founder/Notes |
|---|---|---|---|---|---|
| Acton Camp | Campbellsville | I... | O | 1900 | Rev. E. R. Bennett |
| Adairville Camp | Adairville | I... | R | | |
| Aliceton Camp | Gravelswitch | I... | O | 1897 | |
| Asbury Summer Assembly | Wilmore | I... | O | 1991 | |
| Aspen Grove Camp | Alexandria | I... | O | 1909 | Rev. & Mrs. Redman |
| Bethel Camp | Clayhole | D; Mennonite Church | | | |
| Beulah Heights Camp | Beulah Heights | D; Bible Missionary Church | O | 1894 | Rev. Martin Wells Knapp |
| Blackford Camp | Blackford | D; Church of God (Servant) | O | 1910 | |
| Callis Grove Camp | Bedford | I... | O | 1909 | Mr. R. E. Callis donated land |
| Camargo Camp | Camargo | D; Church of God (Anderson) | O | 1900 | Rev. W. F. Chapel et al. |
| Carthage Holiness Camp | California | I... | O | 1908 | Joseph R. Moore donated land |
| Corbin Camp | Corbin | I... | O | 1930 | Rev. Warner Davis, L. Rounds |
| Eagle Ridge Center | Bowling Green | I... | | | |
| Eastern Assembly Camp | Lowmansville | D; Church of God (Anderson) | R | 1952 | Rev. Moses Kitchen |
| Eastern Kentucky District Camp | Flemingsburgh | D; Church of the Nazarene | O | 1909 | |
| Eastern Kentucky District Camp | Maysville | D; Wesleyan Church | O | 1939 | Rev. Leadingham et al. |
| Glen Eden Camp | West Bend | D; Church of God (Anderson) | O | 1950 | |

| Name | City | Affiliation | O/R | Year | Founder |
|---|---|---|---|---|---|
| Holiness Pilgrims Camp | Tollesboro | I ... | R | 1990 | Rev. Arthur Ray Music |
| Hurricane Camp | Tolu | I ... | O | 1889 | Rev. S. K. Breeding |
| Kavanaugh Camp | Crestwood | D; United Methodist Church | O | 1875 | |
| Kentucky Camp | Lexington | D; Church of God of Prophecy | O | | |
| Kentucky Conference Camp | Fern Creek | D; Wesleyan Church | O | 1939 | |
| Kentucky District Camp | Crestwood | D; Assembly of God Church | | | |
| Kentucky District Camp | Summersville | D; United Pentecostal Church | | | |
| Liberty Camp | Liberty | D; Church of God (Anderson) | | | |
| Morrison Park Camp | Glasgow | I ... | O | 1900 | Dr. Henry Clay Morrison |
| Mount Carmel Camp | Jackson | I; Kentucky Mountain Holiness Asociation | O | 1923 | Dr. Lela G. McConnell |
| Mt. Vernon Camp | Flemingsburg | D; Kentucky Christian Conference | O | 1941 | |
| Mt. Zion Holiness Camp | Sewell | I ... | O | 1950 | |
| Oaks Camp | Paducah | D; Church of God (Anderson) | | | |
| R. G. Finch Memorial Camp | Maysville | D; Emmanuel Association | O | 1951 | R. G. Finch et al. |
| Richmond Road Camp | Lexington | I; Smiley Memorial Community Church | O | 1966 | Rev. T. T. May |
| Ruggles Camp | Tollesboro | D; United Methodist Church | O | 1873 | |
| State Camp | Winchester | D; Church of God (Anderson) | O | 1900 | |
| Terril's Creek Camp | Datha | I ... | O | 1945 | Dr. Andrew Johnson |
| Union Camp | Lexington | I; Evangelical Christian Fellowship | R | 1980 | |

| Wilmore Camp | Wilmore | I; Central Kentucky Holiness Association | O | 1889 | Rev. John Wesley Hughes |
|---|---|---|---|---|---|

## Louisiana

| | | | | | |
|---|---|---|---|---|---|
| Acadia Holiness Camp | Crawley | I . . . | | | |
| BMA Conference Center | Ringgold | I . . . | | | |
| Camp Okaloosa | Monroe | D; Baptist | | | |
| District Camp | DeRidder | D; Bible Missionary Church | O | 1960 | |
| Ebenezer Camp | Montgomery | I . . . | O | 1895 | Revs. W. B. Godbey, W. T. Curry, and J. L. Morrill |
| Fort Jessup Camp | Many | D; Church of the Nazarene | O | 1898 | |
| Free Methodist Camp | Pollock | D; Free Methodist Church | R | | Rev. Josh Sanders |
| Friendship Camp | Friendship | I . . . | | | |
| General Southern Camp | Hammond | D; Church of God (Servant) | O | 1907 | Francis M. Williamson |
| Hudson Camp | Winnfield | I . . . | O | 1898 | I. B. Payne, Sr., et al. |
| Hudson Retreat Center | Jackson | D; Baptist Church | | | |
| Lake Arthur Camp | Lake Arthur | I . . . | O | 1897 | Rev. J. R. Morrill |
| Louisiana Camp | Baton Rouge | D; Church of God of Prophecy | R | | |
| Louisiana Camp | Eros | D; Methodist Protestant Church | | | |
| Louisiana Conference Camp | Pleasant Hill | D; Congregational Methodist Church | O | 1940 | |
| Louisiana Conference Camp | Pollock | D; Free Methodist Church | R | | |
| Louisiana District Camp | Tioga | D; United Pentecostal Church | | | |

| Name | City | Affiliation | O/R | Year | Founder |
|---|---|---|---|---|---|
| Marthaville Camp | Marthaville | D; Original Congregational Methodist Church | O | 1895 | |
| Pineville Camp | Pineville | D; Church of the Nazarene | O | 1937 | |
| Pollack Camp | Pollack | D; Church of God (Anderson) | O | | |
| State Camp | Palmetto | D; Church of God (Anderson) | O | | |
| Summerfield Camp | Summerfield | I . . . | O | 1897 | |
| Summerville Camp | Olla | D; Free Methodist Church | O | | |
| Tall Timbers Conference Center | Alexandria | D; Baptist Church | O | | |

## Maine

| Name | City | Affiliation | O/R | Year | Founder |
|---|---|---|---|---|---|
| Big Lake Camp | Princeton | | | | |
| Camp Berea | North Turner | | | | |
| Camp Wakonda | Washington | D; Church of the Nazarene | | | |
| Carmel Bible Conference | Carmel | I . . . | O | | |
| East Livermore Camp | East Livermore | I . . . | | 1847 | |
| Empire Grove Camp | East Poland | D; United Methodist Church | O | 1834 | |
| Etna Spiritualist Camp | Etna | D; Spiritualist | O | 1876 | Daniel Buswell, Jr. |
| Ferry Beach Park | Saco | D; Universalist | O | 1882 | Dr. Quillen H. Shinn |
| Jacksonville Camp | East Machias | D; United Methodist Church | O | 1865 | |
| Lakeside Camp | Belgrade | | | | |
| Maine District Camp | Richmond | D; Church of the Nazarene | O | 1870 | |
| Mechanic Falls Camp | Mechanic Falls | | | | |

| Camp | Location | Denomination | | Year | Founders |
|---|---|---|---|---|---|
| Northern New England Camp | Hinkley | D; Church of God of Prophecy | O | | |
| Northern New England Conference Camp | Freeport | D; Seventh Day Adventist Church | O | | |
| Ocean Park Association [Chautauqua] | Ocean Park | I... | O | 1881 | Free Baptist |
| Old Orchard Beach Camp | Old Orchard Beach | D; Salvation Army | O | 1870 | |
| Pine Tree Camp | Old Town | D; United Pentecostal Church | | | |
| Piscataquis Valley Camp | Dover-Foxcroft | I... | | | |
| Riverside Camp | Robinson | D; Wesleyan Church | O | 1902 | |
| Temple Heights Spiritualist Camp | Northport | D; Spiritualist | O | 1883 | |
| Washington Camp | Washington | | | | |

## Maryland

| Camp | Location | Denomination | | Year | Founders |
|---|---|---|---|---|---|
| CDP District Camp | Lonham | D; Church of God (Anderson) | | | |
| Chesapeake Conference Camp | Hagerstown | D; Seventh Day Adventist Church | O | | |
| Conference Camp | Silver Spring | D; Free Methodist Church | R | | |
| Conference Camp | Spencerville | D; Free Methodist Church | O | | |
| Damascus Camp | Damascus | I... | O | 1931 | William Beall, Rev. J. R. Parker et al. |
| Deal Island Camp | Deal Island | | | | |
| Denton Camp | Denton | D; Wesleyan Church | O | 1899 | |
| Drayton Retreat Center | Worton | D; United Methodist Church | O | 1965 | Local United Methodists |
| Eastern Shore Camp | Fruitland | D; Evangelical Christian Church (Wesleyan) | O | 1950 | |

| Name | City | Affiliation | O/R | Year | Founder |
|---|---|---|---|---|---|
| Emory Grove | Glyndon | I; Emory Grove Camp Meeting Association | O | 1868 | |
| Glen Echo Park [Chautauqua] | Glen Echo | I . . . | O | | |
| Hagerstown Camp | Hagerstown | D; Church of God (Universal) | | 1960 | |
| Laymen's Camp | Lothian | I; Lothian Laymen's Interdenominational Evangelistic Association | | | |
| Living Word Camp | Owings Mills | I; Living Word Christian Center | O | | |
| Maryland/Delaware Camp | Columbia | D; Church of God of Prophecy | O | | |
| Morris Tabernacle Camp | Sudlersville | I . . . | O | 1947 | Virgil Morris |
| Mountain Lake Park Camp | Mountain Lake Park | I . . . | R | 1882 | Rev. John Thompson |
| Mountain Lake Park Chautauqua | Mountain Lake Park | I . . . | | | |
| Peach Orchard Retreat Center | Silver Spring | | | | |
| Philadelphia District Camp | Northeast | D; Church of the Nazarene | R | | |
| Pine Mar Camp | Taneytown | D; Evangelical Christian Church (Wesleyan) | O | | |
| Sandy Cove Bible Conference | North East | I . . . | O | | Rev. George Palmer |
| Union Grove Camp | Cumberland | I . . . | | | |
| Washington District Camp | Northeast | D; Church of the Nazarene | O | 1908 | |
| Wilson-Butler Camp | Smith Island | D; United Methodist Church | O | 1886 | Dr. William Butler |

## Massachusetts

| Camp | Location | Denomination | | Year | Notes |
|---|---|---|---|---|---|
| Asbury Grove Camp | South Hamilton | D; United Methodist Church | O | 1859 | |
| Bement Conference Center | Charlton Depot | | | | |
| Buzzard's Bay Camp | Wareham | D; Reorganized Church of Jesus Christ | O | 1911 | |
| Central New England District Camp | Hamilton | D; United Pentecostal Church | | | |
| Craigville Camp | Craigville | D; Christian Church | O | | |
| District Camp | North Redding | D; Church of the Nazarene | O | 1920 | |
| Douglas Camp | Douglas | I . . . | O | 1875 | Dr. E. M. Levy |
| Grotonwood Conference Center | Groton | D; American Baptist Church | | | |
| Laurel Park Camp | Northampton | I; Laurel Park Camp Association | O | 1872 | |
| Martha's Vineyard Camp | Martha's Vineyard | D; United Methodist Church | O | 1835 | |
| Martha's Vineyard Chautauqua | Oak Bluffs | D; United Methodist Church | R | | |
| New England Keswick | Monterey | I . . . | | | |
| Roaring Brook Camp | Conway | D; Church of God (Anderson) | O | | |
| Silver Lake Camp | Tewksbury | I . . . | O | 1890 | |
| Smith Mills Camp | New Bedford | I . . . | O | 1907 | |
| South Lancaster Camp | South Lancaster | | | | |
| Southern New England Campground | South Lancaster | D; Seventh Day Adventist Church | O | | |
| Sterling Camp | Sterling | I . . . | O | 1852 | |
| Tremont Camp | Wareham | D; Advent Christian Church | O | 1890 | |
| Yarmouth Camp | Yarmouth | I . . . . | | 1819 | |

| Name | City | Affiliation | O/R | Year | Founder |
|------|------|-------------|-----|------|---------|
| **Michigan** | | | | | |
| Albright Camp | Reed City | D; United Methodist Church | O | 1901 | |
| Allendale Camp | Allendale | I . . . | | | |
| American Holiness Camp | West Branch | I; American Holiness Camp Meeting Association | O | 1949 | |
| Athens Indian Holiness Camp | Union City | A; All Tribes Missionary Indian Council | O | 1945 | Rev. Charles Pamp, Indian evangelist |
| Bair Lake Bible Camp | Jones | | | | |
| Bay Shore Assembly | Sebewaing | D; United Methodist Church | O | 1911 | |
| Bay View Assembly | Petrosky | D; United Methodist Church | O | 1875 | |
| Bay View Assembly, The [Chautauqua] | Bay View | D; United Methodist Church | R | 1876 | |
| Bethel Camp | Deerfield | A; Lower Light Mission Association | | | |
| Bethel Park Camp | Flint | D; Free Methodist Church | O | | |
| Boyne City Camp | Boyne City | I; North Michigan Holiness Association | O | 1910 | Rev. Strait, Rev. B. Monker, Edwin Bradley, et al. |
| Brooklyn Camp | Brooklyn | D; Free Methodist Church | | | |
| Brown City Camp | Brown City | D; The Missionary Church | O | 1882 | |
| Burlington Camp | Burlington | D; Church of God (Anderson) | O | | |
| Camp Amigo | Sturgis | | O | | |
| Camp Arcadia | Arcadia | D; Lutheran Church | O | | |
| Camp Friedenswald | Cassopolis | I . . . | | | |
| Camp Living Waters | Luther | I . . . | | | |

| Name | Location | Affiliation | | Year | Contact |
|---|---|---|---|---|---|
| Camp Michindoh | Hillsdale | I; Michindoh Ministries, Inc. | O | | |
| Cedar Campus | Cedarville | A; InterVarsity Christian Fellowship | O | 1953 | |
| Christian Pilgrim Camp | Vicksburg | D; Christian Pilgrim Church | O | 1938 | |
| Conference Center | Grand Haven | D; Christian Reformed Church | | | |
| Covenant Hills Camp | Davison | D; Free Methodist Church | O | 1860 | |
| Crystal Springs Camp | Dowagiac | D; United Methodist Church | O | 1960 | |
| District Camp | Sunfield | D; Bible Missionary Church | O | 1951 | |
| East Michigan District Camp | Howell | D; Church of the Nazarene | O | | |
| Eastern Michigan District Camp | Vassar | D; Wesleyan Church | O | | |
| Eaton Rapids Camp | Eaton Rapids | I; Michigan State Holiness Campmeeting Association | O | 1885 | |
| Ebenezer Camp | Vestaburg | I; Ebenezer Chapel Association | O | 1954 | Rev. C. E. Morgan |
| Epworth Assembly, The | Ludington | | | | |
| Evangelical Wesleyan Camp | Remus | D; Evangelical Wesleyan Church | O | 1965 | |
| Evangelistic Tabernacle Camp | Ypsilanti | D; Wesley Temple | O | 1940 | Rev. Baughey |
| Family Camp | Charlevoix | D; Church of God (Anderson) | O | 1930 | |
| Family Camp | Jackson | D; Free Methodist Church | | | |
| Five Pines Family Center | Berrien Center | | | | |
| Fleming Grove Camp | Gladwin | I; . . . | | | |
| Geneva Camp and Conference Center | Holland | I; . . . | O | 1911 | Rev. Val Buxton |
| German District Camp | Bridgman | D; Assembly of God Church | | | |

| Name | City | Affiliation | O/R | Year | Founder |
|------|------|-------------|-----|------|---------|
| Good News Camp | Gladwin | | | | |
| Gull Lake Bible Conference | Hickory Corners | I . . . | O | 1919 | |
| Hastings Camp | Hastings | D; Wesleyan Church | O | 1883 | |
| Holiness Missionary Camp | Clio | I . . . | O | | |
| Hopkins Camp | Hopkins | D; Wesleyan Church | O | 1899 | |
| Huron Forest Camp Cherith | Oscoda | I . . . | | | |
| Indian Lake Camp | Vicksburg | D; Church of the Nazarene | O | 1926 | Rev. Starr et al. |
| Isabella County Holiness Camp | Mt. Pleasant | I . . . | O | 1919 | |
| Lael Camp | Lapeer | D; Baptist Church | | | |
| Lake Ann Baptist Camp | Lake Ann | D; Baptist Church | | | |
| Lake Ann Camp | Lake Ann | I; Lake Ann Holiness Association | O | 1925 | Rev. C. E. Myers |
| Lake Ellen Baptist Camp | Crystal Falls | D; Baptist Church | | | |
| Lake Louise Baptist Camp | Boyne Falls | D; Baptist Church | | | |
| Lake Region Conference Camp | Brownsville | D; Seventh Day Adventist Church | O | | |
| Life Action Ranch | Buchanan | O | | | |
| Living Waters Camp | Cassapolis | I . . . | | | |
| Lower Light Camp | Petersburg | A; Lower Light Mission Association | O | 1935 | |
| Mancelona Camp | Mancelona | D; The Missionary Church | O | 1922 | |
| Maranatha Conference | Muskegon | D; Christian Missionary Alliance Church | O | | |

| Camp | Location | | Affiliation | Type | Year | Notes |
|---|---|---|---|---|---|---|
| Maybee Camp | Maybee | I; | Southeast Michigan Holiness Association | O | 1910 | |
| Michigan Camp | Beaverton | D; | Church of Daniel's Band | O | 1892 | |
| Michigan Camp | Fenton | D; | Church of God of Prophecy | O | | |
| Michigan Camp | Flint | D; | Churches of Christ in Christian Union | O | 1946 | |
| Michigan Camp | Napoleon | D; | Pilgrim Holiness Church | | | |
| Michigan Camp | Remus | D; | Conservative Free Methodist Church | R | 1969 | |
| Michigan Conference Camp | Escanaba | D; | Seventh Day Adventist Church | R | | |
| Michigan District Camp | Fa-Ha-Lo | D; | Assembly of God Church | | | |
| Michigan District Camp | Lost Valley | D; | Assembly of God Church | | | |
| Michigan District Camp | Marshall | D; | United Pentecostal Church | | | |
| Miracle Camp | Lawton | | | | | |
| North Michigan Camp | Cadillac | D; | Wesleyan Church | O | 1915 | |
| North Michigan District Camp | Manton | D; | Church of the Nazarene | R | | |
| North Michigan District Camp | Manton | D; | Free Methodist Church | O | 1912 | |
| Oak Grove Camp | Lum | I; | Lapeer County Holiness Association | O | | |
| Ogden Camp | Blissfield | I . . . | | O | | |
| Ola Camp | Gratiot | I; | Gratiot County Holiness Association | O | 1918 | Rev. Ed Drummond |
| Onsted Camp | Onsted | D; | Free Methodist Church | | | |
| Pilgrim Bible Camp | Carson City | I . . . | | | | |

| Name | City | Affiliation | O/R | Year | Founder |
|---|---|---|---|---|---|
| Pilgrim Evangelistic Camp | Adrian | D; Pilgrim Evangelistic Church | O | 1931 | Rev. Donald Baughey |
| Port Huron District Camp | Decker | D; Free Methodist Church | O | | |
| Riverside Camp | Big Rapids | I; Central Michigan Holiness Association | O | 1940 | Revs. Sam Stanger, Harold Armin, Jay Dobbin, et al. |
| Riverside Camp | Buchanan | D; United Methodist Church | O | 1891 | |
| Rock Lake Assembly | Vestaburg | | | | |
| Rock Lake Camp | Edmore | D; United Holiness Church | R | 1970 | |
| St. Louis Camp | St. Louis | D; Church of God (Anderson) | O | | |
| Salvation Camp | Waldron | I . . . | O | | |
| Simpson Park Camp | Romeo | I . . . | O | 1864 | Methodist ministers |
| Skyline Retreat Center | Almont | I . . . | O | | |
| Somerset Beach Camp | Somerset Center | | R | | |
| Somerset Beach Camp | Somerset Center | D; Free Methodist Church | O | | |
| Trinity Holiness Camp | Hudson | D; Trinity Holiness Church | O | 1965 | |
| Tuscola County Camp | Cairo | I; Tuscola County Holiness Association | O | 1913 | |
| Warner Memorial Camp | Grand Junction | D; Church of God (Anderson) | O | 1883 | |
| Wesley Fellowship Church Camp | Napoleon | D; Wesley Fellowship Church | O | 1944 | Rev. O. G. Sprague |
| Wesleyan Holiness Camp | Remus | A; Wesleyan Holiness Association of Churches | | | |
| Wilson Camp | Alpena | D; Free Methodist Church | O | | |

## Minnesota

| Camp | Location | Denomination | | Year |
|---|---|---|---|---|
| Bethel Camp | Montevedeo | D; Evangelical Church of North America | O | 1916 |
| Big Sandy Camp | McGregor | D; Christian Missionary Alliance Church | O | 1959 |
| Camp Arrowhead | Deerwood | D; Church of God (Anderson) | O | |
| Camp Galilee | St. Paul | D; United Pentecostal Church | O | |
| Camp Lebanon | Upsala | | | |
| Camp Shamineau | Motley | | | |
| Covenant Pines Camp | McGregor | D; Evangelical Covenant Church | O | |
| District Camp | Paynesville | D; Church of the Nazarene | R | |
| Family Camp | Paynesville | D; Free Methodist Church | R | 1980 |
| Hartland Camp | Dodge City | D; Seventh Day Adventist Church | | |
| Lake Beauty Camp | Minneapolis | | | |
| Lake Geneva Bible Camp | Alexandria | D; Free Methodist Church | O | |
| Lake Koronis Assembly | Paynesville | I . . . | | |
| Lake Shetec Camp | Slayton | I . . . | | |
| Methodist Camp | Frontenac | D; United Methodist Church | O | 1935 |
| Minnesota Camp | Bloomington | D; Church of God of Prophecy | R | |
| Minnesota District Camp | Lake Geneva | D; Assembly of God Church | | |
| Mimi-I-Kota Conference Camp | Paynesville | D; Free Methodist Church | R | |
| Motley Family Camp | Motley | D; Free Methodist Church | O | |

| Name | City | Affiliation | O/R | Year | Founder |
|---|---|---|---|---|---|
| Oylen Camp | Oylen | D; Christian Missionary Alliance Church | O | 1895 | |
| Pioneer Camp | Wabasha | | | | |
| Red Rock Camp | Paynesville | I . . . | R | 1868 | |
| Silver Lake Camp | Minneapolis | D; Salvation Army | O | | |
| Solid Rock Bible Camp | Cushing | I . . . | O | 1940 | Rev. H. G. Swenson |
| Strawberry Lake Retreat | Ogema | I; Gospel Crusade, Inc. | O | | |
| Timber Bay Camp | Onamia | I . . . | | | |
| Wing River Tabernacle Camp | Verndale | I . . . | O | 1927 | Fred Barnett |

## Mississippi

| Name | City | Affiliation | O/R | Year | Founder |
|---|---|---|---|---|---|
| Adams Camp | Auburn | I . . . | O | 1815 | |
| Camp Farmhaven | Farmhaven | D; Church of God (Anderson) | O | | |
| Camp Lancaster | Florence | D; Church of Nazarene | | | |
| Central Hills Retreat | Kosciusko | D; Baptist Church | | | |
| Felder's Camp | McComb | D; United Methodist Church | O | 1810 | |
| Frost Bridge Camp | Waynesboro | I . . . | O | 1850 | |
| Gulf States Conference Camp | Lumberton | D; Seventh Day Adventist Church | O | | |
| Gulfside Assembly | Waveland | D; United Methodist Church | O | | |
| Lake Forest Ranch | Macon | | | | |
| Mississippi Camp | Jackson | D; Church of God of Prophecy | O | | |
| Mississippi Camp | Sandersville | D; Congregational Methodist | O | 1942 | Rev. J. E. Holder Church |

| Name | Location | Denomination | Status | Year | Notes |
|---|---|---|---|---|---|
| Mississippi Camp | Wynndale | D; The Sanctified Church | O | 1946 | Rev. Josh Green |
| Mississippi Conference Camp | | D; International Pentecostal Holiness Church | O | 1909 | |
| Mississippi District Camp | Jackson | D; United Pentecostal Church | R | | |
| Nazarene Camp | Prentiss | D; Church of the Nazarene | | | |
| New Prospect Camp | Jackson County | D; United Methodist Church | O | 1879 | |
| Old Lebanon Camp | Ackerman | D; Presbyterian Church | O | 1850 | |
| Old Salem Camp | | D; United Methodist Church | | | |
| Oxford Camp | | D; United Methodist Church | | | |
| Palmer Creek Camp | Handsboro | D; United Methodist Church | O | 1883 | |
| Perry Camp | Perry | I; Perry Camp Meeting Association | O | 1896 | Rev. W. W. Hopper |
| Salem Camp | Jackson County | D; United Methodist Church | O | 1826 | |
| Seashore Methodist Assembly | Biloxi | D; United Methodist Church | O | 1870 | |
| Shiloh Camp | Pilahatchie | D; United Methodist Church | O | 1832 | |
| South Union Camp | Ackerman | D; United Methodist Church | O | 1872 | |
| Southern Camp | Lauderdale | D; Church of God (Independent Holiness People) | O | | |
| State Camp | Dixon | D; Church of God (Anderson) | O | | |
| Twin Lakes Conference Center | Florence | | | | |

## Missouri

| Name | Location | Denomination | Status | Year | Notes |
|---|---|---|---|---|---|
| Barry County Camp | Butterfield | D; Church of God (Holiness) | O | 1889 | |
| Central Missouri Camp | Flat | D; Church of God (Anderson) | O | | |
| Central States Conference Center | Kansas City | D; Seventh Day Adventist Church | O | | |

| Name | City | Affiliation | O/R | Year | Founder |
|------|------|-------------|-----|------|---------|
| District Camp | Niangua | D; Bible Missionary Church | O | 1958 | |
| Epworth Among the Hills | Arcadia | D; United Methodist Church | O | 1908 | |
| Flaming Spirit Camp | Fillmore | D; Church of God (Anderson) | | | |
| Friendview Camp | Greenfield | D; Church of God (Holiness) | O | | |
| General Camp | Halltown | D; Fundamental Methodist Church | O | 1954 | |
| Granby Camp | Granby | D; Fire Baptized Holiness Church | | 1971 | |
| Harriman Chapel Camp | El Dorado Springs | D; Church of God (Holiness) | | | |
| Hepzibah Holiness Camp | Dixon | I . . . | | | |
| Joplin District Camp | Cassville | D; Church of Nazarene | R | | |
| Kirksville Camp | Kirksville | D; Church of God (Holiness) | | | |
| Lake Creek Camp | Smithton | D; United Methodist Church | O | 1843 | |
| Light and Life Center | El Dorado Springs | D; Free Methodist Church | | | |
| Logan Valley Christian Retreat | Ellington | | | | |
| Miracle Hills Ranch | Bethany | I . . . | | | |
| Missouri Camp | Leadwood | D; Church of God of Prophecy | O | | |
| Missouri Conference Camp | Mt. View | D; International Pentecostal Holiness Church | O | 1939 | |
| Missouri District Camp | Florissant | D; United Pentecostal Church | | | |
| Missouri State Camp | Niangua | D; Free Will Baptist Church | O | | |
| Mt. Zion Camp | Ava | D; Church of God (Holiness) | R | 1913 | |
| National Camp | Neosho | D; Church of God (Servant) | O | 1938 | |

| Camp | Location | Affiliation | | Year |
|---|---|---|---|---|
| Nevada Camp | Nevada | D; Church of God (Holiness) | | |
| North Missouri Camp | College Mound | D; Church of God (Holiness) | O | 1888 |
| North Missouri Camp | Columbia | D; Church of God (Anderson) | | |
| North Missouri Camp | Excelsior Springs | D; Assembly of God Church | | |
| North Missouri Camp | Paris | D; Church of God (Independent Holiness People) | | |
| Ozark Conference Camp | Chillicothe | D; Free Methodist Church | | |
| Pine Crest Camp | Fredericktown | D; Church of the Nazarene | O | 1947 |
| Rogersville Camp | Rogersville | D; Church of God (Holiness) | | |
| Rose of Sharon Camp | Bloomfield | | | |
| St. Clair County Camp | Lowry City | D; Church of God (Holiness) | | |
| Silvermoon Camp | Diamond | D; Church of God (Holiness) | O | 1975 |
| Southeast Missouri Camp | East Prairie | D; Church of God (Anderson) | | |
| Southern Missouri District Camp | Rocky Mount | D; Assembly of God Church | | |
| Southwest Missouri Camp | Mountain Grove | D; Church of God (Anderson) | | |
| State Camp | Myrtle | D; Church of God (Servant) | O | 1945 |
| Troy Holiness Camp | Troy | D; Fire Baptized Holiness Church | O | 1934 |
| Windermere Assembly | Roach | D; Baptist Church | | |

## Montana

| Camp | Location | Affiliation | | Year |
|---|---|---|---|---|
| Alliance Bible Camp | Lambert | D; Christian Missionary Alliance Church | | |
| Big Sky Bible Camp | Bigfork | A; BCM International, Inc. | O | |
| Bitterroot Lake Camp | Kalispell | D; Church of God (Anderson) | O | |

| Name | City | Affiliation | O/R | Year | Founder |
|------|------|-------------|-----|------|---------|
| Caldwell Springs Camp | Ridge | | | | |
| Church of God Camp | Paradise | D; New Testament Church of God | | | |
| Dickey Lake Bible Camp | Kalispell | D; Christian Missionary Alliance Church | | | |
| Glacier Bible Camp | Hungry Horse | D; Church of God (Anderson) | O | | |
| Indian Camp | Alberton | D; Allegheny Wesleyan Methodist Connection | R | 1970 | |
| Mizpah Conference Center | White Sulphur Springs | I . . . | | | |
| Montana Camp | Bozeman | D; Church of God of Prophecy | R | | |
| Montana Conference Camp | Bozeman | D; Seventh Day Adventist Church | O | | |
| Montana District Camp | Hungry Horse | D; Assembly of God Church | | | |
| Rocky Mountain District Camp | Big Timber | D; United Pentecostal Church | R | | |
| Trails End Ranch | Ekalaka | | | | |
| United Methodist Camp | Big Timber | D; United Methodist Church | O | | |
| Western Conference Camp | Reedpoint | D; Evangelical Church of North America | R | | |
| Yellowstone Bible Camp | Bozeman | C; Christian Missionary Alliance Church | | | |

## Nebraska

| Camp | Location | Affiliation | | Year | Ministers |
|---|---|---|---|---|---|
| Ansley Camp | Ansley | D; Free Methodist Church | | | |
| Calvin Crest Camp and Conference Center | Fremont | | | | |
| Camp Rockhaven | Cozad | D; Church of God (Anderson) | | | |
| Christian Life Campground | Polk | D; United Pentecostal Church | | | |
| District Camp | O'Niel | D; Wesleyan Church | | | |
| Family Camp | Weeping Water | D; The Missionary Church | O | 1895 | |
| Gordon Camp | Gordon | I . . . | O | 1925 | Various ministers |
| Holdredge Camp | Holdredge | D; Church of the Nazarene | | | |
| Imperial Valley Camp | Imperial | I; Imperial Valley Holiness Association | O | 1890 | Levi Harmon, Galen Harmon, et al. |
| Iowa-Nebraska Camp | Omaha | D; Church of God of Prophecy | R | | |
| Maranatha Bible Camp | North Platte | I . . . | | | |
| Mitchell Camp | Mitchell | D; Immanuel Missionary Church | O | | |
| Nebraska District Camp | Kearney | D; Church of the Nazarene | O | 1903 | |
| Nebraska District Camp | Lexington | D; Assembly of God Church | | | |
| Nysted Camp | Dannebrog | D; Evangelical Wesleyan Church | O | 1963 | |
| Rivercrest Bible Camp | Fremont | D; Christian Missionary Alliance Church | | | |
| Sandhill Holiness Camp | North Platte | I . . . | | | |
| Whispering Cedars Camp | Genoa | D; Baptist Church | | | |

| Name | City | Affiliation | O/R | Year | Founder |
|------|------|-------------|-----|------|---------|
| **Nevada** | | | | | |
| District Camp | Elko | D; Church of the Nazarene | O | 1946 | |
| **New Hampshire** | | | | | |
| Alton Bay Conference Center | Alton Bay | I . . . | O | 1863 | |
| Brookwoods/Deer Run | Alton | | | | |
| Camp Fireside | Rochester | | | | |
| Camp Monomonac | Rindge | | | | |
| Camp Spofford | Spofford Lake | | | | |
| Claremont Union Camp | Claremont | I . . . | | 1873 | |
| Hedding Camp | Epping | D; United Methodist Church | O | 1862 | |
| Holdredge Camp | Holdredge | D; Church of the Nazarene | | | |
| Lakeside Camp | Pitsburg | D; United Methodist Church | R | 1984 | Local Methodists |
| Monadnock Bible Conference | Jaffrey Center | I . . . | | | |
| Pilgrim Pines Conference Center | Swanzey | D; Evangelical Covenant Church of America | O | | |
| Rumney Bible Conference | Rumney | | | | |
| Rumney Camp | Rumney | D; Christian Missionary Alliance Church | | | |
| Singing Hills Conference Center | Plainfield | I; Singing Hills Christian Fellowship, Inc. | | | |
| Windsor Hills Family Camping Center | Hillsboro | D; Church of the Nazarene | O | | |

| Winnepesaukee Camp | The Weirs, Lacoina | I; Winnepesaukee Camp Meeting Association | O | 1868 | |
|---|---|---|---|---|---|
| **New Jersey** | | | | | |
| America's Keswick | Whiting | I . . . | O | | |
| Aura Camp | Aura | I; Aura Holiness Camp Meeting Association | O | 1919 | Rev. Hammel |
| Baptist Conference Center | Lebanon | D; Baptist Church | | 1962 | |
| Bonnie Brae Camp | Millington | I . . . | | | |
| Camp Washington | Waymouth | D; Church of God (Anderson) | O | | |
| Delanco Camp | Vincentown | I; Delanco Camp Meeting Association | O | 1898 | Dr. G. W. Ridout |
| Erma Camp | Erma | I; Cape May Holiness Association | O | 1911 | Rev. William Briddle et al. |
| Fellowship Conference Center | Liberty Corner | | | | |
| Ghost Lake Christian Camp | Great Meadows | I . . . | | | |
| Glassboro Camp | Glassboro | D; Wesleyan Church | O | 1921 | H. Marshall, Edgar Zulker, William Gallagher, et al. |
| Harvey Cedars Bible Conference | Harvey Cedars | | O | 1941 | |
| Liebenzell Retreat Center and Camp | Schooley's Mountain | | | | |
| Malaga Camp | Newfield | D; United Methodist Church | O | 1869 | Rev. J. P. Connelly, Joshua Richman, et al. |

| Name | City | Affiliation | O/R | Year | Founder |
|---|---|---|---|---|---|
| Mt. Tabor Camp | Mt. Tabor | I; Mt. Tabor Camp Meeting Association | O | 1866 | |
| New Jersey Camp | Long Branch | D; Church of God of Prophecy | R | | |
| New Jersey Conference Camp | Tranquility | D; Seventh Day Adventist Church | O | | |
| New Jersey–Delaware District Camp | New Field | D; United Pentecostal Church | | | |
| Ocean City Camp | Ocean City | D; United Methodist Church | O | 1879 | |
| Ocean Grove Camp | Ocean Grove | D; United Methodist Church | O | 1869 | Rev. William B. Osborn |
| Ocean Grove Chautauqua | Ocean Grove | D; United Methodist Church | R | 1885 | |
| Pillar of Fire Camp | Zeraphath | D; Pillar of Fire Church | O | 1908 | Bishop Alma White |
| Pine View Grove Camp | Pleasantville | D; Christian Welfare Church | O | 1937 | Rev. Palmer |
| Pitman Grove Camp | Pitman | D; United Methodist Church | O | 1870 | |
| Seaville Camp | South Seaville | D; United Methodist Church | O | 1864 | |
| South Jersey Camp | Deerfield | D; Church of the Nazarene | O | | |
| Tri-State Bible Conference | Montague | | | | |
| Warren Camp | Warren | D; Free Methodist Church | | | |
| Wesley Grove Camp | Trenton | D; Wesleyan Church | O | 1934 | |
| Wiley Camp | Camden | A; Wiley Mission | O | 1935 | |

## New Mexico

| Name | City | Affiliation | O/R | Year | Founder |
|---|---|---|---|---|---|
| All Tribes Indian Camp | Bernalillo | I; All Tribes Indian School | O | 1970 | |
| Bonita Park Camp | Capitan | D; Church of the Nazarene | | | |

| | | | |
|---|---|---|---|
| Central Latin America District Camp | Chama | D; Assembly of God Church | |
| District Camp | Rudiso | D; Church of the Nazarene | 1938 |
| Glorieta Conference Center | Glorieta | D; Southern Baptist Convention | O |
| Lone Tree Bible Ranch | Capitan | | |
| Mesa Redondo Cowboy Camp | Tucumcari | I; Ranchmen's Camp Meetings in the Southwest | 1977 |
| Mogal Mesa Camp | Carrizozo | I; Ranchmen's Camp Meetings in the Southwest | 1939 |
| Navajo Mission Camp | Sheep Springs Mountain | A; Free Trinity Navajo Mission | O 1970 |
| New Mexico Camp | Albuquerque | D; Church of God of Prophecy | R |
| New Mexico District Camp | Mountainair | D; Assembly of God Church | |
| Sacramento Methodist Assembly | Sacramento | D; United Methodist Church | O |
| Sierra Grande Rancher's Camp | Des Moines | I; Ranchmen's Camp Meetings in the Southwest | 1951 |
| Southwest Indian Camp | Manuelito | D; Church of God of Prophecy | O |
| Texico Conference Camp | Corrales | D; Seventh Day Adventist Church | O |
| White Mesa Indian Camp | White Mesa | A; Society of Indian Missions, Inc. | O 1988 |

## New York

| | | | |
|---|---|---|---|
| Beulah Park Camp | Richland | I; Richland Holiness Camp Meeting Association | O 1901 |

| Name | City | Affiliation | O/R | Year | Founder |
|---|---|---|---|---|---|
| Binghamton Camp | Binghamton | D; Pilgrim Holiness Church of New York | O | 1904 | |
| Brushton Camp | Brushton | I; Brushton Holiness Camp Meeting Association | O | 1880 | |
| Burk County Camp | Malone | D; Standard Church of America | O | | |
| Camp Berkshire | Wingdale | D; Seventh Day Adventist Church | O | | |
| Camp Findley | Findley Lake | D; United Methodist Church | O | 1935 | |
| Camp Pinnacle | Vorheesville | | | | |
| Camp Victory Lake | Hyde Park | D; Seventh Day Adventist Church | O | | |
| Camp Woods | Ossining | I . . . | O | 1804 | |
| Camp-of-the-Woods | Speculator | I; Gospel Volunteers, Inc. | O | 1900 | Mr. and Mrs. George F. Tibbitts |
| Cassadaga Lake Camp | Lilly Dale | D; Spiritualist | O | 1879 | |
| Catskill Christian Assembly | Prattsville | | | | |
| Cattaraugus Camp | Cattaraugus | D; Free Methodist Church | | | |
| Chambers Wesleyan Camp | Beaver Dams | D; Wesleyan Church | O | 1919 | Rev. Shea (father of George Beverly Shea) |
| Chautauqua Institution, The | Chautauqua | I . . . | O | 1874 | Lewis Miller and Rev. John Vincent |
| Conference Camp | Adams Center | D; Free Methodist Church | O | | |
| Conference Camp | Corning | D; Free Methodist Church | | | |
| Conference Camp | West Bangor | D; Free Methodist Church | | | |

| Name | Location | Status | Year | Affiliation | Leader |
|---|---|---|---|---|---|
| Covenant Acres Retreat Center | Pike | | | | |
| Delta Lake Bible Camp | Rome | O | | D; Christian Missionary Alliance Church | |
| Delta Lake Bible Conference | Rome | O | | D; Christian Missionary Alliance Church | |
| Dempster Grove Camp | New Haven | O | 1875 | D; United Methodist Church | |
| District Camp | Northville | O | 1957 | D; Evangelical Wesleyan Church | |
| Elim Bible Institute Camp | Lima | | | I. . . | |
| Fort Edwards Camp | Fort Edwrads | O | 1943 | I. . . | |
| Freeport Camp | Freeport, Long Island | O | 1885 | I; Long Island Holiness Camp Meeting Association | Rev. Charles Powell |
| Good Tidings Bible Conference | Cornwallville | | | I; Good Tidings Fellowship, Inc. | |
| Grandview Camp | Brooktondale | O | 1900 | D; Church of the Nazarene | |
| Groveville Park Camp | Red Hook | O | 1909 | D; Church of the Nazarene | |
| Hispanic Family Camp | Saratoga Springs | R | | D; Free Methodist Church | |
| Hoosick Camp | Hoosick Falls | | | D; Seventh Day Adventist Church | |
| Houghton Camp | Houghton | O | 1890 | D; Wesleyan Church | |
| Indian Holiness Camp | Versailles | O | 1944 | I. . . | |
| Lakeside Bible Conference | Redfield | | | | |
| Letourneau Christian Conference | Rushville | | | D; Christian Missionary Alliance Church | |
| Lewis M. Fowler Conference Center | Speculator | | | | |

| Name | City | Affiliation | O/R | Year | Founder |
|---|---|---|---|---|---|
| Lighthouse Christian Camp | Barker | D; Free Methodist Church | O | 1935 | Rev. W. J. Parmeter |
| Lilly Lake Camp | Port Crane | D; Churches of Christ in Christian Union | O | 1896 | |
| Lisbon Camp | Lisbon | I; Lisbon Camp Meeting Association | O | 1927 | |
| Mooers Camp | Mooers | I . . . | O | | |
| New York Conference Camp | Union Springs | D; Seventh Day Adventist Church | O | 1902 | |
| New York District Camp | Berne | D; United Pentecostal Church | | | |
| New York District Camp | Watson Homestead | D; Assembly of God Church | | | |
| Odosagh Bible Conference | Machias | | | | |
| Ontario Bible Conference | Oswego | | | | |
| Peniel Bible Conference | Lake Luzerne | | | | |
| Pine Grove Camp | Saratoga Springs | D; Free Methodist Church | O | | |
| Potter's Grove Camp | Hudson Falls | I . . . | | | |
| Rensselaer Falls Camp | Rensselaer Falls | I . . . | | 1903 | |
| Rome Camp | Rome | I . . . | | | |
| Round Lake District | Round Lake | I . . . | O | 1867 | Joseph Hillman et al. |
| Sacandaga Bible Conference | Broadalbin | | | | |
| Saratoga District Camp | Saratoga Springs | D; Free Methodist Church | R | | |
| Seven Oaks Camp | Latham | I; Eastern New York Holiness Association | O | 1905 | |
| Sharon Park Camp | Hancock | D; Free Methodist Church | | | |
| Silver Bay Association Complex | Silver Bay | D; Y.M.C.A. | O | 1880 | |

| Camp | Location | Affiliation | | Founded | Leader |
|---|---|---|---|---|---|
| Stony Creek Camp | Stony Creek | I . . . | O | 1925 | |
| Thousand Island Park | Orleans | I; Thousand Island Park Corporation | O | 1875 | Rev. John F. Dayan |
| Trenton Camp | Trenton | D; United Methodist Church | O | | |
| Union Springs Camp | Union Springs | D; Seventh Day Adventist Church | O | | |
| Utica Camp | Utica | D; Seventh Day Adventist Church | O | | |
| Vermontville Camp | Vermontville | D; Pilgrim Holiness Church of New York | O | | |
| Victory Grove Camp | Albany | D; Pilgrim Holiness Church of New York | O | 1918 | |
| Village of Faith Camp | Farmingville | I; Faith of God's Word Ministry | O | | Rev. Dan Cotrone |
| Waterbrook Retreat Center | Cornwall | | | | |
| West Chazy Camp | West Chazy | D; Wesleyan Church | O | 1842 | |
| Western New York Camp | Houghton | D; Church of God (Anderson) | O | | |
| Wildwood Christian Camp | East Freetown | D; Free Methodist Church | O | | |
| Word of Life Conference Center | Schroon Lake | I; Word of Life | O | 1947 | Jack Wyrtzen |

## North Carolina

| Camp | Location | Affiliation | | Founded | Leader |
|---|---|---|---|---|---|
| Ball's Creek Camp | Maiden | D; United Methodist Church | O | 1853 | |
| Bethlehem Camp | Climax | D; United Methodist Church | O | 1854 | Local Methodists |
| Bible Methodist Camp | Wyo | D; Bible Methodist Church | | | |

| Name | City | Affiliation | O/R | Year | Founder |
|---|---|---|---|---|---|
| Blackburn Memorial Camp | Todd | I . . . | O | | Rev. Ed Blackburn |
| Blue Ridge Camp | Jefferson | I . . . | O | 1959 | Barbara Arnold & Grace Jones |
| Camp Dixie | Fayetteville | D; United Pentecostal Church | O | | |
| Camp Free | Connelly Springs | I . . . | O | 1920 | Rev. Jim Green |
| Camp Hawthornburg | Robbins | D; Evangelical Friends Church | O | | |
| Camp Hope | Canton | D; Free Methodist Church | R | | |
| Camp Lurecrest | Charlotte | | O | 1949 | |
| Camp McCall | Marion | D; United Methodist Church | O | 1940 | |
| Camp Oak Hill | Raleigh | | | | |
| Camp Willow Run | Littleton | | | | |
| Candler Camp | Lake Junaluska | D; United Methodist Church | O | 1950 | |
| Carolina Conference Camp | Lake Junaluska | D; Seventh Day Adventist Church | R | | |
| District Camp | Asheboro | D; Bible Missionary Church | R | | |
| District Camp | Salisbury | D; Wesleyan Holiness Church | O | | |
| Dunn Camp | Dunn | D; Pentecostal Freewill Baptist Church, Inc. | O | | |
| Eastern North Carolina Camp | Kenly | D; Church of God of Prophecy | O | | |
| Eastern Second Blessing Camp | Harkers Island | I . . . | | | |
| Eliada Camp | Asheville | I . . . | | | |
| Falcon Camp | Falcon | D; International Pentecostal Holiness Church | O | 1900 | J. A. Culbreth |
| Free Pilgrim Camp | Thomasville | I . . . | R | 1968 | Rev. Ray Shemrick |

| Camp | Location | Affiliation | | Year | Leaders |
|---|---|---|---|---|---|
| Free Spirit Camp | Mebane | I... | | | |
| Free Spirit Camp | Salisbury | I... | | | |
| General Conference Grounds | Charlotte | D; Advent Christian Church | O | | |
| God's Community Church Camp | Pinnacle | D; Reformed Free Methodist Church | O | 1970 | |
| Hendersonville Camp | Hendersonville | D; Church of the Nazarene | O | 1956 | |
| Hickory Cove Bible Camp | Taylorsville | | | | |
| Indian Camp | Shannon | D; Assembly of God Church | | | |
| John Wesley Camp | High Point | I... | O | 1941 | Revs. John W. Groce, Paul Rayle, C. E. Williams, and A. Burgess |
| John Wesley College Camp | Greensboro | I... | O | 1905 | |
| Lake Junaluska Assembly | Lake Junaluska | D; United Methodist Church | O | 1908 | |
| Laurel Springs Camp | Jefferson | I... | R | | |
| McKenzie's Camp | Catawba County | D; African Methodist Episcopal Zion Church | O | 1850 | |
| Mott's Grove Camp | Catawba County | D; United Methodist Church | O | 1850 | |
| North Carolina Camp | Durham | D; Church of God (Servant) | R | 1979 | |
| North Carolina Camp | Lenour | D; Missionary Methodist Church | O | 1970 | Fred Tyler |
| New Covenant Camp | Mt. Airy | D; International Pentecostal Holiness Church | O | 1940 | |
| North Carolina District Camp | Franklin | D; Assembly of God Church | | | |
| North Carolina District Camp | Windsor | D; Assembly of God Church | | | |
| Piney Grove Camp | Chocowinity | D; International Pentecostal Holiness Church | O | 1909 | Rev. A. H. Butler |
| Pleasant Grove Camp | Mineral Springs | D; United Methodist Church | O | | |

| Name | City | Affiliation | O/R | Year | Founder |
|------|------|-------------|-----|------|---------|
| Redding Springs Camp | Weddington | D; African Methodist Episcopal Zion Church | O | 1854 | |
| Ridgecrest ConferenceCenter | Ridgecrest | D; Southern Baptist Convention | O | 1909 | Bernard W. Spilman |
| Rock Springs Camp | Denver | D; United Methodist Church | O | 1794 | Rev. Daniel Asbury et al. |
| Salter Path Camp | Salter Path | I . . . | | | |
| Shady Grove Camp | Colfax | D; Wesleyan Church | O | 1919 | Revs. W. C. Lovin, T. L. Hill, J. A. Clement, et al. |
| Shingle HollowCamp | Rutherfordton | D; Congregational Holiness Church, Inc. | O | 1932 | |
| Silk Hope Camp | Siler City | I . . . | | | |
| State Camp | Chapel Hill | D; Church of God (Anderson) | O | 1903 | |
| State Camp | Statesville | D; Church of God (Anderson) | | | |
| Torrence Chapel Camp | Troutman | D; AME Zion Church | O | 1867 | |
| Tucker's Grove Camp | Machpelah | D; United Methodist Church | O | 1850 | |
| Upward Kelly Memorial Camp | Flat Rock | D; Holiness Baptist Church | O | 1947 | |
| Western District Camp | Colfax | D; Wesleyan Church | R | 1919 | |
| Western North Carolina Camp | Marshall | D; Church of God (Anderson) | O | | |
| Western North Carolina Camp | Charlotte | D; Church of God of Prophecy | O | | |
| Wilds, The | Brevard | | O | | |

**North Dakota**

| Asbury Camp | Washburn | I . . . | O | 1925 | |

| Camp | Location | Denomination | Status | Year | Leaders |
|---|---|---|---|---|---|
| Beulah Camp | Jamestown | I . . . | O | 1905 | Rev. S. A. Danford and Rev. E. M. Isaac |
| Crystal Springs Camp | Medina | D; Baptist Church | | | |
| Erie Camp | Erie | I . . . | O | 1913 | Mrs. Sarah Brewer |
| German Camp | Ashley | D; Assembly of God Church | | | |
| Hoople Camp | Hoople | I . . . | O | 1893 | |
| Lehr Camp | Lehr | D; United Methodist Church | O | 1921 | |
| Mt. Carmel Camp | Granville | D; Evangelical Church of North America | O | 1906 | |
| Nazarene Indoor Camp | Jamestown | D; Church of the Nazarene | R | 1980 | |
| North Dakota District Camp | Devils Lake | D; Assembly of God Church | | | |
| North Dakota District Camp | Saywer | D; Church of the Nazarene | O | 1910 | |
| State Camp | New Rockford | D; Church of God (Anderson) | O | 1896 | |

## Ohio

| Camp | Location | Denomination | Status | Year | Leaders |
|---|---|---|---|---|---|
| Akron District Camp | Louisville | D; Church of the Nazarene | O | 1954 | |
| Apostolic Camp Ground | Millersport | D; United Pentecostal Church | O | 1943 | |
| Ashley Camp | Ashley | I; Ashley Interdenominational Holiness Camp Meeting Association | | | |
| Ashley Spiritualist Camp | Ashley | Spiritualist | | 1980 | |
| Bethel Camp | Coshocton | I; Bethel Holiness Camp Meeting Association | R | 1913 | |
| Bethel Camp | New Bloomington | I; Bethel Holiness Camp Meeting Association | O | 1948 | Rev. James Maffin and Rev. Jesse Glassburn |

| Name | City | Affiliation | O/R | Year | Founder |
|---|---|---|---|---|---|
| Beulah Beach Camp | Vermillion | D; Christian Missionary Alliance Church | O | | |
| Beulah Camp | Marion | D; Euclid Avenue Mission | O | 1975 | J. F. Maffin |
| Beulah Grove Camp | Mendon | D; Bible Methodist Church | O | 1922 | Local Methodists |
| Bible Church of God Camp | Idaho | D; Bible Church of God | O | 1988 | Rev. Leonard Lacy |
| Bible Missionary Camp | West Milton | D; Bible Missionary Church | R | | |
| Brailey Camp | Swanton | I . . . | O | 1951 | H. E. Greisinger |
| Brush Arbor Camp | Alvada | I . . . | O | 1960 | H. McKee |
| Burning Bush Camp | Marion | D; Home Missionary Holiness Church | O | 1960 | |
| Burning Heart Camp | Bentonville | D; Kentucky Christian Holiness Church | O | 1940 | |
| Butler Springs Assembly | Sinking Spring | I . . . | | | |
| Calvary Christian College Camp | Paris | I; Calvary Christian College | O | 1969 | Rev. Maas |
| Cambridge Indoor Camp | Cambridge | I; Cambridge Holiness Association | R | 1960 | |
| Camp Burton | Burton | | | | |
| Camp Canaan | Oak Hill | D; Bible Methodist Connection of Tennessee | O | 1980 | Rev. Grant Rhodes |
| Camp Carl | Akron | | | | |
| Camp Gideon | Mechanicstown | D; Evangelical Friends Church | O | | |
| Camp Gilead | Cardington | I . . . | O | 1955 | Melvin Sharrock et al. |
| Camp Kaphar | Urichsville | I . . . | O | 1938 | Laity of the area |

| Camp Name | Location | Affiliation | Status | Year | Founder/Leader |
|---|---|---|---|---|---|
| Camp Mohaven Retreat Center | Loudenville | D; Seventh-day Adventist Church | O | 1930 | |
| Camp St. Marys | St. Marys | D; United Methodist Church | O | 1870 | Col. Ephraim Ball et al. |
| Camp Sychar | Mt. Vernon | I; . . . | O | 1938 | Rev. T. P. Roberts et al. |
| Camp Union | York Center | I; . . . | O | 1926 | |
| Central Ohio District Camp | Columbus | D; Church of the Nazarene | O | 1930 | |
| Christian Baptist Camp | Wheelersburg | D; Christian Baptist Church | O | 1930 | Revs. A. L. Baldridge, Hallie Nunley, Van Williams, et al. |
| Christian Community Camp | Washington Court House | D; Christian Community Holiness Church | O | 1947 | Rev. Delbert Harper, Sr. |
| Christian Holiness Camp | Washington Court House | D; Christian Holiness Church | O | 1950 | Rev. C. H. Detty |
| Comargo Camp | Loveland | D; Christian Nation Church | O | 1904 | Rev. Poe, Eugene Light |
| Coolville Camp | Coolville | I; . . . | O | 1880 | |
| Doughty Camp | Millersburg | I; Doughty Camp Meeting Association, Inc. | O | 1921 | |
| Dunkirk Camp | Dunkirk | I; Hardin County Holiness Camp Meeting Association | O | 1902 | Rev. Terry et al. |
| East Ohio District Camp | Coshocton | D; Wesleyan Church | O | | |
| Faith Ranch | Jewett | I; . . . | R | 1990 | |
| Family Camp | Mt. Vernon | D; Church of the Nazarene | O | 1977 | Rev. Hughie Gillespie |
| Fellowship Camp | Oak Hill | D; Bible Brethren Church | O | | |
| Fellowship Holiness Camp | Marysville | D; Wesleyan Holiness Church of North America, Inc. | O | 1963 | Ministers and laity of the denomination |
| God's Acres Camp | Newark | D; Church of God (Universal) | O | | |
| God's Non-Sectarian Tabernacle Camp | Washington Court House | D; House of Prayer | O | 1918 | Rev. Henry Leeth et al. |

| Name | City | Affiliation | O/R | Year | Founder |
|------|------|-------------|-----|------|---------|
| Greenwood Lake Conference Center | Delaware | D; The Salvation Army | O | 1988 | |
| Hancock County Camp | Findlay | I; Hancock County Holiness Association | O | 1892 | Rev. B. W. Day and Rev. E. S. Dunham |
| Hicksville Camp | Hicksville | I . . . | R | 1963 | |
| Hocking Valley Tabernacle | New Straitsville | I; Hocking Valley Tabernacle Association | O | 1963 | Rev. E. V. Baker |
| Holiness Camp | Chillicothe | I; Holiness Ministerial Association | R | 1971 | |
| Holiness Camp | Columbus | D . . . | O | | Rev. Shopshire |
| Holiness Camp | Hannibal | I . . . | | | |
| Holiness Camp | Lucasville | I . . . | O | 1985 | |
| Hollow Rock Camp | Toronto | I; Hollow Rock Camp Meeting Association | O | 1818 | Methodists |
| Indoor Camp | Cambridge | I; Cambridge Holiness Association | R | 1960 | |
| Indoor Camp | De Graff | D; New Testament Church of God | R | 1975 | |
| Indoor Camp | Newark | D; New Testament Church of God | R | 1975 | |
| International Conference Center | London | D; International Pentecostal Church of Christ | O | | |
| Jerusalem Camp | Massieville | D; Household of Faith Missions | O | 1914 | |
| King's Domain Conference Center | Oregonia | I . . . | | | |

| Name | Location | Type | R/O | Year | Founder |
|---|---|---|---|---|---|
| Kirkwood Conference Center | Wilmington | O | | | |
| Koinonia Conference Center | Geneva | I . . . | O | 1872 | Local Methodists |
| Lakeside Assembly Grounds | Lakeside | D; United Methodist Church | R | 1877 | |
| Lakeside Association, The [Chautauqua] | Lakeside | D; United Methodist Church | | | |
| Lancaster Camp | Lancaster | D; United Methodist Church | O | 1872 | Rev. William C. Holliday |
| Lancaster Chautauqua, The | Lancaster | D; United Methodist Church | R | | |
| Lower Light Camp | Rhoads | D; Lower Light Mission | R | 1967 | |
| Serpent Mound Camp | Locust Grove | A; Missionary Worker's Ministerial Association | O | 1927 | |
| Memorial Holiness Camp | West Milton | D; Brethren in Christ Church | O | 1943 | Bishop O. B. Ulery and Harvey Hokee |
| Morristown Camp | Morristown | I . . . | O | 1948 | Rev. King, Rev. Deeker, and Mr. McKinney |
| Mount Lookout Camp | Waynesfield | I; Mount Lookout Holiness Camp Meeting Association | O | 1898 | Hugh Lusk et al. |
| Mount of Blessings Camp | Cincinnatti | I; God's Bible School | O | 1897 | Rev. Martin Wells Knapp |
| Mount of Praise Camp | Circleville | D; Churches of Christ in Christian Union | O | 1918 | Rev. O. L. Ferguson et al. |
| Mt. Vernon Camp | Mt. Vernon | D; Seventh Day Adventist Church | O | | |
| Muskingum Valley Camp | Zanesville | I; Muskingum Valley Holiness Association | R | 1930 | |
| Nelsonville Camp | Nelsonville | I . . . | O | 1930 | Rev. Miniker et al. |
| Nipgen Camp | Nipgen | D; Churches of Christ in Christian Union | O | 1945 | Rev. Russel Knisely et al. |

| Name | City | Affiliation | O/R | Year | Founder |
|------|------|-------------|-----|------|---------|
| Northcentral Ohio District Camp | Mt. Vernon | D; Church of the Nazarene | R | 1985 | |
| Northeast Ohio Camp | Berlin Center | D; Church of God (Anderson) | O | 1950 | |
| Northeastern District Camp | Sebring | D; Wesleyan Holiness Association of Churches | R | 1965 | |
| Northern Ohio Camp | Canton | D; Church of God of Prophecy | R | | |
| Northwest Ohio Camp | Payne | D; Church of God (Anderson) | O | 1885 | |
| Northwestern Ohio District Camp | St. Marys | D; Church of the Nazarene | O | 1949 | Dr. W. E. Albia |
| Oak Side Camp | Hanover | D; Evangelical Christian Church | O | 1960 | |
| Ohio Conference Camp | Mansfield | D; Free Methodist Church | O | 1878 | |
| Ohio District Camp | Big Prairie | D; Assembly of God Church | O | 1878 | |
| Ohio State Camp | Akron | D; Church of God (Servant) | O | 1964 | |
| Ohio State Camp | Springfield | D; Church of God (Anderson) | O | 1910 | |
| Peniel Camp | Benton | I; Peniel Holiness Camp Meeting Association | O | 1954 | Rev. H. L. Ferguson |
| Pillar of Fire Camp | Cincinnati | D; Pillar of Fire Church | O | 1921 | Bishop Alma White |
| Portage Camp | Portage | I; Sandusky Union Holiness Association | O | 1878 | Ministers of the United Brethren Church |
| Quaker Canyon Camp | Damascus | D; Evangelical Friends Church | O | | |
| Rising Sun Camp | Wayne | D; Six Points Mission | O | 1937 | |
| Rutland Camp | Rutland | I . . . | | | |
| Sabina Camp | Sabina | D; United Methodist Church | O | 1893 | Ministers of the Methodist Protestant Church |

| Scioto County Camp | Portsmouth | I; Scioto County Holiness Association | O | 1934 | Rev. John Cross |
|---|---|---|---|---|---|
| Sebring Camp | Sebring | I; Sebring Interdenomination Camp Meeting Association | O | 1904 | Mrs. Will Murphy et al. |
| Sharon Center Camp | Sharon Center | I; Sharon Center Holiness Camp Meeting Association | O | 1900 | |
| Six Mile Turn Camp | Crooksville | I; Six Mile Turn Holiness Association | O | 1935 | |
| Slovak Camp | Hubbard | D; Church of God (Anderson) | O | | |
| Southeast Ohio Camp | Warsaw | D; Church of God (Anderson) | O | 1910 | |
| Southern Ohio Camp | Fairfield | D; Church of God of Prophecy | R | | |
| Southwest Ohio Camp | Lebanon | D; Church of God (Anderson) | O | 1950 | |
| Spencerville Camp | Spencerville | I . . . | O | 1944 | Rev. Roy Johnson |
| Stoutsville Camp | Stoutsville | I; Stoutsville Camp Meeting Association | O | 1897 | Ministers of the Evangelical Association |
| Tent Camp | Locust Grove | I . . . | R | 1972 | Rev. Ed Workman |
| Thornville Camp | Lancaster | D; Seventh Day Adventist Church | O | 1989 | |
| Tri-County Camp | Mt. Vernon | I . . . | R | 1970 | |
| Tri-State Camp | East Liverpool | D; Free Methodist Church | O | 1908 | |
| Tri-State Camp | East Liverpool | I; Tri-State Camp Meeting Association | O | | |
| Tri-State Holiness Tent Camp | West Unity | I . . . | R | | |
| Tri-Township Tabernacle Camp | Minford | A; Tri-Township Sunday School Convention | O | 1955 | David Dealey |

| Name | City | Affiliation | O/R | Year | Founder |
|---|---|---|---|---|---|
| Union Camp | Chillicothe | I; ... | O | 1957 | Rev. Clark Diehl |
| United Missionary Church Camp | Ludlow Falls | D; United Missionary Church District of the Mennonite | O | 1896 | Ministers of the Ohio Brethren in Christ Church |
| United Pilgrim Holiness Camp | Lancaster | D; United Pilgrim Holiness Church | O | 1949 | Rev. James Hicks |
| Victory Camp | Westerville | D; Wesleyan Church Conference of the Wesleyan | O | 1924 | Ministers of the Ohio Methodist Church |
| Waynesville Camp | Waynesville | I; ... | | | |
| Wellston Camp | Wellston | I; United Methodist Camp Meeting Association, Inc. | O | 1947 | Rev. C. Walter |
| West Central District Camp | Columbus | D; Churches of Christ in Christian Union | R | | |
| Winter Camp | Newark | D; Church of God (Universal) | O | 1960 | |
| Wren Camp | Wren | I; ... | O | 1942 | |

## Oklahoma

| Name | City | Affiliation | O/R | Year | Founder |
|---|---|---|---|---|---|
| Ada Camp | Ada | D; International Pentecostal Holiness Church | O | 1925 | |
| Boley Camp | Boley | D; Church of God (Servant) | O | | |
| Camp Bristow | Bristow | | O | | |
| Camp Egan | Tahlequah | D; United Methodist Church | O | 1945 | |
| Church of God Camp | Oklahoma City | D; Church of God (Anderson) | O | | |
| District Camp | Duncan | D; Bible Missionary Church | O | 1960 | |

| Camp | Location | Affiliation | Status | Year | Notes |
|---|---|---|---|---|---|
| Grant County Camp | Medford | I; Grant County Holiness Association | | | |
| Lenapah Cowboy Camp | Nowata | I; Ranchmen's Camp Meetings in the Southwest | O | 1982 | |
| Methodist Canyon Camp | Hinton | D; United Methodist Church | O | 1953 | |
| New Life Ranch | Colcord | | | | |
| Ochelata Camp | Ochelata | D; Fire Baptized Holiness Church | O | 1936 | Rev. Downing |
| Oklahoma Camp | Oklahoma City | D; Church of God of Prophecy | | | |
| Oklahoma Camp | Poteau | D; Assembly of God Church | | | |
| Oklahoma Conference Camp | Oklahoma City | D; International Pentecostal Holiness Church | O | 1909 | |
| Oklahoma Conference Camp | Perkins | D; Free Methodist Church | O | 1898 | |
| Oklahoma District Camp | Mustang | D; United Pentecostal Church | | | |
| Oklahoma District Camp | Oklahoma City | D; Assembly of God Church | | | |
| Oklahoma State Camp | Happy Hill | D; Church of God (Independent Holiness People) | O | | |
| Southeast Oklahoma District Camp | Durant | D; Church of the Nazarene | R | | |
| Southwest Oklahoma District Camp | Anadarko | D; Church of the Nazarene | O | 1952 | |
| State Camp | Bristow | D; Church of God (Anderson) | O | 1902 | |
| State Camp | Guthrie | D; Church of God (Servant) | O | 1934 | |
| Tri-County Camp | Vici | I; Tri-County Holiness Association | O | | |
| Tulsa Camp | Tulsa | D; Church of God (Servant) | O | 1974 | |
| Tulsa Camp | Tulsa | I; Kenneth Hagin Ministries | R | | Kenneth Hagin Ministries |

| Name | City | Affiliation | O/R | Year | Founder |
|---|---|---|---|---|---|
| Turner Falls Camp | Turner Falls | D; Assembly of God Church | O | 1919 | Ardmore District, Methodist |
| West Oklahoma Camp | Cordell | D; Church of God (Anderson) | O | | |
| West Oklahoma Conference Camp | Clinton | D; International Pentecostal Holiness Church | | 1945 | |
| Wewoka Woods Adventist Center | Wewoka Woods | D; Seventh Day Adventist Church | O | | |

## Oregon

| Name | City | Affiliation | O/R | Year | Founder |
|---|---|---|---|---|---|
| Aldersgate Bible Camp | Turner | D; Free Methodist Church | O | 1920 | |
| Ashland Holiness Camp | Ashland | D; Fire Baptized Holiness Church | O | 1960 | |
| Bundy Bridge Camp | Corvallis | I; Willamette Holiness Association | O | 1920 | |
| Camp Arrah Wanna | Portland | D; American Baptist Church | O | | |
| Camp Morrow Bible Conference | Wamic | | | | |
| Camp Tadmor | Lebanon | | | | |
| Canby Grove Camp | Clackamas | D; Church of God (Anderson) | O | | |
| Cannon Beach Conference Center | Cannon Beach | I . . . | O | | |
| Canyonview Camp | Silverton | | | | |
| Church of God Camp | Canby | D; Church of God (Universal) | R | | |
| Crestview Manor Conference Center | Corbett | | | | |

| Name | Location | Affiliation | O/R | Year | Director |
|---|---|---|---|---|---|
| Evangelical Center | Milwaukie | | | | |
| Evangelical Summer Assembly | Jennings Lodge | D; Evangelical Church of North America | O | 1914 | |
| Fircroft Camp | Langlois | I . . . | O | 1950 | |
| German Camp | Salem | D; Assembly of God Church | | | |
| Gladstone Campground | Gladstone | D; Seventh-day Adventist Church | O | 1878 | |
| Multnomah County Camp | Portland | I; Multnomah County Holiness Association | O | 1925 | |
| Northwest Conference Camp | Turner | D; Wesleyan Church | R | | |
| Northwest Region Camp | Portland | D; Fellowship of Bible Churches | R | | |
| Oregon Conference Camp | Aurora | D; Wesleyan Church | O | 1930 | |
| Oregon District Camp | Salem | D; Assembly of God Church | | | |
| Oregon District Camp | Turner | D; United Pentecostal Church | R | | |
| Oregon State Camp | Jefferson | D; Church of God (Servant) | O | 1950 | |
| Oregon–Pacific Northern District Camp | Jennings Lodge | D; Church of the Nazarene | O | | |
| Oregon–Pacific Southern District Camp | Rogue River | D; Church of the Nazarene | R | | |
| Pacific Northwest Camp | Portland | D; Church of God of Prophecy | R | | |
| Rogue River Camp | Rogue River | D; Church of God (Holiness) | O | 1908 | Joel F. Milton |
| Southern Oregon Camp | Medford | D; Seventh Day Adventist Church | R | | |
| State Camp | Brooks | D; Church of God (Anderson) | O | | |
| Tilkum Retreat Center | Newberg | I . . . | | | |
| Twin Rocks Conf. Center | Rockaway | D; Friends Church | | | |

| Name | City | Affiliation | O/R | Year | Founder |
|------|------|-------------|-----|------|---------|
| Yamhill County Holiness Camp | Yamhill | I; Yamhill County Holiness Association | O | 1950 | |
| **Pennsylvania** | | | | | |
| Allegheny East Conference Camp | Pine Forge | D; Seventh Day Adventist Church | O | | |
| Armstrong County Camp | Kittaning | I . . . | O | 1930 | |
| Auburn Camp | Auburn | D; German Eldership of the Church of God | O | 1914 | |
| Barnsboro Camp | Barnsboro | I . . . | | | |
| Belsano Camp | Belsano | I; Cambria and Indiana County Holiness Association | O | 1925 | |
| Bentleyville Camp | Bentleyville | I; Bentleyville Union Holiness Association | O | 1867 | Rev. T. C. McClure et al. |
| Berrysburg Camp | Berrysburg | I . . . | | | |
| Bethel Camp | Center Valley | D; Evangelical Christian Church | R | 1981 | |
| Bethel Camp | Center Valley | I . . . | R | 1981 | Mrs. S. E. Hilbert |
| Bethel Park Camp | New Paris | D; United Methodist Church | O | 1906 | |
| Beulah Camp | Gordon | D; God's Missionary Church | O | 1940 | Rev. Charles Wolfgang |
| Bible Brethren Camp | Kittany | D; Bible Brethren Fellowship | O | 1976 | |
| Bible Club Camp | Erie | I . . . | | | |
| Bible Truth Camp | Dunbar | I . . . | | | |

| Camp Name | Location | Affiliation | | Year | Director |
|---|---|---|---|---|---|
| Big Knob Camp | Rochester | I; . . . | | 1943 | |
| Bit of Heaven Camp | Franklin | I; . . . | | | |
| Black Rock Retreat Center | Quarryville | D; Mennonite Church | O | | |
| Blue Mountain Retreat | Ringgold | I; . . . | O | 1974 | Chris Dornbeirer |
| Bowman Park Camp | Bowmantown | D; United Methodist Church | O | 1891 | |
| Bradford County Camp | Sayre | I; . . . | | | |
| Brandywine Summit Camp | Delaware County | D; United Methodist Church | O | 1865 | |
| Brookville Camp | Brookville | D; Free Methodist Church | O | | |
| Brush Valley Retreat | Homer City | | | | |
| Bucktail Camp | Cranberry | I; . . . | O | | |
| Camp Allegheny | Monroeville | I; . . . | | | |
| Camp Allegheny | Stoystown | D; United Methodist Church | O | | |
| Camp Andrews | Holtwood | D; Mennonite Church | | | |
| Camp Hebron | Halifax | I; Camp Hebron Association | O | | |
| Camp Innabah | Downingtown | D; United Methodist Church | O | 1929 | |
| Camp Iriquoiana | Halsted | | | | |
| Camp Joy-El | Greencastle | | | | |
| Camp Lambec | Mercer | | O | | |
| Camp Men-O-Lan | Quakertown | D; Mennonite Church | O | 1941 | |
| Camp Shiloh | Montrose | D; Shiloh Apostolic Temple of Philadelphia | O | 1950 | |
| Camp Timberedge | Beach Lake | D; Free Methodist Church | O | | |
| Carsonville Camp | Halifax | I; . . . | | | |
| Central Holiness Camp | Belleville | I; . . . | | | |
| Central Manor Camp | Mountville | D; Churches of God in North America (General Eldership) | O | 1892 | Dr. I. A. MacDonald |

| Name | City | Affiliation | O/R | Year | Founder |
|---|---|---|---|---|---|
| Central Oak Heights Camp | Milton | I; Central Oak Heights Association | O | 1894 | |
| Cherry Run Camp | Rimersburg | D; United Methodist Church | O | 1862 | Local Methodists |
| Chester Heights Camp | Chester Heights | I . . . | O | 1872 | |
| Christ's Rescue Mission Camp | Center Valley | A; Christ's Rescue Mission | R | | |
| Cleona Camp | Cleona | D; United Christian Church | O | 1896 | |
| Conservative Brethren Camp | Clinton | D; Conservative Brethren | R | 1980 | |
| Crystal Spring Camp | Crystal Spring | D; United Methodist Church | O | 1885 | |
| Dimock Camp | Dimock | D; United Methodist Church | O | 1862 | Local Methodist pastors |
| Doubling Gap Center | Newville | I; Doubling Gap Center, Inc. | | | |
| Drums Camp | Drums | D; United Methodist Church | R | 1991 | Rev. Wesley Stanton-Light and Dr. Kenneth O. Brown |
| Duncannon Camp | Duncannon | D; Church of God (Servant) | O | 1980 | |
| Edinboro Family Camp | Edinboro | D; Christian Missionary Alliance Church | | | |
| Elizabethville Camp | Elizabethville | D; United Methodist Church | O | 1879 | |
| Elkland Camp | Forksville | I; Elkland Holiness Camp Meeting Association | O | 1906 | |
| Erie District Camp | Erie | D; Free Methodist Church | O | | |
| Fairview Village Camp | Fairview | I . . . | | | |
| Family Camp | Kane | A; Association of Evangelical Churches | R | 1980 | |
| Fellowship Camp | Hanover | D; God's Missionary Church | O | 1952 | Rev. Ralph Rudisill |
| Fellowship Camp | Hanover | I . . . | O | 1951 | |

| Camp | Location | Affiliation | | Year | Notes |
|---|---|---|---|---|---|
| Fellowship of the Cross Camp | Lake Pleasant | I . . . | | | |
| Fink Ridge Camp | Titusville | D; National Association of Holiness Churches | O | 1970 | |
| First Bible Holiness Camp | Venus | D; First Bible Holiness Church | O | 1957 | Rev. L. F. Stroud |
| Full Gospel Assemblies Family Camp | Coatesville | D; Full Gospel Assemblies International | R | 1965 | Dr. A. M. Strauser |
| General Assembly Camp | Boyertown | D; Church of God (Anderson) | O | | |
| God's Bible Holiness Church Camp | Center Valley | D; God's Bible Holiness Church | R | 1960 | |
| Goodrich Camp | Goodrich | I . . . | O | 1960 | |
| Gospel Missionary Camp | Hughesville | A; Gospel Missionary Association | R | 1970 | |
| Grace Brethren Retreat Center | Denver | D; Grace Brethren Church | O | | |
| Greenwood Hills Bible Conference | Fayetteville | | | | |
| Harvest Time Camp | Center Valley | D; God's Missionary Church | R | | |
| Hayes Grove Camp | Dawson | I . . . | O | 1950 | |
| Herndon Camp | Herndon | D; Evangelical Congregational Church | O | 1874 | |
| Hickory Grove Camp | Greenville | D; International Pentecostal Holiness Church | O | 1925 | |
| Highland Park Camp | Sellersville | D; United Methodist Church | O | 1893 | |
| Holiness Gospel Camp | Newberrytown | I . . . | O | 1957 | |
| Hughesville Camp | Hughesville | I; Hughesville Camp Meeting Association | O | 1904 | |
| Hyndman Camp | Hyndman | D; United Methodist Church | O | | |

| Name | City | Affiliation | O/R | Year | Founder |
|---|---|---|---|---|---|
| Judson Camp and Retreat Center | Springfield | D; Baptist Church | | | |
| Jumonville Conference Center | Hopwood | D; United Methodist Church | O | | |
| Kane Camp | Kane | D; Free Methodist Church | O | | |
| Kenbrook Bible Camp | Lebanon | D; Brethren in Christ Church | O | 1950 | Fairland Brethren in Christ Church |
| Kiski Valley Camp | Apollo | D; Free Methodist Church | O | | |
| Kiski Valley Camp | Apollo | I . . . | R | | |
| Ladore Conference Center | Waymart | D; Salvation Army | O | 1967 | |
| Lamar Camp | Lamar | D; Free Methodist Church | O | | |
| Landisville Camp Meeting | Landisville | I; Landisville Camp Meeting Association | O | 1867 | Methodist clergy and laity |
| Laurel Highlands Camp | Aliquippi | D; Baptist Church | | | |
| Laurel Lake Camp | Reading | D; Seventh Day Adventist Church | O | | |
| Laurel Lake Family Camp | Rossiter | D; Seventh Day Adventist Church | O | | |
| Laurelville Mennonite Center | Mt. Pleasant | D; Mennonite Church | | | |
| Lavelle Camp | Lavelle | D; Evangelical Methodist Church | O | 1929 | |
| Lebanon Valley Holiness Camp | Ono | I; Lebanon Valley Holiness Camp Meeting Association | O | 1929 | |
| Lewistown Valley Camp | Tamaqua | I . . . | O | 1905 | Jay Heisler |
| Life Line Hour Camp | Sellersville | I . . . | | 1970 | |

| Camp | Location | Affiliation | Type | Year | Leader |
|---|---|---|---|---|---|
| Mahaffey Camp | Mahaffey | D; Christian Missionary Alliance Church | O | 1920 | |
| Manahath Camp | Williamsburg | D; Evangelical Methodist Church | O | 1954 | |
| Milford Park Camp | Zionsville | I . . . | O | 1927 | |
| Monteagle Sunday School Assembly [Chautauqua] | Monteagle | I . . . | O | 1882 | |
| Montrose Bible Conference | Montrose | I; Montrose Bible Conference Association | O | 1908 | Dr. Reuben A. Torrey |
| Mt. Gilead Conference Center | Abington | | | | |
| Mt. Gretna Camp | Mt. Gretna | D; United Methodist Church | O | 1892 | |
| Mt. Joy Camp | Milmont | I . . . | O | 1950 | |
| Mt. Lebanon Camp | Lebanon | D; United Methodist Church | O | 1892 | |
| Mount of Blessings Camp | Carroll | D; God's Missionary Church | O | 1948 | Rev. Joe Hoffman |
| Mt. Olivet Camp | Dillsburg | I . . . | O | 1862 | |
| National Association Camp | West Middlesex | D; Church of God (Anderson) | O | 1917 | |
| New Castle District Camp | New Castle | D; Free Methodist Church | O | | |
| New Castle Indoor Camp | New Castle | D; Free Methodist Church | R | 1975 | |
| Oak Hill Camp | Franklin | D; United Brethren Church | O | 1936 | |
| Oakland Mills Camp | Oakland | D; Evangelical Methodist Church | O | 1960 | |
| Oil City District Camp | Pleasantville | D; Free Methodist Church | O | 1897 | |
| Paradise Lake Retreat Center | Bushkill | I . . . | | | |
| Patterson Grove Camp | Huntington Mills | D; United Methodist Church | O | 1835 | |
| Peniel Camp | Conneautville | I; Peniel Holiness Association | O | 1896 | |
| Penns Creek Camp | Penns Creek | D; God's Missionary Church | O | 1935 | Rev. George Stroub |

| Name | City | Affiliation | O/R | Year | Founder |
|---|---|---|---|---|---|
| Pennsylvania Camp | Hamburg | D; Seventh Day Adventist Church | | | |
| Pennsylvania Camp | Somerset | D; Church of God of Prophecy | | | |
| Pennsylvania Chautauqua, The | Mt. Gretna | D; United Methodist Church | R | | |
| Pennsylvania District Camp | Redrock | D; United Pentecostal Church | | | |
| Pennsylvania-Delaware District Camp | Carlisle | D; Assembly of God Church | | | |
| Penn-York Camp | Ulysses | I; . . . | O | 1969 | |
| Perkasie Park Camp | Perkasie | D; United Methodist Church | O | 1882 | Local Methodists |
| Pine Ridge Camp | Franklin | I; . . . | O | 1970 | |
| Pine Valley Conference Center | Ellwood | | | | |
| Pinebrook Bible Conference | Stroudsburg | D; Bible Fellowship Church, Inc. | O | 1933 | |
| Pineridge Holiness Camp | Lickingville | D; Pilgrim Holiness Church of New York | O | 1966 | Rev. Al Payea et al. |
| Pittsburgh District Camp | Butler | D; Church of the Nazarene | O | 1944 | |
| Pleasant Ridge Camp | McConnelsburg | I; . . . | | 1960 | |
| Pleasant Ridge Nazarene Camp | Harrisonville | D; Church of the Nazarene | | 1990 | |
| Pocono Mountain Bible Conference | Gouldsboro | D; Primitive Methodist Church | O | 1954 | |
| Pocono Plateau | Cresco | D; United Methodist Church | O | | |
| Port Matilda Camp | Port Matilda | I; Bald Eagle Valley Holiness Association | R | 1949 | |

| Name | Location | Affiliation | O/R | Year | Notes |
|---|---|---|---|---|---|
| Randolph County Camp | Randolph | I; ... | | 1970 | Rev. William T. Swindells |
| Rawlinsville Camp | Rawlinsville | D; United Methodist Church | O | 1885 | |
| Reading Holiness Camp | Reading | I; Reading Holiness Association | O | 1900 | |
| Reformed Free Methodist Camp | Flatwoods | D; Reformed Free Methodist Church | O | 1965 | |
| Refreshing Mountain Camp | Stevens | I; Refreshing Mountain Camp, Inc. | | | |
| Revival Time in America Camp | Center Valley | I; ... | R | 1991 | |
| Rhodes Grove Camp | Chambersburg | I; ... | O | 1960 | |
| Roberts Memorial Camp | Dallas | D; Free Methodist Church | O | 1960 | |
| Rome Camp | Titusville | I; Rome Interdenominational Camp Association | | 1960 | |
| Rosedale Grove Camp | Lauerdale | D; Evangelical Congregational Church | O | 1924 | |
| Roxbury Holiness Camp | Roxbury | D; Brethren in Christ Church | O | 1935 | Local ministers and laity of the denomination |
| Schwartz Valley Holiness Camp | Richfield | I; ... | O | 1950 | |
| Seneca Hills Bible Conference | Franklin | I; ... | | | |
| Seyfert Camp | Gibralter | D; Evangelical Christian Church | O | 1893 | |
| Spruce Lake Retreat | Canadensis | D; Mennonite Church | O | | |
| Stabler's Grove Camp | Salladasburg | I; ... | | 1936 | |

| Name | City | Affiliation | O/R | Year | Founder |
|---|---|---|---|---|---|
| Stoneboro Camp | Stoneboro | D; Original Allegheny Conference of the Wesleyan Methodist Church | O | 1900 | Rev. P. B. Campbell et al. |
| Stoverdale Camp | Hummelstown | I... | O | 1872 | |
| Strout's Holiness Camp | Franklin | I... | O | 1950 | |
| Summit Camp | Cooperstown | I... | | 1970 | |
| Summit Camp | Titusville | D; Evangelical Wesleyan Church | O | 1963 | Rev. N. J. McCleery |
| Summit Grove Camp | New Freedom | D; Christian Missionary Alliance Church | O | 1900 | |
| Sunbury Camp | Hummel's Wharf | I; God's Holiness Grove Camp Meeting Association | O | 1919 | |
| Tarentum Camp | Natrona Heights | I; Pittsburgh-Tarentum Camp Meeting Association | O | 1849 | |
| Tarentum Camp | Tarentum | D; United Methodist Church | O | 1849 | |
| Tel Hai Camp and Conference Center | Honey Brook | D; Mennonite Church | O | | |
| Transylvania Bible School | Freeport | I; Transylvania Bible School | O | 1960 | Dr. Henry Shilling |
| Tri-State Camp | Clinton | I; Tri-State Holiness Association | O | 1924 | |
| Tri-State District Camp | Cherry Town | D; Bible Missionary Church | R | 1960 | |
| Tuscarara Resource Center | Mt. Bethel | I; Mt. Bethel Christian Ministries, Inc. | O | | |
| Twin Pines Bible Conference | Stroudsburg | I... | O | | |

| | | | | |
|---|---|---|---|---|
| Twin Pines Camp | Shamokin | D; Evangelical Congregational Church | O | 1964 | |
| Twin Pines Camp | Snydersville | I . . . | | 1970 | |
| Uniontown Area Camp | Fairchance | D; Free Methodist Church | O | 1956 | Bishops Lehman and Gress |
| United Zion Camp | Manheim | D; United Zion Church | O | | |
| Visitation Evangelism Camp | Center Valley | I . . . | R | | |
| Waldenheim Camp | Allentown | D; Evangelical Congregational Church | O | 1904 | |
| Warfordsburg Camp | Warfordsburg | D; Free Methodist Church | O | | |
| Wesley Woods | Grand Valley | D; United Methodist Church | ☉ | | |
| Wesleyan Bible Holiness Camp | Roxbury | D; Wesleyan Bible Holiness Church | R | 1965 | |
| Western Pennsylvania District Camp | Lamar | D; Wesleyan Church | O | | |
| Westminster Highlands | Mercer | D; Presbyterian Church | | | |
| White Hall Camp | Emlenton | D; Church of God (Anderson) | O | 1891 | |
| York County Camp | Hanover | I; York County Holiness Association | O | 1894 | |

**Rhode Island**

| | | | | |
|---|---|---|---|---|
| Camp Greene | Greene | D; Advent Christian Church | O | 1871 | |
| Camp Greene | Greene | D; Free Methodist Church | R | | |
| Canonicus Camp and Conference Center | Exeter | | | | |
| Portsmouth Camp | Portsmouth | I; Portsmouth Camp Meeting Association | O | 1890 | Rev. Seth C. Rees |

| Name | City | Affiliation | O/R | Year | Founder |
|---|---|---|---|---|---|
| **South Carolina** | | | | | |
| Beech Springs Camp | Pelzer | D; International Pentecostal Holiness Church | O | 1935 | |
| Cattle Creek Camp | Branchville | D; United Methodist Church | O | 1790 | |
| Church of God Camp | Darlington | D; Church of God (Anderson) | O | | |
| Columbus County Camp | Tabor City | D; Pentecostal Fire Baptized Holiness Church | O | 1943 | Rev. S. B. Norton |
| Community Lighthouse Camp | Pickens | I; ... | O | 1984 | |
| Cypress Camp | Ridgeville | I; United Methodist Church | O | 1794 | |
| Ebenezer Holiness Baptist Camp | Columbia | I; Holiness Baptist Church | O | 1964 | |
| Elgin Camp | Elgin | D; Congregational Holiness Church, Inc. | O | 1965 | |
| Epworth Camp | Ninety-Six | I; ... | O | 1905 | Rev. W. P. B. Kinard |
| Hemingway Camp | Hemingway | I; ... | O | 1962 | |
| Holly Hill Camp | Holly Hill | D; Church of God (Servant) | O | 1970 | |
| Holmes Bible School Camp | Greenville | D; International Pentecostal Holiness Church | O | 1912 | Rev. N. J. Holmes |
| Indian Field Camp | St. George | D; United Methodist Church | O | 1795 | |
| Longridge Retreat Center | Ridgeway | | | | |
| Look-Up Retreat | Travelers Rest | | | | |
| Mayo Tabernacle Camp | Spartansburg | I; ... | O | | |
| Mt. Carmel Camp | Fort Mill | I; ... | | | |
| Prospect Camp | Rowesville | D; United Methodist Church | O | | |

| Camp | Location | Denomination | | Year | |
|---|---|---|---|---|---|
| St. Luke Camp | Reeseville | D; United Methodist Church | O | | |
| St. Paul's Camp | Harleyville | D; United Methodist Church | O | 1860 | |
| Shady Grove Camp | Harleyville | D; United Methodist Church | O | 1860 | |
| South Atlantic Camp | Orangeburg | D; Seventh Day Adventist Church | O | | |
| South Carolina Camp | Mauldin | D; Church of God of Prophecy | O | | |
| South Carolina Camp | Westminster | D; Pentecostal Fire Baptized Holiness Church | O | 1947 | B. O. McClain et al. |
| South Carolina Conference Camp | Greer | D; Wesleyan Church | O | 1900 | |
| South Carolina Conference Camp | Lake City | D; International Pentecostal Holiness Church | O | 1935 | |
| South Carolina District Camp | Batesburg | D; Church of the Nazarene | O | | |
| South Carolina District Camp | Batesville | D; United Pentecostal Church | R | | |
| State Camp | Bishopville | D; Church of God (Anderson) | O | | |

## South Dakota

| Camp | Location | Denomination | | Year | |
|---|---|---|---|---|---|
| Allen Camp | Allen | D; Church of God (Independent Holiness People) | O | 1970 | |
| Allen Sioux Indian Camp | Allen | D; Church of God (Independent Holiness People) | R | 1970 | |
| Beulah Holiness Camp | Brookings | I; . . . | R | 1900 | |
| Black Hills Indian Camp | Hot Springs | D; Wesleyan Church | O | 1930 | |
| Byron Bible Camp | Huron | | | | |
| Cedar Canyon Camp | Rapid City | D; Wesleyan Church | O | 1940 | |
| Church of God Camp | Tuthill | D; Church of God (Holiness) | R | 1970 | |

| Name | City | Affiliation | O/R | Year | Founder |
|---|---|---|---|---|---|
| Church of God Camp | Brookings | D; Church of God (Anderson) | O | 1904 | |
| Indian Holiness Camp | Spring Creek | A; Society of Indian Missions Inc. | O | 1950 | |
| Midwest Bible Camp | Watertown | A; Midwest Evangelistic Association | O | 1955 | Keith Williams |
| North Dakota–South Dakota Camp | Bismarck | D; Church of God of Prophecy | R | | |
| Prairie Home Church Bible Camp | Faith | I... | | 1975 | |
| Riverside Camp | Mitchell | I; South Dakota Holiness Association | O | 1893 | Rev. J. E. Norvell et al. |
| South Dakota District Camp | Rapid City | D; Assembly of God Church | | | |
| Tuthill Camp | Tuthill | I; Southwest South Dakota Holiness Association | O | 1940 | |
| Whetstone Valley Camp | Wilmot | I; Whetstone Valley Holiness Association | O | 1925 | |
| Woodland Holiness Camp | Willow Lake | I... | O | 1950 | |

### Tennessee

| Name | City | Affiliation | O/R | Year | Founder |
|---|---|---|---|---|---|
| Bible Methodist Camp Camp Ridgedale | Knoxville Vableer | D; Bible Methodist Church | O | 1970 | |
| Cedine Bible Camp and Conference | Spring City | I... | O | 1946 | |
| Church of God Camp | Greenville | D; Church of God (Anderson) | O | 1900 | |

| Camp | Location | Affiliation | | Year | Founder/Notes |
|---|---|---|---|---|---|
| Church of God Camp | Sugar Tree | D; Church of God (Anderson) | O | 1935 | |
| Cumberland Grove Camp | Jamestown | D; United Methodist Church | O | 1987 | |
| Doe River Gorge Conference Center | Elizabethton | I . . . | | | |
| Eagle Ridge Renewal Center | McMinnville | D; Free Methodist Church | O | 1970 | |
| East Tennessee District Camp | Knoxville | D; Church of the Nazarene | R | 1915 | Rev. J. O. McClurkan |
| Eleazer Camp | Madisonville | D; United Methodist Church | O | 1840 | |
| Flint Gap Mission Camp | Knoxville | I . . . | | 1950 | |
| Forest Chapel Camp | Westmoreland | D; Free Methodist Church | O | 1890 | Rev. J. W. W. Kelly et al. |
| Georgia-Cumberland Conference | Collegedale | D; Seventh Day Adventist Church | O | | |
| Hillmont Retreat Center | White Bluff | | | | |
| Joyner's Camp | Somerville | D; United Methodist Church | O | 1892 | |
| Kentucky-Tennessee Camp | Portland | D; Seventh Day Adventist Church | O | | |
| Kern Camp | Beersheba Springs | D; United Methodist Church | O | 1941 | |
| Kleey's Chapel Camp | Burlison | D; Church of God (Holiness) | O | 1960 | |
| Lighthouse Christian Camp | Smithville | | | | |
| Louisville Camp | Louisville | I . . . | O | 1887 | |
| Mountain Lake Ranch | Dandridge | | | | |
| National Camp | Glendale | I; National Campground Association | O | 1873 | Members of several local denominations |
| Overton Camp | Rock Island | D; Church of God (Anderson) | | | |
| Southeast Tennessee Camp | Englewood | D; Church of God (Anderson) | | | |
| Spring Creek Camp | | D; United Methodist Church | O | 1850 | |
| Sulphur Springs Camp | Morristown | D; United Methodist Church | O | 1820 | |

| Name | City | Affiliation | O/R | Year | Founder |
|------|------|-------------|-----|------|---------|
| Tabernacle Camp | Brownsville | D; United Methodist Church | O | 1826 | |
| Tennessee Camp | Cleveland | D; Church of God of Prophecy | | | |
| Tennessee Camp | Lawrenceburg | D; Congregational Methodist Church | O | 1960 | |
| Tennessee District Camp | Parsons | D; United Pentecostal Church | | | |
| Tennessee District Center | Dickson | D; Church of the Nazarene | O | 1970 | |
| Tennessee State Holiness Camp | Dayton | I; Tennessee State Holiness Association | O | 1940 | Rev. George Blanchard |
| Tri-State Conference Camp | Memphis | D; International Pentecostal Holiness Church | O | | |
| Wears Valley Retreat | Sevierville | | | | |
| West Tennessee Camp | Big Rock | D; Church of God (Anderson) | | 1970 | |
| West Tennessee Camp | Savannah | D; Bible Methodist Church | | 1970 | |
| Western District Camp | Jamestown | D; Bible Methodist Connection of Churches | R | 1970 | |

Texas

| Name | City | Affiliation | O/R | Year | Founder |
|------|------|-------------|-----|------|---------|
| Abilene District Camp | Plainview | D; Church of the Nazarene | O | 1890 | |
| Alto Frio Camp | San Antonio | I . . . | O | | |
| Aubrey Camp | Aubrey | D; Congregational Methodist Church | | | |
| Bethel Camp | Carthage | D; United Methodist Church | O | 1860 | |
| Bloy's Cowboy Camp | Ft. Stockton | I; Ranchmen's Camp Meetings in the Southwest | O | 1890 | Rev. W. B. Bloys |

| Name | Location | Status | Affiliation | Year | Owner |
|---|---|---|---|---|---|
| Blue Barn Retreat | Alba | | | | |
| Brookhaven Retreat | Hawkins | | | | |
| Camp Arrowhead | Cleburne | O | D; Church of the Nazarene | 1941 | |
| Camp Copass | Denton | O | D; Baptist Church | | |
| Camp Inspiration | Eastland | | D; Church of God (Anderson) | | |
| Center for Christian Growth | New Braunfels | | | | |
| Central Latin American Camp | Cleburne | R | D; Church of the Nazarene | 1970 | |
| Circle 6 Ranch | Stanton | | D; Baptist Church | | |
| Cowboy Camp | Mason | R | A; Ranchmen's Camp Meetings in the Southwest | 1990 | |
| East Texas Camp | Nacadoches | | D; Church of God (Anderson) | | |
| Evangelical Brethren Camp | Mt. Calm | | D; Evangelical Brethren Church | | |
| Forest Glen Camp | Houston | | | | |
| Harambe Oaks Ranch | Fischer | | D; Baptist Church | | |
| Heart of Texas Camp | Brownwood | | | | |
| H. E. Butt Foundation Camp | Kerrville | O | I; H. E. Butt Foundation | | |
| Hidden Acres Conference Center | Kauffman | | | | |
| His Hill Conference Center | Comfort | | | | |
| Houston District Camp | Huntsville | R | D; Church of the Nazarene | 1950 | |
| Jan-Kay Ranch | Detroit | | I; Jan-Kay Ranch, Inc. | 1947 | |
| Lakeview Methodist Assembly | Palestine | O | D; United Methodist Church | | |
| Little George Havens' Cowboy Camp | Coleman | O | I; Ranchmen's Camp Meetings in the Southwest | 1966 | Mr. & Mrs. George Havens |

| Name | City | Affiliation | O/R | Year | Founder |
|---|---|---|---|---|---|
| Lone Star Camp | Athens | D; Seventh Day Adventist Church | O | 1858 | |
| Methodist Camp Grounds | Chappel | D; United Methodist Church | O | 1923 | |
| Mt. of Blessings Camp | Atlanta | I . . . | | 1898 | Rev. W. T. Currie |
| Noonday Camp | Hallsville | I . . . | O | | |
| North Texas District Camp | Irving | D; Assembly of God Church | R | | |
| Paisano Baptist Assembly | Paisano Mountain | D; Baptist Church | O | 1921 | Rev. L. R. Millican |
| Panhandle Camp | Amarillo | D; International Pentecostal Holiness Church | O | 1935 | |
| Pine Cove Conference Center | Tyler | | | | |
| Pineywoods Camp | Woodlake | D; Baptist Church | | | |
| Pleasant Hill Camp | Franklin County | D; United Methodist Church | O | 1873 | |
| Sandy Springs Camp | Center | I . . . | | 1954 | |
| Scottsville Nazarene Camp | Scottsville | D; Church of the Nazarene | O | 1886 | Rev. F. T. Browning |
| South Central Spanish Camp | San Antonio | D; Church of God of Prophecy | | | |
| South Texas District Camp | Kerrville | D; Assembly of God Church | | | |
| State Camp | Hallettsville | D; Church of God (Anderson) | | | |
| Sunshine Valley Holiness Camp | Donna | I . . . | O | 1970 | Rev. A. H. Clark and Rev. Hunter |
| Texas Baptist Camp | Palacios | D; Baptist Church | | | |
| Texas Camp | Weatherford | D; Church of God of Prophecy | O | | |
| Texas Conference Camp | Dallas | D; International Pentecostal Holiness Church | R | | |
| Texas Conference Camp | Garrison | D; Congregational Methodist Church | O | 1950 | |

| Texas Conference Camp | Keene | D; Seventh Day Adventist Church | O | | |
| Texas District Camp | Lufkin | D; United Pentecostal Church | | | |
| Texico District Camp | Amarillo | D; United Pentecostal Church | | | |
| Timberline Conference Center | Lindale | D; Baptist Church | | | |
| Union Camp | Waco | I . . . | O | 1879 | |
| West Texas District Camp | Lubbock | D; Assembly of God Church | | | |
| Woodland Hills Retreat | Whitesboro | | | | |
| Y L Cowboy Camp | Canadian | I; Ranchmen's Camp Meetings in the Southwest | O | 1981 | |
| Zephyr Baptist Camp | Sandia | D; Baptist Church | | | |

## Utah

| Nevada-Utah Conference Camp | Springville | D; Seventh Day Adventist Church | O | | |

## Vermont

| Ithiel Falls Camp | Johnson | I; Ithiel Falls Campground Association | O | 1898 | Rev. Ithiel T. Johnson; land donated by Mr. Rice |
| Lyndonville Camp | Lyndonville | I . . . | | | |
| White River Camp | White River Junction | D; Advent Christian Church | O | 1887 | |

## Virginia

| Bloxom Camp | Bloxom | I . . . | O | | |

| Name | City | Affiliation | O/R | Year | Founder |
|---|---|---|---|---|---|
| Blue Ridge Camp | Chatham | I; Blue Ridge Christian Ministries, Inc. | O | 1977 | |
| Blue Ridge Second Blessing Camp | Check | D; Evangelical Wesleyan Church | O | 1984 | |
| Blue Ridge Second Blessing Holiness Camp | Copperhill | I . . . | O | 1970 | |
| Buckingham Tabernacle Camp | Buckingham | D; Wesleyan Church | O | 1900 | Rev. Leroy Banks, Mr. Garnett, and Jimmy Jones |
| Camp Bethel | Wise | I . . . | R | | |
| Camp Bethel | Wise | I; Bible Mission of Southwest Virginia, Inc. | O | 1939 | |
| Camp Blue Ridge | Montebello | | | | |
| Camp Christi | Christiansburg | D; Church of God (Anderson) | O | | |
| Camp Shenandoah Springs | Madison | | | | |
| Camp Wakefield | Wakefiled | D; Evangelical Friends Church | O | | |
| Chesapeake Camp | Matthews | I; Chesapeake Interdenominational Holiness Camp Meeting Association | O | 1879 | E. T. Adams, Wilbur Diggs, et al. |
| Chesapeake Camp | Onemo | I . . . | O | | |
| Christiansburg Camp | Christiansburg | I . . . | O | 1959 | |
| Church of God Camp | Bedford | D; Church of God (Anderson) | O | 1945 | |
| Church of God Camp | Manassas | D; Church of God (Universal) | O | 1945 | |
| Church of God Camp | Roanoke | D; Church of God (Anderson) | O | 1920 | |

| Name | Location | Status | Year | Affiliation |
|---|---|---|---|---|
| Covenant Village Conference Center | Vienna | | | |
| Dogwood Lake Conference Center | Winchester | | | |
| Dranesville Camp Association | Herndon | O | 1895 | I; Dranesville Camp Meeting |
| East Virginia Conference Camp | Hopewell | O | 1948 | D; International Pentecostal Holiness Church |
| Grace Bible Camp | Goshen | | | I . . . |
| Grace Bible Camp and Retreat Center | Goshen | | | |
| Hallelujah Echo Camp | Pearisburg | | 1975 | I . . . |
| Highland Retreat | Bergton | | | |
| Holy Ghost Campmeeting | Ashland | O | 1954 | I; Calvary Pentecostal Tabernacle |
| Jonesville Camp | Jonesville | O | 1810 | D; United Methodist |
| Liberty Oaks Camp | Lynchburg | O | | |
| Master's Inn, The | Altavista | | | I . . . |
| Missionary Methodist Community Camp | Buckingham | R | 1988 | D; Missionary Methodist Church |
| Patomac Conference Camp | New Market | O | | D; Seventh Day Adventist Church |
| Piedmont Camp | Shawsville | O | 1950 | D; International Pentecostal Holiness Church |
| Pourtsmouth Camp | Pourtsmouth | O | 1947 | D; International Pentecostal Holiness Church |
| Robert Sheffey Memorial Camp | Trigg | O | 1979 | D; United Methodist Church |

| Name | City | Affiliation | O/R | Year | Founder |
|------|------|-------------|-----|------|---------|
| Saluda Camp | Saluda | I . . . | O | 1902 | |
| Southside Holiness Camp | Wakefield | I; Southside Virginia Holiness Association | O | 1897 | Rev. John T. Moore |
| Southwest Virginia Holiness Camp | Salem | I; Southwest Virginia Holiness Camp Meeting Association | O | 1896 | D. B. Strouse, Clarence Strouse, Mrs. Fanny Camden, Mrs. C. B. LeFevre, J. J. Tene, and J.L. Early |
| Spotsylvania Camp | Spotsylvania | I; Spotsylvania Holiness Association | O | 1903 | |
| Virginia Camp | Roanoke | D; Church of God of Prophecy | | | |
| Virginia District Camp | Buckingham | D; Church of the Nazarene | O | 1946 | |
| Virginia District Camp | Sprouses Corner | D; United Pentecostal Church | | | |
| Wesleyan Camp | Roanoke | D; Wesleyan Church | O | 1950 | |
| Whyteville Camp | Whyteville | D; International Pentecostal Holiness Church | O | | |
| Williamsburg Christian Retreat Center | Toano | | | | |

**Washington**

| Name | City | Affiliation | O/R | Year | Founder |
|------|------|-------------|-----|------|---------|
| Black Lake Camp | Olympia | D; Church of God (Anderson) | O | | |
| Black Lake Conference Center | Olympia | | | | |
| Camp Berachah | Auburn | | | | |
| Camp Casey Conference Center | Coupeville | | | | |

| Camp | Location | Association | Type | Year | Founders / Notes |
|---|---|---|---|---|---|
| Cedar Lake Camp | Harrah | D; Grace Brethren Church | | | |
| Cedar Springs Conference Center | Lake Stevens | | R | | |
| Church of God Camp | Spokane | D; Church of God (Anderson) | O | 1911 | Rev. E. B. Reese, local Methodist pastor |
| Clark County Camp | Orchards | I; Clark County Holiness Association | | | |
| Crista Camps | Poulsbo | I . . . | | | |
| Discovery Bay Camp | Port Townsend | I; Jefferson County Holiness Association | O | 1924 | Rev. A. O. Quall, Mrs. W. A. Neville, Rev. J. E. Bradley, Mrs. E. Cowgill, and Rev. A. P. Arnold |
| Eatonville Camp | Eatonville | D; Seventh-day Adventist Church | | | |
| Emanuel Camp | Tacoma | I; Pierce County Holiness Association | O | 1913 | |
| Entiat Camp | Entiat | I; Chelean County Holiness Association | O | 1927 | Ida Brown, Arthur Barcart, F. W. Carpher. Rev. P. A. Cohagen, George Davis, Mrs. Harry Johnson, and Rev. and Mrs. Everett Scotten |
| Ferndale Camp | Ferndale | I; Northwest Washington Holiness Association | O | 1895 | Carl J. Kallgren, C. W. Jones, C. C. Hoskens, A. Warren, William Creasey, Sherman Johnson, and W. M. Cissons |
| Firs Conference Center, The | Bellingham | | | | |
| Fruitland Indian Camp | Fruitland | D; Assembly of God Church | | | |

| Name | City | Affiliation | O/R | Year | Founder |
|---|---|---|---|---|---|
| Green Mountain Camp | Lacamas | I . . . | O | 1923 | B. G. Clemens |
| Inland Empire Camp | Deer Lake | D; Church of God (Anderson) | O | | |
| Kolbe Kamp | Spokane | D; United Methodist Church | O | 1909 | |
| Lake Retreat Camp | Ravensdale | D; Baptist Church | | | |
| Lynnwood Nazarene Camp | Lynnwood | D; Church of the Nazarene | | | |
| Malo Camp | Malo | D; Seventh Day Adventist Church | | | |
| Mt. Baker Conference Center | Denning | D; Baptist Church | | | |
| Native American Family Camp | Seattle | D; United Methodist Church | R | | |
| Northwest District Camp | Camp Bethel | D; Assembly of God Church | | | |
| Northwest District Camp | Cedar Springs | D; Assembly of God Church | | | |
| Northwest District Camp | Fruitland | D; Assembly of God Church | | | |
| Northwest District Camp | Silver Lake | D; Assembly of God Church | | | |
| Okanagan County Camp | Concully | I; Okanagan County Holiness Association | O | | |
| Pacific Northwest Family Camp | Easton | D; Church of God (Anderson) | | | |
| Pinelow Camp | Spokane | D; Church of the Nazarene | O | | |
| Royal Ridges Retreat | Battle Ground | | O | | |
| Upper Columbia Conference Camp | College Place | D; Seventh Day Adventist Church | O | | |
| Warm Beach Camps and Conference Center | Stanwood | D; Free Methodist Church | O | 1955 | |

| Camp | Location | Affiliation | Status | Year | Contact |
|---|---|---|---|---|---|
| Washington Conference Camp | Auburn | D; Seventh Day Adventist Church | O | | |
| Wesleyan Camp | Clarkston | D; Wesleyan Church | O | 1945 | |

## West Virginia

| Camp | Location | Affiliation | Status | Year | Contact |
|---|---|---|---|---|---|
| Ambassadors for Christ Camp | Huntersville | A; Ambassadors for Christ | O | 1966 | Rev. & Mrs. James Maharaj |
| Appalachian District Camp | Ghent | D; Assembly of God Church | O | 1935 | |
| Black Hills Camp | Grafton | D; Free Methodist Church | O | 1940 | |
| Camp Caesar | Webster Springs | D; Apostolic Christian Church | O | | |
| Camp Towels | Clarksburg | I . . . | | | |
| Camp Victory | Elkview | I . . . | | 1974 | |
| Church of God Camp | Charleston | D; Church of God (Anderson) | | | |
| Church of God Camp | Green Bank | D; Church of God (Servant) | O | 1979 | |
| Craigsville Camp | Cattle | D; Church of God (Anderson) | | | |
| Hartford Camp | Hartford | D; Churches of Christ in Christian Union | O | 1946 | |
| Howell's Mill Assembly | Ona | | | | |
| Indoor Bible Camp | Institute | D; Church of the Nazarene | R | 1965 | |
| Mission Camp | Pt. Pleasant | I . . . | O | 1924 | Rev. C. A. Maddy |
| Morgantown Camp | Morgantown | I; Morgantown Holiness Association | R | 1937 | |
| Mt. Nebo Camp | Mt. Nebo | I; Nicholas County Holiness Association | O | | |
| Mt. Olivet Camp | Hinton | D; Christian Nation Church | O | 1915 | Rev. John W. Harris |

| Name | City | Affiliation | O/R | Year | Founder |
|---|---|---|---|---|---|
| Mt. Salem Revival Grounds | West Union | | | | |
| Mountain State Holiness Camp | Clintonville | I. . . . | | | |
| Peyton's Camp | Hinton | I. . . . | | 1945 | Harry Peyton |
| Pilgrim Faith Camp | Princeton | D; Original Allegheny Conference of the Wesleyan Methodist Church | O | 1955 | |
| Pleasant District Tabernacle Camp | Bruceton Mills | I; Pleasant District Holiness Association | O | 1939 | |
| Potomac District Camp | Falling Waters | D; Assembly of God Church | | | |
| Potomac Park Conference Center | Falling Waters | | | | |
| Rippling Waters Camp | Romance | D; Church of God (Anderson) | | | |
| Susie Chapel Camp | Huntington | D; Church of God (Holiness) | O | 1950 | |
| Valley Vista Adventist Center | Huttonsville | D; Seventh Day Adventist Church | O | | |
| Valley Vista Camp | Elkins | D; Seventh Day Adventist Church | | | |
| Valley Vista Camp | Huttonsville | | | | |
| Wesleyan Chapel Camp | Prosperity | I. . . | | | |
| West Virginia Camp | Charleston | D; Church of God of Prophecy | R | | |
| West Virginia District Camp | Culloden | D; Wesleyan Church | O | 1940 | |
| West Virginia District Camp | Point Pleasant | D; United Pentecostal Church | | | |
| West Virginia District Camp | Summersville | D; Church of the Nazarene | O | 1930 | |

| Name | Location | Affiliation | O/R | Year | Directors |
|---|---|---|---|---|---|
| White Pines Camp | Arbovale | I; White Pines Camp Meeting Association | O | 1938 | Glenn Arbogast, J. B. Orndorff, Mrs. Dessa Tracy, Mrs. Lillian Sutton, and Mrs. David E. Woods |

## Wisconsin

| Name | Location | Affiliation | O/R | Year |
|---|---|---|---|---|
| Arc, The | Osceola | | | |
| Bryan Methodist Camp Grounds | Fon du Lac | D; United Methodist | O | 1890 |
| Burr Camp | Hillsboro | D; Wesleyan Church | O | 1890 |
| Camp Forest Springs | Westboro | I . . . | | 1957 |
| Camp Witwen | Prarie du Sac | D; United Methodist Church | O | 1853 |
| Camp Wonderland | Camp Lake | D; Metropolitan Church Association | R | |
| Church of God Campground | Milwaukee | D; Church of God of Prophecy | O | |
| Covenant Harbor Retreat Center | Lake Geneva | D; Evangelical Covenant Church | | |
| Dells Baptist Camp | Middleton | D; Baptist Church | | |
| Forrest Assembly Grounds | Forrest Junction | D; United Methodist Church | O | 1900 |
| Fort Wilderness | McNaughton | | | |
| Green Lake Conference Center | Green Lake | D; American Baptist | O | 1944 |
| Lake Geneva Conference Center | Lake Geneva | D; Evangelical Covenant Church | O | |
| Lake Waubesa Bible Camp | McFarland | I . . . | | |
| Phantom Ranch Bible Camp | Mukwonago | | | |
| Racine Camp | Racine | I . . . | O | 1909 |

| Name | City | Affiliation | O/R | Year | Founder |
|------|------|-------------|-----|------|---------|
| Riverside Bible Conference | Amherst | | | | |
| Rock Springs Camp | Rock Springs | D; Church of God (Anderson) | O | 1925 | |
| Shell Lake Camp | Shell Lake | D; Church of God (Evening Light) | O | 1975 | |
| Silver Birch Ranch | White Lake | | | | |
| Sky Lodge Camp | Montello | | | | |
| Sky Lodge Christian Camp | Montillco | D; Free Methodist Church | O | 1975 | |
| Spencer Lake Bible Camp | Waupaca | D; Church of the Nazarene | R | | |
| Timber-Lee Center | East Troy | | | | |
| Wesley Woods Conference Center | Williams Bay | D; United Methodist Church | O | | |
| Wisconsin Camp | Milwaukee | D; Church of God of Prophecy | R | | |
| Wisconsin Conference Camp | Westfield | D; Seventh Day Adventist Church | O | | |
| Wisconsin District Camp | Shawano | D; United Pentecostal Church | | | |
| Wisconsin District Camp | Waupaca | D; Assembly of God Church | | | |
| Wonderland Conference Center | Camp Lake | D; The Salvation Army | | | |
| Wood Lake Camp | Grantsburg | D; Baptist Church | | | |

## Wyoming

| | | | | | |
|------|------|-------------|-----|------|---------|
| Camp Story | | | | | |
| Lone Tree Bible Ranch | Glendo | D; Church of God (Anderson) | | | |

| Camp | Location | Affiliation | | Year |
|---|---|---|---|---|
| Mills Spring Camp | Casper | D; Seventh Day Adventist Church | O | |
| Mills Springs Camp | Casper | D; Church of God (Anderson) | | |
| Palo Duro Cowboy Camp | Gruver | I; Ranchmen's Camp Meetings in the Southwest | O | 1985 |
| Prune Creek Camp | | D; Church of God (Anderson) | | |
| Rocky Mountain Lodge | Jackson Hole | | | |
| Wyoming Church | Casper | D; Church of God of Prophecy | R | |
| Wyoming District Camp | Camp Beard | D; Assembly of God Church | O | |

## Foreign Countries

### Canada—Alberta

| Camp | Location | Affiliation | | Year |
|---|---|---|---|---|
| Alberta District Camp | Didsbury | D; The Missionary Church | O | 1905 |
| Alix Camp | Alix | D; Free Methodist Church | O | 1931 |
| Canada West District Camp | Harmatten | D; Church of the Nazarene | | |
| Church of God Camp | Camrose | D; Church of God (Anderson) | | |
| Foothills Camp | Red Deer | D; Seventh Day Adventist Church | | |
| Newbrook Camp | Newbrook | D; Standard Church of America | | |
| Sunchild Indian Camp | Sunchild | A; Society of Indian Missions | O | 1989 |
| Sunnyside Camp | Sylvan Lake | D; Pentecostal Assemblies of Canada | O | 1937 |

| Name | City | Affiliation | O/R | Year | Founder |
|------|------|-------------|-----|------|---------|
| **Canada—British Columbia** | | | | | |
| Camp Hope | Hope | D; Seventh Day Adventist Church | | | |
| Canada Pacific District Camp | Vancouver | D; Church of the Nazarene | | | |
| Fraser Valley Camp | Abbotsford | D; Pentecostal Assemblies of Canada | O | 1933 | |
| Nelson Camp | Nelson | D; Pentecostal Assemblies of Canada | | | |
| Pine Grove Camp | Winfield | D; Free Methodist Church | O | 1950 | |
| Vancouver Island Camp | Nanaimo | D; Pentecostal Assemblies of Canada | O | | |
| **Canada—Manitoba** | | | | | |
| Killainey Camp | Killainey | D; Free Methodist Church | O | 1896 | |
| Manhattan Beach Camp | Manhattan Beach | D; Pentecostal Assemblies of Canada | O | 1919 | |
| Manitoba District Camp | Roblin | D; Free Methodist Church | O | 1925 | |
| **Canada—New Brunswick** | | | | | |
| Beulah Camp | Browns Flats | D; Wesleyan Church | O | 1894 | |

## Canada—Newfoundland

| Woody Acres Camp | St. Johns | D; Seventh Day Adventist Church | | |
|---|---|---|---|---|

## Canada—Nova Scotia

| Berwick Camp | Berwick | D; United Church of Canada | O | 1872 |
|---|---|---|---|---|
| Maritime Conference Camp | Pugwash | D; Seventh Day Adventist Church | | |

## Canada—Ontario

| Bethel Camp | Odessa | D; Standard Church of America | | |
|---|---|---|---|---|
| Braeside Camp | Paris | D; Pentecostal Assemblies of Canada | O | 1934 |
| Brethren in Christ Camp | Niagara Falls | D; Brethren in Christ Church | O | |
| Cedardale Camp | Pefferlaw | D; Church of the Nazarene | O | 1946 |
| Church of God Camp | Arthur | D; Church of God (Anderson) | | |
| Clarksburg Camp | Clarksburg | D; The Wesleyan Church | O | 1900 |
| Cobden Camp | Cobden | D; Free Methodist Church | O | 1920 |
| Independent Holiness Churches Camp | Roblin | D; Independent Holiness Churches | | 1937 |
| Inland Camp | Petersboro | D; Free Methodist Church | O | 1946 |
| Ivanhoe Camp | Ivanhoe | D; Standard Church of America | | |
| Kakabeka Falls Bible Camp | Kakabeka Falls | D; Free Methodist | | 1952 |
| Kitchner Camp | Kitchner | D; The Missionary Church | O | 1887 |
| Lake Elioda Camp | Athens | D; Standard Church of America | | |

| Name | City | Affiliation | O/R | Year | Founder |
|---|---|---|---|---|---|
| Lakeshore Camp | Cobourg | D; Pentecostal Assemblies of Canada | O | 1936 | |
| Light and Life Camp | Elginburg | D; Free Methodist Church | | 1919 | |
| Manitoulin Island Camp | Manitoulin Island | D; Pentecostal Assemblies of Canada | O | 1941 | |
| Muskoka Camp | Severn Bridge | D; Free Methodist Church | O | 1948 | |
| Niagara Camp | Fort Erie | I . . . | | 1982 | |
| Ottowa District Camp | Stittsville | D; Free Methodist Church | O | | |
| Pine Orchard Camp | Newmarket | D; Free Methodist Church | O | 1947 | |
| Reformed Free Methodist Camp | Yarker | D; Reformed Free Methodist Church | | | |
| Rest Acres | Brantford | D; Church of the Nazarene | | | |
| Silver Birches Camp | Kirkland Lake | D; Pentecostal Asssemblies of Canada | O | 1949 | |
| Silver Lake Camp | Maberly | D; Wesleyan Church | O | 1957 | |
| Stayner Camp | Stayner | D; The Missionary Church | O | 1881 | |
| Sydenham Camp | Sydenham | D; Independent Holiness Churches | O | 1920 | |
| Thamesford Bible Camp | London | I . . . | | | |
| Thamesford Camp | Thamesford | D; Free Methodist Church | | | |
| Thunder Bay Camp | Thunder Bay | I . . . | | | |
| Wesley Acres | Picton | D; Free Methodist Church | | | |
| Winchester Camp | Winchester | I . . . | O | 1974 | |
| Zion Hill Camp | Forresters Falls | D; Standard Church of America | | | |

## Canada—Quebec

| | | | | |
|---|---|---|---|---|
| Bois Francs Camp | Saint Clothilde | D; Seventh Day Adventist Church | | |
| Cobden Camp | Shawville | D; Free Methodist Church | | |

## Canada—Saskatchewan

| | | | | |
|---|---|---|---|---|
| Arlington Beach Camp | Cymric | D; Free Methodist Church | O | 1918 |
| Camp Whitesand | Theodore | D; Seventh Day Adventist Church | O | |
| Echo Camp | Echo | D; United Methodist Church | | |
| Independent Holiness Churches Camp | Admiral | D; Independent Holiness Churches | 1937 | |
| Independent Holiness Churches Camp | Napawin | D; Independent Holiness Churches | O | 1957 |
| Indian Camp | Broadview | D; Free Methodist Church | | |
| Living Waters Camp | Watrous | D; Pentecostal Assemblies of Canada | O | 1943 |
| Sault Ste. Marie Camp | St. Joseph's Island I.... | | O | 1918 |

## England

| | | | |
|---|---|---|---|
| Wesleyan Camp | Birmingham | D; Wesleyan Church | 1980 |

| Name | City | Affiliation | O/R | Year | Founder |
|------|------|-------------|-----|------|---------|
| **Guatemala** | | | | | |
| General Camp | Monjas | A; Evangelistic Faith Missions | R | 1980 | |
| Grace Tabernacle Camp | | D; Grace Tabernacle Church | O | 1970 | |
| **Malawi** | | | | | |
| Mpaso Camp | Mpaso | D; Church of God (Remnant) | | | |
| **Mexico** | | | | | |
| Church of God Camp | Ajas Negras | D; Church of God (Evening Light) | R | | |
| Church of God Camp | Ensenada | D; Church of God (Servant) | R | 1980 | |
| **Nigeria** | | | | | |
| Apostolic Faith Camp | Lagos | D; Apostolic Faith Mission | O | 1960 | |

# INDEX

| Name | Location | Affiliation | | Year |
|---|---|---|---|---|
| Canyon Meadows Conference Center | Lake Hughes | D; American Baptist | | |
| Capital Christian Center | Weimar | I . . . | | |
| Cedar Falls Camp | Angelus Oaks | D; Seventh Day Adventist Church | O | |
| Central California Conference Camp | Soquel | D; Seventh Day Adventist Church | O | |
| Christian Encounter Camps and Retreats | Grass Valley | I; Christian Encounter Ministries | | |
| Church of God Camp | Oakland | D; Church of God (Servant) | | |
| Church Prayer Ministry International | Fremont | I . . . | | |
| Community Covenant Church Camp | West Point | I . . . | | |
| Corralitos Conference Center | Watsonville | I . . . | | |
| Diamond Arrow Camp | Nevada City | D; Church of God (Anderson) | | 1960 |
| Echo Mountain Ranch Retreat Center | Los Gattos | I . . . | | |
| Emerald Cove Camp | Bass Lake | I . . . | | |
| Esther Christian Conference Center | Wrightwood | I . . . | | |
| Forest Home Conference Center | Forest Falls | I . . . | | 1938 |
| Forward Bible Conference, Inc. | Placerville | I . . . | | |
| Fresno Camp | Fresno | D; Church of God (Servant) | | 1970 |
| Golden Valley Camp | Stockton | D; Evangelical Methodist Church | O | 1963 |

| Name | City | Affiliation | O/R | Year | Founder |
|---|---|---|---|---|---|
| Harmony Pines Christian Center | Wrightwood | I ... | | | |
| Hartland Camp and Conference Center | Badger | I ... | | | |
| Hartstone Bible Conference | Potter Valley | I; Hartstone Bible Conference, Inc. | | | |
| Hidden Lakes Retreat | Fremont | I ... | | | |
| Hume Lake Camp | Fresno | I ... | | | |
| Idyllwild Pines Camp and Conference Center | Idyllwild | I ... | O | 1923 | Christian businessmen from the Los Angeles area |
| Interstate Camp | Hanford | D; Church of God (Anderson) | | | |
| Kidder Creek Orchard Camp | Greenview | I ... | O | | |
| King's Retreat, The | Tahoe City | | O | | |
| Koinonia Conference Grounds | Watsonville | I ... | | | |
| LaHolla Camp | Valley Center | I ... | | | |
| Lake Avenue Congregation Church Camp | Pasadena | D ... | | | |
| Laurel Pines Camp and Conference | Redlands | I ... | | | |
| Long Beach Camp | Long Beach | D; Salvation Army | R | 1957 | Lt. Commissioner William J. Perkins |
| Los Angeles District Camp | Pasadena | D; Church of the Nazarene | | | |
| Meteor Ranch Bible Conference | Upper Lake | I ... | | 1911 | |
| Mile High Pines Camp | Moreno Valley | | | | |

| Name | Location | Affiliation | | Notes |
|---|---|---|---|---|
| Mission Springs Conference Center | Scotts Valley | D; Evangelical Covenant Church | O | |
| Mt. Gilead Bible Conference | Sebastopol | I; . . . | | |
| Mount Hermon Christian Conference Center | Mount Hermon | I; Mount Hermon Association, Inc. | O | 1906 |
| Mt. Hope Bible Conference Center | Forbestown | I; . . . | | |
| Mountain Meadows Conference | Shingletown | I; . . . | | |
| North California-Nevada District Camp | Mount Lassen | D; Assembly of God Church | O | |
| Oak Glen Christian Conference Center | Yucaipa | I; . . . | | |
| Oak Glen Pines Camp | Yucaipa | D; Free Methodist Church | O | 1956 |
| Oakbridge Camp | Ramona | A; Young Life | | |
| Oakhurst Conference Center | Coarsegold | I; . . . | | |
| Old Oak Ranch Conference Center | Sonora | I; . . . | | |
| Pacific Conference Spiritual Life Center | Upland | D; Brethren in Christ Church | O | 1964 Bishop Alvin C. Barkholder, Dr. Jesse F. Lady |
| Palomar Baptist Camp | Palomar Mountain | D; Baptist Church | | |
| Paradise Springs Conference Center | Valyermo | I; . . . | | |
| Pine Springs Ranch | Mountain Center | D; Seventh Day Adventist Church | O | |
| Pine Summit Christian Conference Center | Big Bear Lake | I; . . . | O | 1965 |
| Pine Valley Bible Conference | Pine Valley | I; . . . | | |

| Name | City | Affiliation | O/R | Year | Founder |
|---|---|---|---|---|---|
| Pinecrest Conference Center | Twin Peaks | I... | O | | |
| Ponderosa Pines Camp | Running Springs | I... | O | | |
| Rancho Capistrano Renewal Center | San Juan Capistrano | I... | | | |
| Redwood Christian Camp | Boulder Creek | I; Redwood Christian Association | O | 1942 | Dr. J. C. McPheeters et al. |
| Redwood Christian Park | Boulder Creek | I... | | | |
| Redwood Glen Baptist Camp | Loma Mar | D; Baptist Church | | | |
| Shady Nook Camp | Sacramento | A; World Gospel Mission (Peniel Mission) | O | 1952 | Dr. James Bishop, former director of Peniel Mission |
| Sierra Conference Grounds | Groveland | I; Sierra Christian Conference, Inc. | | | |
| Sierra Pines Baptist Camp | Little Norway | D; Baptist | | | |
| Silver Spur Conference Center | Tuolumne | I... | | | |
| Sky Mountain Camp | Emigrant Gap | | | | |
| Southern California Camp | El Monte | D; Church of God (Holiness) | | 1960 | |
| Southern California Camp | Palmdale | D; Fire Baptized Holiness Church | O | 1967 | |
| Southern California Camp | Riverside | I... | O | 1936 | C. C. Cunningham, W. H. Howard, H. M. Shaw, et al. |
| Southern California District Camp | Costa Mesa | D; Church of the Nazarene | R | | |
| Southwestern State Camp | Azusa | D; Church of God (Anderson) | R | 1960 | |
| Springs of Living Waters | Richardson Springs | I; Springs of Living Waters | | | |

| Name | Location | Affiliation | | Year |
|---|---|---|---|---|
| Tahquitz Conference Ground | Idyllwild | I; Tahquitz Conference Association, Inc. | | |
| Thousand Pines Center | Crestline | D; American Baptist | | |
| Victory Ranch | Moreno | | | |
| Wesleyan Park Camp | Santa Cruz | D; Free Methodist Church | O | 1960 |
| West Coast Holiness Camp | Vallejo | D; Church of the Bible Covenant | | 1975 |
| Western District Camp | Santa Cruz | D; United Pentecostal Church | | |
| Westminster Woods | Occidental | | | |
| Wolf Mountain Conference | Grass Valley | I; Wolf Mountain Conference Association | O | |
| Wynola Bible Conference | Julian | I . . . | | |

## Colorado

| Name | Location | Affiliation | | Year |
|---|---|---|---|---|
| Bear Trap Ranch | Colorado Springs | | | |
| Black Forest Camp and Conference Center | Colorado Springs | I . . . | | |
| Camp Coy | Indian Hills | D; Church of God (Anderson) | O | 1960 |
| Camp Elim | Woodland Park | I . . . | | |
| Camp ID-RA-HA-JE | Bailey | | O | |
| Camp ID-RA-HA-JE West | Somerset | | | |
| Camp Joy | Cedar Edge | D; Church of God (Anderson) | | |
| Colorado Camp | Canon City | D; Free Methodist Church | O | |
| Colorado Camp | Canon City | D; Wesleyan Holiness Association | R | |

| Name | City | Affiliation | O/R | Year | Founder |
|---|---|---|---|---|---|
| Colorado Camp | Colorado Springs | D; Christian Missionary Alliance Church | | | |
| Colorado Camp | Colorado Springs | D; Emmanuel Association | O | 1936 | |
| Colorado Chautauqua Association | Boulder | I . . . | O | | |
| Colorado Christian Service Camp | Colorado Springs | I . . . | | | |
| Colorado Conference Camp | Woodland Park | D; International Pentecostal Holiness Church | O | | |
| Colorado Cowboy Camp | Kiowa | A; Ranchmen's Camp Meeting of the Southwest | O | 1964 | |
| Colorado District Camp | Denver | D; Church of the Nazarene | O | 1904 | |
| Colorado District Camp | Larkspur | D; United Pentecostal Church | R | | |
| Colorado-Utah Camp | Denver | D; Church of God of Prophecy | R | | |
| Covenant Heights Camp | Estes Park | I . . . | | | |
| Crested Butte Family Life Camp | Crested Butte | I . . . | | | |
| Estes Park Center | Estes Park | I . . . | | | |
| Four Corners Camp | Mancos | A; Ranchmen's Camp Meeting of the Southwest | O | 1965 | |
| Glorious Freedom Camp | Cedar Edge | D; Church of God (Holiness) | O | | |
| Grace Tabernacle Camp | Colorado Springs | D; Grace Tabernacle | O | 1950 | |
| Highlands Camp | Allenspark | D; Presbyterian Church | | | |
| Horn Creek Conference | Westcliffe | I . . . | | | |
| Inter-Mountain District Camp | Elizabeth | D; Bible Missionary Church | O | 1965 | |

| Camp | Location | Affiliation | | Year | Notes |
|---|---|---|---|---|---|
| Lamar Camp | Lamar | D; Church of God (Holiness) | O | | |
| Living Rock Retreat | South Fork | I; Spiritual Fitness Ministries | O | 1985 | |
| Meadowdale Ranch Conference Center | Estes Park | I . . . | | | |
| Pike's Peak Wesleyan Camp | Colorado Springs | D; Wesleyan Church | O | 1913 | People's Mission Church, Rev. William H. Lee |
| Pillar of Fire Camp | Denver | D; Pillar of Fire Church | O | 1901 | Bishop Alma White |
| Rainbow Falls Park Camp | Woodland Park | | | | |
| Rocky Mountain Camp | Morrison | D; Church of God (Holiness) | | | |
| Rocky Mountain District | Cedaredge | D; Assembly of God Church | | | |
| Rocky Mountain Mennonite Camp | Divide | D; Mennonite Church | | | |
| San Luis Valley Cowboy Camp | Del Norte | A; Ranchmen's Camp Meeting of the Southwest | O | 1988 | |
| Southern Baptist Assembly | | D; Southern Baptist Convention | O | | |

## Connecticut

| Camp | Location | Affiliation | | Year | Notes |
|---|---|---|---|---|---|
| Camp Bethel | Haddam | I; Camp Bethel Association, Inc. | O | 1878 | |
| Connecticut Camp | Southington | D; Advent Christian Church | O | 1869 | |
| Evangelical Baptist Camp | Ashford | D; Baptist | | | |
| Mountain Lake Bible Conference | New Preston | I; Christian Youth Fellowship, Inc. | O | 1947 | |
| Pine Grove Camp | Canaan | I . . . | | | |
| Plainville Camp | Bristol | I . . . | | | |

| Name | City | Affiliation | O/R | Year | Founder |
|---|---|---|---|---|---|
| Plainville Camp | Plainville | I... | O | 1865 | |
| Southern New England Camp | New Britain | D; Church of God of Prophecy | | | |
| Willimantic Camp Meeting | Willimantic | I; Willimantic Camp Meeting Association | O | 1860 | Dr. W. K. Otis et al. |

## Delaware

| Name | City | Affiliation | O/R | Year | Founder |
|---|---|---|---|---|---|
| AME Zion Camp | Frankford | D; African Methodist Episcopal Zion Church | O | 1910 | |
| Antioch Camp | Frankford | D; African Methodist Episcopal Zion Church | O | 1900 | |
| Carey's Camp | Philips Hill | D; United Methodist Church | O | 1875 | |
| Del-Mar-Va District Camp | Laurel | D; Wesleyan Church | O | 1960 | |
| Eastern Shore Camp | Laurel | D; Churches of Christ in Christian Union | R | 1973 | |

## Florida

| Name | City | Affiliation | O/R | Year | Founder |
|---|---|---|---|---|---|
| Avon Park Holiness Camp | Avon Park | I... | O | 1939 | Dr. H. C. Morrison, John Taylor, Rev. S. Haynes |
| Bethlehem Camp | Bonifay | I... | O | 1930 | Dr. W. J. Hughes |
| Bible Methodist Camp | Florilla | D; Bible Methodist Church | O | 1985 | |
| Bible Town Ministries | Boca Raton | D; Boca Raton Community Church | | | |
| Breezewood Missionary Camp | Summerfield | I... | O | 1958 | Rev. G. T. Bustin |

| Name | Location | Denomination | | Year | Notes |
|---|---|---|---|---|---|
| Bristol Camp | Bristol | D; International Pentecostal Holiness Church | O | 1905 | Rev. and Mrs. C. M. Wheeler |
| Camp Aldersgate | Kissemee | I; ... | R | 1961 | Rev. Richard Fullerton |
| Camp Freedom | St. Petersburg | D; Brethren in Christ Church | O | 1953 | Rev. Baughey |
| Camp Moon | Leesburg | D; Church of God (Anderson) | O | 1905 | |
| Camp Suwanee Retreat Center | Dowling Park | I; ... | | | |
| Canaveral Retreat Center | Merrit Island | I; ... | | | |
| Cassadaga Camp | Lake Helen | D; Spiritualist | O | 1894 | |
| Central Florida Camp | Orlando | D; Church of the Nazarene | O | 1975 | |
| Christian Life Center Camp | Lakewood | A; Christ's Ambassadors | O | 1974 | Rev. G. T. Bustin |
| DeFuniak Chautauqua | DeFuniak Springs | I; ... | | | |
| Florida Camp | Century | D; Apostolic Faith Church | O | 1951 | |
| Florida Camp | Goulds | D; Church of God (Servant) | O | | |
| Florida Camp | Lakeland | D; Church of God of Prophecy | R | | |
| Florida Conference Camp | Apopka | D; Seventh Day Adventist Church | O | | |
| Florida District Camp | Ocala | D; United Pentecostal Church | | | |
| Florida District Camp | Orange City | D; God's Missionary Church | O | 1971 | |
| Florida Holiness Camp | Lakeland | I; Florida Holiness Camp Ground, Inc. | O | 1925 | Local laity and ministers |
| Florida Regional Camp | Taft | D; Churches of Christ in Christian Union | O | 1967 | |
| Glen St. Mary Camp | Glen St. Mary | D; Congregational Holiness Church, Inc. | O | 1951 | |
| John Wesley Memorial Camp | Tampa | I; ... | | | |
| Lake Aurora Christian Assembly | Lake Wales | I; ... | | 1970 | |

| Name | City | Affiliation | O/R | Year | Founder |
|------|------|-------------|-----|------|---------|
| Leesburg Life Enrichment Center | Leesburg | D; United Methodist Church | O | 1980 | |
| Light and Life Camp | Lakeland | D; Free Methodist Church | O | | |
| Lord's Barn Retreat, The | Homestead | I . . . | | | |
| Mid-Florida Holiness Camp | Intercession City | I . . . | O | 1940 | |
| Mid-Winter Camp | Brooksville | D; Wesleyan Church | O | 1950 | |
| Nazarene Camp | Carol City | D; Church of the Nazarene | O | | |
| North Florida Christian Service Camp | Keystone Heights | I . . . | | | |
| Odum Camp | Sopchoppy | D; Congregational Holiness Church, Inc. | O | 1965 | |
| Palmetto Victory Camp | Palmetto | I . . . | | 1965 | |
| Peace Valley Camp | Bowling Green | I; Florida State Holiness Association | O | 1951 | J. R. Gilbert, J. W. Hughes, et al. |
| Pleasant Grove Camp | Durant | D; Assembly of God Church | O | 1885 | |
| Sea Breeze Camp | Hobe Sound | I . . . | O | 1948 | Rev. & Mrs. H. Robb French et al. |
| South Eastern Spanish Camp | Wimauma | D; Church of God of Prophecy | | | |
| Southeastern Conference Camp | Hawthorne | D; Seventh Day Adventist Church | O | | |
| Southeastern Spanish District Camp | Lake Wales | D; Assembly of God Church | | | |
| Suwanne Camp | White Springs | D; Church of the Nazarene | O | 1900 | |
| Voice in the Wilderness | Brookville | D; Elim Fellowship | | | |
| West Florida District Camp | Maianna | D; Assembly of God Church | | | |

## Georgia

| Name | Location | Affiliation | | Year | Director |
|---|---|---|---|---|---|
| Antioch Camp | Gainesville | I . . . | | | |
| Bethel Camp | Carrolton | D; United Methodist Church | O | 1868 | Rev. John Murphy |
| Beulah Heights Camp | Atlanta | A; International Pentecostal Association | O | 1908 | |
| Bible Memory Conference Center | Cleveland | A; Bible Memory Association | | | |
| Calvin Center | Hampton | | | | |
| Camp Hamby | Summerville | D; United Methodist Church | O | 1968 | |
| Camp Westminster | Atlanta | D; Presbyterian Church | | | |
| Candler Camp | Atlanta | D; United Methodist Church | O | 1950 | |
| Church of God Camp | Doraville | D; Church of God of Prophecy | O | | |
| Church of God Camp | Tifton | D; Church of God of Prophecy | O | | |
| Cohutta Springs Adventist Center | Sylvania | D; Seventh Day Adventist Church | O | | |
| Cullasaja Camp | Cullasaja | D; Assembly of God Church | O | 1920 | |
| Dublin District Camp | Adrian | D; United Methodist Church | O | | |
| Epworth-by-the-Sea | Clarkesville | D; United Methodist Church | O | 1948 | |
| Fellowship Valley Retreat | Clarkesville | I; Faith Ventures, Inc. | | | |
| Flat Rock Camp | Franklin | D; United Methodist Church | O | 1876 | |
| Fountain Camp | Washington | D; United Methodist Church | | | |
| Franklin Springs Camp | Franklin Springs | D; International Pentecostal Holiness Church | O | 1918 | |
| Gaskin Springs Holiness Camp | Douglas | I . . . | O | 1946 | |

| Name | City | Affiliation | O/R | Year | Founder |
|------|------|-------------|-----|------|---------|
| Georgia Camp | Toccoa Falls | D; Christian Missionary Alliance Church | R | 1980 | |
| Georgia Conference Camp | Atlanta | D; International Pentecostal Holiness Church | O | 1950 | |
| Georgia Conference Camp | Butler | D; Congregational Methodist Church | R | | |
| Georgia Conference Camp | Taccoa Falls | D; Free Methodist Church | R | 1970 | |
| Georgia District Camp | Adrian | D; Church of the Nazarene | O | 1918 | |
| Georgia District Camp | Barnsville | D; United Pentecostal Church | O | | |
| Georgia District Camp | Union Point | D; Wesleyan Church | O | 1930 | Rev. Frank Graham |
| Great Love Camp, A | Atlanta | I; A Great Love | | | |
| Hartwell Camp | Hartwell | D; Seventh Day Adventist Church | | | |
| Holbrook Camp | Holbrook | D; United Methodist Church | O | 1838 | |
| Hortense County Camp | Hortense | I . . . | O | 1903 | |
| Indian Springs Holiness Camp | Flovilla | I . . . | O | 1890 | Rev. George Matthews, Rev. W. A. Dodge |
| Lawrenceville Camp | Lawrenceville | D; United Methodist Church | O | 1832 | |
| Lebanon Camp | Lebanon | D; United Methodist Church | O | 1845 | |
| Little Rock Camp | Leesburg | I; Wesleyan Church | O | 1907 | |
| Loudsville Camp | Cleveland | D; United Methodist Church | O | 1838 | |
| Lumpkin Camp | Dawsonville | D; United Methodist Church | O | 1830 | |
| Marietta Camp | Marietta | D; United Methodist Church | O | 1837 | |
| Morrison Camp | Rome | D; United Methodist Church | O | 1868 | |
| Mossy Creek Camp | Cleveland | D; United Methodist Church | O | 1833 | |

| Camp | Location | Denomination | | Date | Leaders |
|---|---|---|---|---|---|
| Mt. Gilead Camp | Atlanta (Ben Hill) | D; United Methodist Church | O | 1824 | |
| Mount Moriah Camp | Matthews | I. . . . | O | 1827 | Rev. Pharah, William Parker |
| Mt. Zion Camp | Griffin | D; United Methodist Church | O | 1834 | |
| Mountain Gap Camp | Mountain Gap | D; International Pentecostal Holiness Church | O | 1930 | |
| Okefenokee Holiness Camp | Waycross | I. . . . | O | 1900 | |
| Perry Camp | Perry | I. . . . | | | |
| Pine Log Camp | Dalton | D; United Methodist Church | O | 1842 | |
| Pine Mountain Camp | Zebulon | I. . . . | O | 1940 | Rev. C. P. East, Rev. S. M. Haynes, et al. |
| Pinelog Camp | Cartersville | I. . . . | | | |
| Pirkle Memorial Camp | Griffin | D; Congregational Holiness Church, Inc. | O | 1950 | |
| Poplar Springs | Canon | D; United Methodist Church | O | 1832 | |
| Regional Camp | Atlanta | I; Operation P.R.E.A.C.H., International | R | | |
| Rockridge Baptist Assembly | Franklin | D; Baptist Church | | | |
| Salem Camp | Covington | D; United Methodist Church | O | 1828 | |
| Shiloh Camp | Carrolton | D; United Methodist Church | O | 1867 | |
| Shingleroof Camp | McDunnough | D; United Methodist Church | O | 1831 | |
| Southeastern Holiness Camp | Lizella | D; Evangelistic Groups, Inc. | O | 1957 | Rev. J. Acie Raquemore, Rev. Frank Chapman |
| State Camp | Hamilton | D; Church of God (Anderson) | R | | |
| State Camp | La Grange | D; Church of God (Anderson) | O | | |
| State Camp | Wadley | D; Church of God (Anderson) | O | | |
| Tattnal County Camp | Reidsville | D; United Methodist Church | O | 1820 | |

| Name | City | Affiliation | O/R | Year | Founder |
|---|---|---|---|---|---|
| Taylor County Holiness Camp | Butler | I... | O | 1938 | Rev. S. F. Andrews, Rev. M. J. Wood |
| Toccoa Camp | Toccoa | D; Pentecostal Fire Baptized Holiness Church | O | 1919 | Rev. A. C. Craft |
| Toccoa Wilderness Ministries | Blue Ridge | I... | | | |
| Trader's Hill Camp | Falkaton | D; United Methodist Church | O | 1987 | Rev. Lawrence A. Lemmons |
| Tygart Camp | Ray City | D; United Methodist Church | O | 1968 | |
| Union Camp | Waco | I... | O | 1876 | |
| Union Grove Camp | Cleveland | D; Congregational Holiness Church, Inc. | O | 1925 | |
| Union Grove Camp | White County | I... | | | |
| Whispering Pines Camp | Holly Springs | D; Church of God (Anderson) | O | | |
| White Oak Camp | Thomson | D; United Methodist Church | O | 1842 | |

## Hawaii

| Name | City | Affiliation | O/R | Year | Founder |
|---|---|---|---|---|---|
| Hawaii District Camp | Hilo | D; Assembly of God Church | | | |

## Idaho

| Name | City | Affiliation | O/R | Year | Founder |
|---|---|---|---|---|---|
| Alacca Bible Conference | Grangeville | I... | | | |
| Camp Sanders | Sanders | D; Free Methodist Church | O | | |
| Central Idaho Camp | Heyburn | D; Christian Missionary Alliance | O | | |
| Daystar Conference Center | Donnelly | I... | | | |